PIETIES IN TRANSITION

For Andrew Butcher

Pieties in Transition
Religious Practices and Experiences, *c*.1400–1640

Edited by

ROBERT LUTTON
University of Nottingham, UK

and

ELISABETH SALTER
University of Wales-Aberystwyth, UK

ASHGATE

Published by
Ashgate Publishing Limited
Gower House
Croft Road
Aldershot
Hampshire GU11 3HR
England

Ashgate Publishing Company
Suite 420
101 Cherry Street
Burlington, VT 05401-4405
USA

Ashgate website: http://www.ashgate.com

British Library Cataloguing in Publication Data
Pieties in transition: religious practices and experiences, c.1400–1640
   1. Christian life – England – Kent – History – To 1500 2. Christian life – England – Kent
   – History – 16th century 3. Christian life – England – Kent – History – 17th century
   4. Reformation – England – Kent 5.Kent (England) – Church history
   I. Lutton, Robert II. Salter, Elisabeth, 1972-
   274.2'2306

Library of Congress Cataloging-in-Publication Data
Pieties in transition: religious practices and experiences, c.1400–1640 / [edited by] Robert
   Lutton and Elisabeth Salter.
      p. cm.
   Includes bibliographical references and index.
   ISBN-13: 978-0-7546-5616-6 (alk. paper)
   ISBN-10: 0-7546-5616-0 (alk. paper)
   1. Pietism – England – Kent – History. 2. England – Religious life and customs.
   I. Lutton, Robert. II. Salter, Elisabeth.

BR1652.G7P54 2007
274.2'05–dc22

                                                      2006020593

ISBN-13: 978-0-7546-5616-6

BR
763
.K46
P54
2007

Printed and bound in Great Britain by MPG Books Ltd, Bodmin, Cornwall.

Contents

Part III   Reading and Representation: Material Cultures of Piety

List of Maps, Figures and Plates

List of Tables

Notes on Contributors

Claire Bartram is Lecturer in Renaissance Studies at Canterbury Christ Church University and is currently working on several publications concerning book culture in early–modern society.

G.M. Draper teaches landscape and urban history for the University of Kent, carries out historical consultancy for archaeological units and is leading a three-year project on Rye, Sussex, for the Romney Marsh Research Trust.

Andrew Hope was educated at Cranbrook School and Cambridge University. He has taught at the Universities of Oxford and Reading and in a number of schools and colleges. He has published articles on Lollardy and on William Tyndale.

Robert Lutton is Lecturer in Medieval History at the University of Nottingham. He is the author of *Lollardy and Orthodox Religion in Pre-Reformation England*. He is currently working on a major project investigating Christocentric pieties in the late medieval and early modern periods.

Emily Richards studied in Berlin before completing an MA in Medieval and Tudor Studies at the University of Kent with Andrew Butcher and Peter Brown. She is currently working as a legal assistant while researching Carthusian manuscripts and the English body–soul debate in her spare time. She hopes to return to PhD study in October 2006 at York.

Elisabeth Salter is Lecturer in Medieval and Renaissance Literatures in the Department of English, University of Wales, Aberystwyth. She works on creativity, identity, and the uses of text. She is author of *Cultural Creativity in the Early English Renaissance* (Palgrave, 2006) and *Six Renaissance Men & Women*, (Ashgate, 2006), and is currently developing a large-scale project on the history (and ethnography) of reading.

Paula Simpson completed her PhD at the University of Kent in 1997. She worked as a Research Associate on the *Taxatio* Project at the University of Manchester between 1997 and 2000 and is currently an Honorary Research Fellow at the same university.

Annemarie Speetjens (Utrecht, The Netherlands) studied History and Medieval Studies in Utrecht and Rome. She is working on a PhD thesis entitled 'A Quantitative Study of the Transformations of Two Forms of Late Medieval Memorial Piety: The Foundations of Chantries and Charitable Piety in the Northern Low Countries, 1400–1580' at the Vrije Universiteit, Amsterdam. She currently teaches history at the Stedelijk Gymnasium, Schiedam.

Sheila Sweetinburgh is an Honorary Research Fellow at the University of Kent. She has published a monograph and several articles on the medieval English hospital.

Alexandra Walsham is Professor of Reformation History at the University of Exeter. She is the author of *Church Papists: Catholicism, Conformity and Confessional Polemic in Early Modern England* (Boydell, 1993), *Providence in Early Modern England* (Clarendon, 1999) and *Charitable Hatred: Tolerance and Intolerance in England, 1500-1700* (Manchester University Press, 2006), and has also co-edited (with Julia Crick), *The Uses of Script and Print, 1300-1700* (CUP, 2004) and (with Peter Marshall), *Angels in the Early Modern World* (CUP, 2006). She is currently working on a monograph to be entitled *The Reformation of the Landscape: Religion, Memory and Legend in Early Modern Britain.*

Acknowledgements

The editors would like to thank all the people who have helped to shape this volume. We held a colloquium at the University of Kent in September 2004 in which the contributors whose chapters are published here presented early drafts of their work. We would like to thank each of them for their contribution to this volume, as well as others who attended the colloquium and participated in the discussions on that day. Our particular thanks go to Andrew Butcher for his general inspiration in this, as in so many other areas of research, and for his insightful presentation at the colloquium concerning the future of studies in piety. Elisabeth would also like to thank her new colleagues at Aberystwyth for their support in this year of changes; and Rob would also like to thank his colleagues at London College of Fashion for granting him the time to continue with his own research and writing.

List of Abbreviations

AC	*Archaeologia Cantiana*
BIHR	*Bulletin of the Institute of Historical Research*
BL	British Library
CCAL	Canterbury Cathedral Archives and Library
CKS	Centre for Kentish Studies
CPR	*Calendar of Patent Rolls*
CUP	Cambridge University Press
HMC	*Royal Commission on Historical Manuscripts*
LP	*Letters and Papers Foreign and Domestic in the Reign of Henry VIII*, ed. J.S. Brewer, J. Gairdner and R.H. Brodie (21 vols, London, 1862–1965)
NA: PRO	The National Archive, Public Record Office (Kew)
ODNB	*Oxford Dictionary of National Biography,* ed. H.C.G. Matthew and B. Harrison, 60 vols (Oxford, 2004)
OUP	Oxford University Press
SCH	*Studies in Church History*
VCH Kent	*The Victoria History of the County of Kent*, ed. W. Page (London, 1926)

Introduction

Robert Lutton and Elisabeth Salter

This collection explores the changing pieties of townspeople and villagers before, during and after the Reformation. It brings together an interdisciplinary range of scholars with the purpose of presenting new research on a subject of importance to historians of society and religion in late medieval and early modern Europe.

Our aim is to examine the diverse evidence for transitions in piety across a period traditionally understood to be one of immensely significant ideological change in England, and in Europe more generally. Largely shunning more traditional approaches to the subject of piety in local society, which have tended to foreground the parish as the dominant lay religious institution, the chapters look at a variety of different units that all suggest their own trajectories and narratives of transition. In so doing the individual essays and the volume as a whole raise important issues which are relevant to historical reconstruction more generally concerning the different types of evidence available, the different histories each provides, and how best to interpret them. This volume therefore represents an intervention in the study of the dynamics of late medieval and early modern pieties.

The way this volume approaches the task is to engage in detailed examinations and re-examinations of the empirical evidence for piety in this period. The chapters employ a broad range of source – including manuscript and printed devotional texts; instructional and polemical writings; spiritual biography, history writing and sermons; funeral monuments; the records of ecclesiastical courts and administration; last wills and testaments; parish records; hospital and confraternal materials; municipal records and a wide range of documentation relating to local society – and a broad range of approaches including those associated with social, cultural, and religious history, literary and manuscript studies, social anthropology and the interpretation of the material culture of religion.

Because of the attention to detailed reconstruction, the geographical focus of the contributions examines evidence pertaining to a region defined by the county of Kent and, in one case, the Low Countries. The inclusion of this last essay by Annemarie Speetjens might, at first sight, seem incongruous, if it were not for the likelihood that comparison between Kent and the Low Countries may be just as rewarding and pertinent as comparison between Kent and a number of other English counties. There was considerable contact and cultural exchange between Kent and the Low Countries in this period and the chapters by Rob Lutton, Annemarie Speetjens and Sheila Sweetinburgh collectively demonstrate that these two northern European regions, or at least certain centres and districts within them, may have undergone remarkably similar cultural changes in the late fifteenth and early sixteenth centuries, all of which had an important bearing on piety and subsequent reformation. There is, however, nothing provincial about the implications of the individual contributions and the findings of the volume as a whole. This is because the various contributions employ a common or comparative geographical focus as a means to explore issues of method and conceptualization rather than to provide coherent and exhaustive historical description of a defined region. We would like to propose that further collections of this kind, focusing on other geographical areas, are essential to furthering understandings of piety, and its transitions, in this period of both radical changes and surprising continuities. But before further introductory discussion of the approaches taken and evidences used, perhaps a consideration of some definitions of terms such as 'piety' and 'transition' may be useful.

One of the results of bringing this collection together (and indeed one of the initial purposes of producing such a volume) is to problematize any easy definition of a term such as piety. What the contributions indicate is the instability of definitions of 'piety', and the many ramifications of the practices and experiences associated with being pious, across the time span of *c.* 1400–1640. These encompass those categories of behaviour, belief and experience that have traditionally been associated with the term 'piety' and that might be described as religiosity or spirituality, but they also concern *pietas* or family duty; notions of moral and immoral behaviour, and the memorialization and commemoration of the dead; attitudes to reading and education, to the church, its personnel and to the poor; customary action and collective or individual assent to, or dissent from, doctrinal beliefs or the conventions of previous generations.

For the two chapters under the heading 'Orthodoxies and Heterodoxies' the problem of how to interpret the nature of heterodox pieties and their relationships to broader contexts of orthodox and heterodox beliefs and practices is approached in quite different ways. Both chapters share a concern with teasing out individual and family pieties, but whereas Rob Lutton sees the expectations of family as a constraint upon the range of pious choices available to the individual and seeks to locate transitions in piety within a vertical model of cultural transmission, Andrew Hope explores the ways in which two individuals departed from expected conventions of behaviour '… by attending to how religious convictions worked themselves out in particular circumstances of networks of social or family ties'.[1] The geographical propinquities and shared family and social networks of Joan Bocher and Elizabeth Barton reconstructed so carefully by Hope, provide a means to problematize crude conceptualizations of the social determination of piety and religious dissent. Hope's model of transition highlights the psychological imperatives that cause certain types of individuals – in this case young women – under certain pressures and at particular moments in time to set themselves on extreme courses of action. Martyrdom, in this sense, becomes a self-conscious

[1]   Andrew Hope, this volume, p. 45; Robert Lutton, this volume, p. 30.

pious category in the sixteenth century and a means to obtaining a voice. Lutton, on the other hand, is concerned with explaining enduring contrasts in the religious cultures of the two Wealden towns and parishes of Cranbrook and Tenterden through reconstruction of their social and economic dynamics and material cultures, and also with exploring how the deep structures of lived religion were related to traditions of dissent and responses to reform. Both chapters emphasize the ways in which interaction between élite learned and popular uneducated cultural milieus and discourses gave rise to innovations in belief and new ways of being pious.

For the group of chapters under the heading 'Institutions as Evidence for Transitions in Piety', the examination of official structures, such as various educational institutions, the hospital and the ecclesiastical court, reveal the extent to which the official requirements for pious behaviour were mediated by individual and collective behaviour, as well as other traditions and practices. Paula Simpson, for example, shows the ways that individuals used official sites of pious behaviour, such as the parish church, to perform their resistance to tithe payment; and the repeated choice of an occasion immediately following a church service for the public airing of these grievances. The notion of how to practise piety here becomes mixed with the civic and communal issues of customary practice and community knowledge. And it is a mix of religious and civic concerns which are taken into the forum of the ecclesiastical court for public discussion and resolution.[2] G.M. Draper's detailed investigation of sites for the provision of education – chantries, hospitals, colleges of priests as well as grammar schools – also adds great depth to the ways we understand the mechanisms through which pious practice is accessed at the specific level of local society. Draper's contribution also emphasizes the role of lay benefaction in funding these institutions as, similarly, Sheila Sweetinburgh's analysis of charitable giving to hospitals indicates the important role of benefaction as a site for pious practice. Even if charitable giving for education was, as Draper suggests 'episodic', the extent of the giving tends to indicate the perceived importance of learning and teaching in local society. Here, education becomes a vehicle for developing knowledge about piety, through pious benefaction which is itself provided as a form of pious act by members of the local community. In all these chapters, piety is at once structured by institutions and transformed by the specific acts of individuals and groups at the level of locality, parish, and family.

For the group of chapters under the heading 'Reading and Representation: Material Cultures of Piety', the cultural products which express or disseminate ideas about piety are shown to be affected by a number of ideological influences, and to have the potential for a multiplicity of interpretations. Although represented through solid objects, the practice and display of pious sentiments is found to evade homologous definitions of piety. Claire Bartram's discussion of styles of representation in post-reformation monuments, for example, indicates the important interactions between the monumental display of the social self and the

---

[2]   Paula Simpson, this volume, p. 104.

moral and spiritual (or pious) self in the process of defining and displaying identity, particularly in a gentry context. She stresses the importance of contextualizing these forms of representation in relation to the textual circulation of ideas based in both humanist and puritan discourses. The mixing of '… Puritan self-examination and the social activism of Christian humanism', she suggests, defined the pious, self-controlled, industrious lay person, active in civic and ecclesiastical affairs.[3] Elisabeth Salter and Emily Richards both examine the use of books in the promulgation and formation of ideas about piety and in the practice of pious behaviour. Emily Richards shows how important it is to be aware of the ways piety was defined by different audience groups when analysing the meanings attributed to pious concepts in devotional literature. She demonstrates the very important role of language in the reception and the transmission of spiritual meaning. Her detailed analysis based on one Carthusian manuscript indicates that questions need to be asked about the meanings of pious vocabularies for spiritual writings circulated beyond the contexts of their production in contemplative orders to the very different contexts of their reception amongst the lay religious in local society. Elisabeth Salter is also concerned with the process of making meaning in the use of devotional books, specifically at the level of popular culture. She indicates the ways that elements of popular discourses of rhyme and proverb are structured into popular devotional texts as well as being present in the evidence left by reader annotations. This, she suggests, has implications for the 'oral' processes involved in imagining pious concepts, and so implications for the nature of popular conceptions of 'piety'.

And what of transition? The volume itself, as a whole, constitutes a re-examination of transition. Some chapters make specific reference to instances of transition in pious practices and concepts, or/and continuities in practice despite changes in official definitions of what is appropriate piety. G.M. Draper's analysis of educational provision, for example, uses a traditional historiography of transition between the medieval and early modern period – that of education and literacy – as a vehicle for indicating the persuasive evidence for extensive literate activity, education and the pious provision of this in the two centuries before the official Reformation. Her findings do however indicate that there were some specific changes in the sites at which education took place, and this involved a move from education being focused on individual teachers, to the foundation of specific school buildings. Simpson also finds strong and quantifiable evidence for continuity in the 'enduring forms dispute over tithe took in the period 1500–1600' despite the ideological changes of this century.[4] This is reflected in the continued use of particular symbolic sites for performing grievances. The chancel, for example, was still used even though its meanings as a pious space had changed from the sacramental and sacerdotal to a place for the demarcation of social superiority. There was, however, also some transition in the nature of the

---

[3]   Claire Bartram, this volume, pp. 137–8.
[4]   Paula Simpson, this volume, p. 101.

grievances raised, and this appears to reflect ideological change: in the later sixteenth century, confrontations over tithe often also addressed rights concerning seating positions.[5] And Sweetinburgh demonstrates how 'The appropriation of an apparently ancient vocabulary of charitable provision in the late sixteenth century enabled contemporaries to highlight the advancement of the new faith'.[6] Elisabeth Salter's analysis of devotional reading also makes a case for continuities in pious practice across the official Reformation. She shows evidence for the continued uses of specific forms of devotional text across the ideological transition, and the continuities, therefore, in the modes of conceptualizing religious ideas as indicated by the continued use of the verses of daily moralization.

Rob Lutton's detailed comparative analyses of two Kent towns makes a significant contribution towards proving the complexity of either transition or continuity. He shows the need to consider the different influences on pious viewpoint and religious practice, indicating that family tradition and specific customs based on local dynamics affected the extents to which there was continuity and transition in the practices of corporate and familial pious giving and commemoration. Annemarie Speetjens's chapter asks whether it is possible to measure transition using the sorts of quantitative methods that were pioneered by Gabriel Le Bras and Jacques Toussaert. These have a vexed legacy in the study of piety in the Low Countries and, ironically, have had a greater influence on work investigating popular religion in England. Indeed, such approaches have been employed in different ways in the analysis of testamentary evidence by Lutton and Sweetinburgh in this volume.[7] Speetjens's detailed re-assessment of the evidence for a sudden crisis in late medieval devotional life in the Low Countries around the year 1520 presents an at once more extended and more complex picture of transition that focuses as much on the transformations within devotional forms as the changes in their popularity over time, and she wisely cautions us about the limitations of quantitative methods without dismissing their worth.

Underlining the different approaches taken by contributors, the chapters are split between those with a geographical focus and those with either theoretical or other empirical basis. Some are micro-studies that deal with particular instances or episodes of transition or are focused on individuals, families, practices or networks; others examine the development and changing roles of religious institutions in the re-shaping of pieties over the period as a whole. All but one of the chapters takes Kent as its geographical focus. The particular geographical position of the County makes it a distinctively important region for the study of change and transition. It was geographically close to the reforming influences of northern Europe as well as being on the hinterland of London. So whilst providing detailed evidence for the nature of piety and how it changed in one region, this

---

[5]   Ibid., p. 102.

[6]   Sheila Sweetinburgh, this volume, p. 73.

[7]   For the influence of Toussaert on work on piety in late medieval England see for example Norman P. Tanner, *The Church in Late Medieval Norwich* (Toronto, 1984), p. xv.

volume also has implications for the study of pieties in transition throughout northern Europe. Indeed, a number of contributors make comparative reference to work on other counties or regions and engage with wider historiographies. One of the benefits of bringing together a body of work on a specific geographical area is that it readily becomes apparent that parts of the country that are traditionally thought of as coherent in fact contained great variety. There may not be anything especially Kentish about the types of pieties that are described in the following chapters, at least not in the sense of their demonstration of any overarching culture of the county. The work of Paul Lee on the diocese of Rochester in the west of the county suggests that pre-Reformation religion was quite different in this part of Kent compared to further east.[8] In this sense comparison with the Low Countries becomes more pertinent and it is the importance of the bearing of locality on piety in fields of behaviour as diverse as non-payment of tithe, educational endowment, reading, devotion to saints or to Christ, commemoration of the dead, charitable giving and religious dissent that comes to the fore as opposed to a coherent regional identity or culture.

The book is an interdisciplinary volume that, we would like to suggest, constitutes a cultural history (although significantly not *The* Cultural History) of changing pieties in the period *c.* 1400–1640. In recent years it has increasingly been the work of Cultural History to look below the level of the highest élites and to focus in detail on process, practice, and even experience at the level of popular culture alongside interactions between the élite and non-élite.[9] This project is being pursued with increasing pace by historians of the various European Reformations.[10] The chapters in this book represent a coherent and concerted effort to apply these preoccupations to the close examination of the nature and dynamics of piety across both the late medieval and early modern periods. There are certain key ways in which the contributors achieve this.

Firstly, both the material used and the approaches taken indicate the contributors' readiness to challenge traditional historiographies. For example, Draper's detailed examination of the implications for pious practice of the extensive levels of literate practice on Romney Marsh and in the Cinque Ports challenges a traditional historiography of rising literacy which sees the foundation of schools and a 'literate revolution' '... indisputably as early–modern events and

---

[8]   Paul Lee, 'Monastic and Secular Religion and Devotional reading in Late Medieval Dartford and West Kent', unpublished Ph.D Thesis, University of Kent (1998) and *Nunneries, Learning and Spirituality in Late Medieval English Society: The Dominican Priory of Dartford* (Woodbridge, 2001).

[9]   See for example Roger Chartier, *Cultural History: Between Practices and Representations* (trans. L.G. Cochrane, Oxford, 1988); Robert Darnton, *The Kiss of Lamourette: Reflections in Cultural History* (London, 1990).

[10]   See for example Andrew Pettegree, *Reformation and the Culture of Persuasion* (Cambridge, 2005) and Ulinka Rublack, *Reformation Europe* (Cambridge, 2005).

part of the Protestant Reformation'.[11] By looking to the evidence provided by a comparison of two towns in near geographical proximity, Rob Lutton's examination of testamentary practices across the Reformation challenges a dominant historiography which proposes that what would come to be seen as Catholic attitudes were consistently thriving on the eve of the Reformation, throughout England.[12]

The second key element which assists contributors in providing new insights, as well as re-assessments of traditional historiographies, is the extent to which they have explored very concentrated bodies of evidence or individual elements including individual people or cultural products. This has enabled a recovery of nuances concerning the processes through which piety is practised and experienced. Of necessity, this mode of investigation requires close reading rather than broad brush approaches, although throughout the volume this is always with an eye to the more generalizable implications of the detailed evidence examined. In some cases the prioritising of individual elements involves a very detailed investigation of one manuscript, as provided in Richards's exploration of the implications for understanding the interactions and tensions between the producers of manuscripts such as British Library Additional 37049 who were engaged in the contemplative life and the lay readers who may have had access to such texts. In other cases, the individual elements are people, as illustrated by Andrew Hope's investigation of Elizabeth Barton and Joan Bocher's particular journeys to martyrdom. Claire Bartram's detailed analysis of Roger Manwood's monument enables the contextualization of this material object within discourses of remembrance and reputation which relate to one individual, as well as showing how that individual illustration helps in the process of 'recomplicating' the interpretation of the Elizabethan effigy monument in order to '... more strongly contextualize the monument within Protestant and humanist–inspired processes of remembrance ...' and, therefore, the formation of identity.[13] For other contributors the attention to detailed analysis involves prioritizing one type of source. Sweetinburgh, for example, uses the last will and testament to analyse communal and familial charitable practices within a particular parish or town;[14] and the evidence of ecclesiastical courts, and more specifically on resistance to tithe payments forms the focus for Simpson. She elegantly indicates how a quantifiable 'prevalence and persistence over time of small-scale resistance to tithe' has

---

[11]   G.M. Draper, this volume, pp. 76–7; see Peter Clark, *English Provincial Society from the Reformation to the Revolution: Religion, Politics and Society in Kent 1500–1640* (Hassocks, 1977), pp. 185, 189–90.

[12]   Robert Lutton, this volume, pp. 14, 24–9; see Eamon Duffy *The Stripping of the Altars: Traditional Religion in England, 1400–1580* (London–New Haven, 1992).

[13]   Claire Bartram, this volume, p. 143.

[14]   Sheila Sweetinburgh, this volume, pp. 60–61.

implications for understanding the ways that continuities of practice exist in a period of massive ideological change and acute social and economic crisis.[15]

The third key element in approaches – an interrogation of the conceptual bases for analysing piety – persists throughout the volume and finds contributors querying traditionally employed terminology as well as customary units of analysis. It is partly the interdisciplinary range of evidences and theoretical approaches across which the contributors are writing that stimulates this inquiry into concepts. Elisabeth Salter, for example, proposes possibilities for a way of understanding devotional reading using a concept of 'oralization', derived from 'ethnographic attitudes to literate practice'. This enables her to examine the imaginative processes involved in the practice of devotional reading in popular culture, and the implications this has for continuities in devotional experience across the ideological transitions of the Reformation.[16] And, Emily Richards proposes that differences between medieval and modern meanings of terms such as 'mysticism' and 'contemplation' may lead to confusion and possibly 'a forgetting of how language both shapes and is shaped by spiritual experience'.[17] The querying of vocabularies and units of analysis on which enquiry is based indicates an area requiring further development, and which might look to recent developments in cognitive psychology and its allied sub-discipline of cognitive anthropology, alongside further interrogations of the mechanisms through which piety is experienced, understood, and mythologized. We would do well to remember that in making our representations of piety we are '… constantly negotiating between the explicit and conscious, on the one hand, and the inexplicit (or tacit) and unconscious, on the other …' and that '… this issue of negotiation is central to our attempts to understand historically what we might call the dynamics of piety'.[18]

---

[15]   Paula Simpson, this volume, p. 108.

[16]   Elisabeth Salter, this volume, p. 150.

[17]   Emily Richards, this volume, p. 164.

[18]   Andrew Butcher, ' "The Micro-Mechanisms of Cognition and Communication" and Changing Modes of Religiosity', unpublished paper given at the 'Pieties in Transition' colloquium, University of Kent, September 2004. And see Maurice E.F. Bloch, *How We Think They Think: Anthropological Approaches to Cognition, Memory, and Literacy* (Boulder, Colorado–Oxford, 1998), p. vii.

PART I
Orthodoxies and Heterodoxies

Chapter 1

Geographies and Materialities of Piety
Reconciling Competing Narratives of Religious Change in Pre-Reformation and Reformation England

Robert Lutton

In his recent *Image and Devotion in Late Medieval England* Richard Marks discusses approaches to the study of images of saints and how they were used in late medieval England:

> The selective and fragmentary nature of the empirical evidence rules out any attempt to write grand narrative, even if one were so inclined. Like the medieval Church itself, image-use was not monolithic; it operated at different levels, reflected different interests and took place in different contexts. A study based on microhistories and polysemic readings in time and place precludes the shoe-horning of the relationships between medieval people and their images into inappropriate and therefore unhistorical structures.[1]

It is perhaps a measure of the influence of the revisionist turn in the historiography of late medieval religion in England that the sort of approach Marks advocates is so rarely followed. Instead, there is now a tendency to emphasize the coherence, uniformity and continuity of piety in England in the decades before the Reformation over and above its contradictions, heterogeneity and dynamics of change. This is illustrated by two further comments by Marks. The first describes the pieties of the residents of the parish of Eaton Bray in Bedfordshire: 'The wills both of these villagers and of their overlords spoke the same discourse of conventional piety. With the exception of a small minority of dissidents (the Lollards), all classes subscribed to the same set of orthodox beliefs and practices, encompassing the liturgy, the sacraments and veneration of the saints'. The second explains the stark contrasts between different parishes' levels of testamentary

---

[1]   Richard Marks, *Image and Devotion in Late Medieval England* (Stroud, 2004), pp. 8–9.

giving to saints' cults within the Bedfordshire archdeanry of Sudbury as being '... determined by parish custom ...' but does not attend to the implications for piety of such differences in customary practice.[2]

Examination of the geography of changing pieties in pre-Reformation England remains fragmentary and without a coherent comparative framework. There is an increasing number of studies of large, medium-sized and small urban centres together with work on counties, dioceses or regions encompassing more rural parishes.[3] These show that significant geographical differences existed between different parts of the country and from one centre to the next. Despite this, national surveys do not generally draw attention to these different trajectories of religious development and change before the 1530s, perhaps because such differences have not generally been seen as important in religious terms.[4]

As a result, the geographical variety of orthodox piety has not informed explanations of the different rates and degrees of compliance with state-sponsored reform in the sixteenth century from one town or county to the next. A.G. Dickens described a 'great crescent' of Protestant heartlands comprising Norfolk, Suffolk, Essex and Kent with London at its centre and a 'spur' running along the Thames valley, including Buckinghamshire, Oxfordshire and Berkshire. In addition, he identified Bristol and its hinterland and towns such as Coventry and Hull as important Protestant centres. In general, Protestants were more likely to be found in the south and the east than in the west and the north and in towns rather than in the countryside.[5] This geographical pattern broadly corresponds to the documented incidence of Lollardy in the fifteenth and early sixteenth centuries.[6] Whether or not

---

[2]   Marks, *Image and Devotion*, pp. 8, 30. The most influential revisionist work is Eamon Duffy, *The Stripping of the Altars: Traditional Religion in England, 1400–1580* (New Haven–London, 1992). His *The Voices of Morebath: Reformation and Rebellion in an English Village* (New Haven–London, 2001) proceeds from the same thesis. On heterogeneity see, for example, Norman P. Tanner, 'The Reformation and Regionalism: Further Reflections on the Church in Late Medieval Norwich', in J.A.F. Thomson (ed.), *Towns and Townspeople in the Fifteenth Century* (Gloucester, 1987), pp. 129–47 and David Aers, 'Altars of Power: Reflections on Eamon Duffy's *The Stripping of the Altars: Traditional Religion in England, 1400–1580*', *Literature & History* 3rd Series, 3 (1994): 90–105.

[3]   For example Norman P. Tanner, *The Church in Late Medieval Norwich* (Toronto, 1984); Robert Lutton, *Lollardy and Orthodox Religion in Pre-Reformation England: Reconstructing Piety* (Woodbridge, 2006); Andrew D. Brown, *Popular Piety in Late Medieval England: the Diocese of Salisbury, 1250–1550* (Oxford, 1995).

[4]   For example Duffy, *Altars*; Christopher Marsh, *Popular Religion in Sixteenth-Century England* (Basingstoke–London, 1998).

[5]   A.G. Dickens, 'The Early Expansion of Protestantism in England, 1520–1558', *Archiv für Reformationsgeschichte*, 78 (1987): 187–90, 197–213; Peter Marshall, *Reformation England, 1480–1642* (London, 2003), pp. 82–3.

[6]   Malcolm Lambert, *Medieval Heresy: Popular Movements from the Gregorian Reform to the Reformation* (3rd edition, Oxford, 2002), pp. 294–300.

local Lollard networks provided a platform or springboard for early Protestantism is, however, a matter of ongoing debate. Richard Rex, in his recent book *The Lollards*, for example, has sought to demolish the view that Lollards in any significant way provided converts to evangelicalism and a ready-made infrastructure for the dissemination of new doctrines.[7]

According to Rex, '... the vast majority of early English Protestants about whom anything is known ... came not from Lollard, but from devout Catholic backgrounds'.[8] Experiences of conversion through reception of Lutheran theology were one of the defining features of early Protestantism in the 1520s and 1530s. However, one of the things this chapter seeks to explore is how transitions in orthodox religious culture may have helped bring individuals to dramatic moments of transformation as well as aiding less violent journeys from old beliefs to new.[9] Without some indication of their specific content, terms such as 'devout' and 'Catholic' merely beg the question.

Christopher Marsh provides a useful summary of the factors that are generally accepted as having ensured that Protestantism flourished in certain areas or contributed to the impression of the geographical pattern described above:

> ... proximity to continental influences; a better supply of Protestant preachers; higher literacy levels; and more advanced economic networks, which provided ready-made channels for the dissemination of new ideas. ... the more vigorous official investigations that seem to have occurred in the counties closer to London, ... that may make the pattern look clearer than it actually was. Some of the same factors help to explain why, even within the southern and eastern counties, Protestant forms of dissent developed most readily in towns (a Europe-wide correlation), and in rural areas characterised by dispersed settlement and proto-industry. The link between the cloth trade and radical dissent has been noted many times.[10]

What is, of course, absent from this set of explanations is geographical variation in orthodox piety. Nevertheless, Marsh does discuss the potential appeal of Protestant doctrines to so-called orthodox Catholics and the continuities that helped pave the way for a gradual cultural and religious transition in the sixteenth century.[11] There is a growing body of work that questions the degree of attachment to some aspects of traditional religion and seeks to identify continuities between pre- and post-Reformation religious life that were not subject to, or survived, the changes

---

[7]   Richard Rex, *The Lollards* (Basingstoke, 2000), pp. 115–42.

[8]   Ibid., pp. 119, 133–7.

[9]   Richard Rex, 'The Friars in the English Reformation', in P. Marshall and A. Ryrie (eds), *The Beginnings of English Protestantism* (Cambridge, 2002) pp. 38–59; Peter Marshall, 'Evangelical Conversion in the Reign of Henry VIII', pp. 14–37, esp. 36–7 and Peter Marshall and Alec Ryrie, 'Protestantisms and their Beginnings', p. 9 all in Marshall and Ryrie, *The Beginnings of English Protestantism*.

[10]   Marsh, *Popular Religion*, p. 159.

[11]   Ibid., pp. 198–201.

imposed by state-sponsored reform. This has begun to sensitively identify gradual pre-Reformation shifts in lay religious practice and belief that, consciously or not, anticipated reform, and reformist critiques of some of the central pillars of traditional religion that may have met with significant support across the countryside.[12]

Kent and the Reformation

Kent is treated as a special case in the historiography of the Reformation. The county is seen as the most responsive in England to evangelical reform and the most precociously Protestant.[13] Explanations for Kent's rapid acceptance of Protestantism have looked largely to the influence of Archbishop Cranmer and his promotion of evangelical preaching with the cooperation of a sympathetic group of magistrates. They suggest a model of cultural dissemination and transformation that was largely clerically driven and worked from the top down. Lollardy in Kent, at least more recently, has been largely dismissed as an important factor in this transition. Discussion of the influence of orthodox pieties on local responses to reform is limited to impressionistic statements that demand further investigation. For example, the collapse in offerings at Becket's shrine at Canterbury by the 1530s was, according to Michael Zell, indicative of the limited role of the saints and their images in the spiritual lives of a significant number of people, particularly in the towns of Kent and on the Weald.[14]

Peter Clark's still definitive account of the Reformation in Kent presents 'popular anti-clericalism' as a key factor in the county's relatively rapid and favourable response to reformist ideas. Anti-clericalism could lead to 'theological radicalism' or 'doctrinal unorthodoxy' in time but Clark does not describe how this transition occurred. Lollardy played only a minor role in the establishment of mainstream Protestantism and was, in Clark's view, more important as an antecedent to the more radical religious groups and networks that he identifies as

---

[12] See, for example, Margaret Aston, *England's Iconoclasts, I: Laws Against Images* (Oxford, 1988); Peter Marshall, *Beliefs and the Dead in Reformation England* (Oxford, 2002); Susan Wabuda, *Preaching During the English Reformation* (Cambridge, 2002); Christine Peters, *Patterns of Piety: Women, Gender and Religion in Late Medieval and Reformation England* (Cambridge, 2003).

[13] For example Christopher Haigh, review of Margaret Bowker, *The Henrician Reformation. The Diocese of Lincoln under John Longland, 1521–1547* (Cambridge, 1981), *English Historical Review*, 48 (1983): 371; Christopher Haigh, 'The Recent Historiography of the English Reformation', *Historical Journal*, 25 (1982): 995–1007.

[14] Diarmaid MacCulloch, *Tudor Church Militant: Edward VI and the Protestant Reformation* (London, 1999), p. 112; Rex, *Lollards*, p. 122. Michael Zell, 'The Coming of Religious Reform', in Michael Zell (ed.), *Early Modern Kent, 1540–1640* (London, 2000), pp. 178–9, 183. For a recent attempt at a more detailed study of the Wealden town of Tenterden see Lutton, *Lollardy*.

the forerunners of separatist Nonconformity in Kent. With regard to Lollardy and Lutheranism, he states: '… the two strains of reform doctrine never completely converged even after the Reformation' and geographical continuities between Lollardy and Protestantism in areas such as the Weald were due more to good communication links and '… the absence of effective ecclesiastical policing …' than continuity of persons. Wealden Lollards are portrayed as 'small peasant farmers and artisans', Lutherans as 'substantial men or clergy'. Protestant ideas are described as '… filtering down to the local level …' and as moving from the more radical towns to the more conservative countryside. The significance of pre-Reformation pieties for the course of reform is, for Clark, confined to the resistance of 'grass-roots' Catholicism, which became increasingly rural, and drew support from 'structural conservatism'.[15] That this model of change requires some correction is suggested by Alec Ryrie's recent re-examination of Cranmer's investigations into heresy in 1543. Whilst this confirms the strength of clerical leadership in the early evangelical conventicles in Kent, it also highlights their radical iconoclasm and suggests the interaction of indigenous dissent, perhaps of Lollard origin or influenced by Lollard ideas, with newer teachings; a model of change proposed some time ago by J.F. Davis.[16]

The Weald is the one extensive area of Kent that is consistently seen as host to religious dissent and radicalism, from Lollardy through to seventeenth- and eighteenth-century Nonconformity. There is less agreement among historians as to the reasons for this apparent propensity for radical dissent or how to relate it to the progress and embedding of Protestantism in the county.[17] To problematize this further Clark describes the Wealden market town of Cranbrook as a conservative stronghold in the 1530s and early 1540s.[18] As a result, Duffy refers to Cranbrook as 'a bastion of traditional religion' in these years and, in turn, Rex writes that '…

---

[15]   Peter Clark, *English Provincial Society from the Reformation to the Revolution: Religion, Politics and Society in Kent, 1500–1640* (Hassocks, 1977), pp. 29–31, 38, 44, 48, 59–62, 77, 101, 177.

[16]   Alec Ryrie, *The Gospel and Henry VIII: Evangelicals in the Early English Reformation* (Cambridge, 2003), pp. 223–38; J.F. Davis, *Heresy and Reformation in the South-East of England, 1520–1559* (London, 1983). See also Zell, 'Coming of Religious Reform', passim, but esp. pp. 180, 183–5, 190, 202 and 'The Establishment of a Protestant Church', in Zell, *Early Modern Kent*, pp. 214–18.

[17]   See, for example, Patrick Collinson, 'Cranbrook and the Fletchers: Popular and Unpopular Religion in the Kentish Weald', in Collinson, *Godly People: Essays in Protestantism and Puritanism* (London, 1983), pp. 399–428; Alan Everitt, 'Nonconformity in Country Parishes', *The Agricultural History Review*, 18, *Land, Church and People: Essays Presented to Professor H. P. R. Finberg*, ed. J. Thirsk (1970 supplement): 178–99; Davis, J.F., 'Lollard Survival and the Textile Industry in the South-East of England', in G.J. Cuming (ed.), *SCH* 3, (1966): 191–201; Christopher Hill, 'From Lollards to Levellers', in *Collected Essays of Christopher Hill*, II: *Religion and Politics in Seventeenth-Century England* (Brighton, 1986), pp. 89–116.

[18]   Clark, *English Provincial Society*, pp. 59–77.

its strong pre-Reformation attachment to Catholicism was at least as significant for its future as its Lollard tradition'.[19] Both neither mention nor explain how, according to Clark, Cranbrook had become a radical stronghold by 1552 and how it could have been a Lollard centre thirty years earlier.

This chapter arises partly out of a desire to begin to explore these more perplexing contradictions in the narratives of reformation change. By comparing pieties in the two principal Wealden centres of Cranbrook and Tenterden *c.* 1450–1640, I hope to shed more light on their relative religious trajectories and their possible underlying causes. In addition to comparing the overall profiles of piety in the two parishes, through analysis of religious giving in wills and churchwardens' accounts, the chapter investigates the pieties of different resident families in order to explore their relative diversities of practice over time. This provides a framework within which to take a fresh look at the progress of reform and reaction and continuities of piety in the two centres. This is not, therefore, intended to be a history of pre-Reformation piety and the Reformation in the Weald, let alone Kent, but one step towards the better understanding of the dynamics of piety in late medieval and early modern England.

Cranbrook and Tenterden: Geography, Demography and Economy

Cranbrook and Tenterden were the two most important market towns in the Kentish Weald, and were both exceptionally large parishes at 10,400 and 8,500 acres respectively (see Map 1.1). Lying ten miles apart, they presided over distinct but interlocking hinterlands: Cranbrook in the central and Tenterden in the eastern parts of the Weald. Both had sizeable urban cores and a number of geographically scattered satellite settlements some of which, like Small Hythe, Tenterden's estuarine port, were important centres in their own right. Perhaps half of the total population of Cranbrook parish resided in 'Cranbrook town' itself and this fraction may have decreased over the course of the sixteenth century as population growth filled up suburban and outlying settlements. Both parishes probably hosted rising populations from the late fifteenth century, which accelerated in the early sixteenth but their demographic experiences were very different. Tenterden's population was around 1,300 in the 1560s and remained stable or even slightly decreased over the course of the sixteenth century. This was due to a net 'natural decrease', in part because of disease stemming from the parish's position on the edge of Walland and Romney marshes. This was only offset by in-migration from its hinterland. With greater opportunities for industrial employment alongside agriculture and less affected by disease, Cranbrook experienced rapid population growth up to the last decades of the sixteenth century when the decline of the broadcloth industry and

---

[19]   Duffy, *Altars*, p. 479; Rex, *Lollards*, p. 122. For criticism of Clark's approach see Collinson, 'Cranbrook and the Fletchers', p. 407.

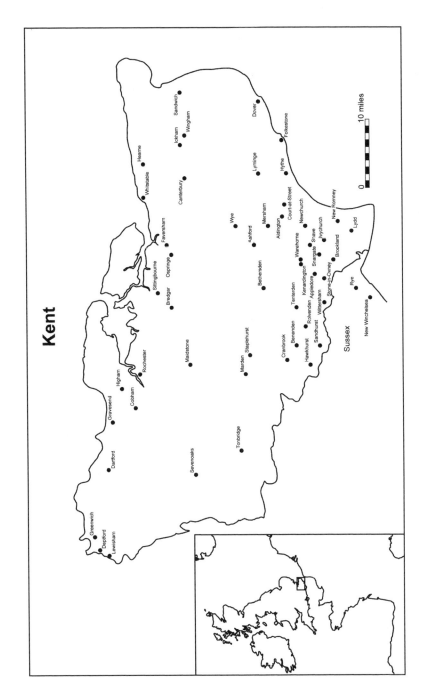

Map 1.1   Showing Locations in Kent (kindly drawn by John Hills)

structural factors may have begun to put a check on family formation and birth rates, and out-migration may have overtaken in-migration. Its parochial population numbered around 2,000 by the 1560s and may have been as large as 3,500 by the 1630s.[20]

More urbanized than Tenterden, by 1600 the population of Cranbrook town as opposed to the parish as a whole was approximately 1,500 and very similar to Dartford and Tonbridge, but smaller than larger centres like Maidstone, Dover, Sandwich and Gravesend. With around 1,000 inhabitants Tenterden town was more comparable to Sevenoaks.[21] Cranbrook was the most densely populated parish in the Weald of Kent by the middle of the sixteenth century and exceptionally wealthy. It was at the centre of Kent's woollen cloth industry, was also host to iron production and was the 'capital' of the administrative unit known as the 'Seven Hundreds' of the Weald with its own leet and civil suit courts.[22]

Tenterden remained the second most important centre of wealth in the Weald next to Cranbrook. Its chief economic role was as a regional agricultural marketing centre redistributing goods flowing in and out of the Weald mainly through Small Hythe and Rye on the coast. To a greater extent than Cranbrook, agriculture formed the backbone of the parish's economy. This was centred on stock-raising and fattening, mainly of cattle, increasingly for the London market. Some truly large fortunes were made in the sixteenth century by large Tenterden graziers, but compared to the semi-industrialized parishes of the central Weald there were fewer opportunities for families to become established in Tenterden.[23] Due to its corporate status as a limb of the Cinque Ports Tenterden was exempt from the jurisdiction of county magistrates. Large noble or gentry estates dominated neither parish and the Church owned little local land compared to other parts of Kent.[24]

Religious Dissent and Responses to Reform

Tenterden was the most important centre in a tradition of Lollard heresy on the Weald that may have been continuous from the 1420s to the Reformation. Cranbrook, on the other hand, does not appear to have been as central to early

---

[20]   Michael Zell, *Industry in the Countryside: Wealden Society in the Sixteenth Century* (Cambridge, 1994), pp. 52–87. Jacqueline Bower, 'Kent Towns, 1540–1640', in Zell, *Early Modern Kent*, pp. 146–50, 161, 168; on Small Hythe see Lutton, *Lollardy*, ch. 3.

[21]   W.K. Jordan, 'Social Institutions in Kent, 1480–1660: A Study of the Changing Pattern of Social Aspiration', *AC*, 75 (1961): 4; Bower, 'Kent Towns', p. 160.

[22]   Zell, *Industry*, pp. 149–50, 153–88; Jordan, 'Social Institutions': 2; Patricia Hyde and Michael Zell, 'Governing the County', in Zell, *Early Modern Kent*, p. 10; Jane Andrewes, 'Industries in Kent, *c.* 1500–1640', in Zell, *Early Modern Kent*, p. 126.

[23]   Zell, *Industry*, pp. 100, 107, 116–21, 147–50.

[24]   Hyde and Zell, 'Governing the County', p. 10; Zell, 'A Wood–Pasture Agrarian Regime: The Kentish Weald in the Sixteenth Century', *Southern History*, 7 (1985): 72; Zell, *Industry*, pp. 30–31.

Lollardy.[25] The heretical networks and conventicles detailed in Archbishop William Warham's investigations into heresy in 1511–12 involved 53 suspects of whom 14 were from Tenterden and another nine came from adjacent parishes. Seven suspects came from Cranbrook and another eight lived in nearby Staplehurst. A substantial majority were, therefore, from the Weald and Tenterden remained at the centre of a network of active dissenters dating from the 1480s. As in other areas where Lollardy was investigated, family and household connections as well as links through trade and artisanal activity and the work of a small number of peripatetic teachers were all important in building a network of dissent. It appears that these Lollards continued to participate in parish religion and some, or at least their kinsfolk, were involved in parish administration and local government at Tenterden. As was the case in other areas of long-term continuity in dissent, it seems that there was widespread sympathy for, or at least tolerance of, Lollardy on the Weald.[26]

The recorded beliefs of these suspects are typically formulaic and shaped by the process of inquisition, but their general character was sacramentarian, anti-sacerdotal and against pilgrimage and the cult of saints. There were, however, no outright attacks on the Church and the expression of beliefs is generally more moderate in tone compared to the Norwich heresy trials of 1428–30 for example.[27]

I have described responses to Henrician reform at Tenterden in detail elsewhere. Zell suggests that '… religious conflict was probably endemic …' in the parish by the 1530s, but this appears to have been limited largely to friction between reformist townsfolk and conservative clergy. The town seems to have entertained radical preaching, but the conservative retrenchment at the end of Henry's reign appears to have made this more difficult. Tenterden was, of course, a limb of the Cinque Port of Rye and its close relations with what was the most precociously Protestant town in East Sussex may have helped foster the cause for reform.[28] However, the parish's incumbent from 1546 to 1555, Dr Richard

[25] See Lutton, *Lollardy*, pp. 149–62; Anne Hudson, *The Premature Reformation: Wycliffite Texts and Lollard History* (Oxford, 1988), p. 121; J.A.F. Thomson, *The Later Lollards, 1414–1520* (Oxford, 1965), p. 175; Margaret Aston, *Lollards and Reformers: Images and Literacy in Late Medieval Religion* (London, 1984), pp. 29, 78–80; *Register of Henry Chichele*, ed. E. F. Jacob (Canterbury and York Series, vol. 47, 1947), vol. 4, pp. 297–301.

[26] *Kent Heresy Proceedings, 1511–12*, ed. Norman P. Tanner (Kent Records, vol. 26, 1997); Lutton, *Lollardy*, pp. 162–71; Thomson, *Later Lollards*, p. 191; Hudson, *Premature Reformation*, p. 121; D. Plumb, 'The Social and Economic Status of the Later Lollards', in Margaret Spufford (ed.), *The World of Rural Dissenters, 1520–1725* (Cambridge, 1995), pp. 103–31.

[27] Anne Hudson, 'The Examination of Lollards', *BIHR*, 46 (1973): 145–59; *Kent Heresy Proceedings, 1511–12*; *Heresy Trials in the Diocese of Norwich, 1428–31*, ed. Norman P. Tanner (Camden 4th Series, 20, 1977).

[28] Graham Mayhew, 'The Progress of the English Reformation in East Sussex, 1530–1559: The Evidence from Wills', *Southern History*, 5 (1983): 50.

Thornden, was religiously conservative. Hugh Price, Cranbrook's vicar from 1534 to 1554 appears to have been non-resident.[29]

The evidence for Cranbrook's conservatism in the early 1540s is, on further examination, not nearly as robust as has been suggested. On 4 August 1542, the Protestant Thomas Dawby, formerly curate of Lenham, had a conversation with one Alexander Plotte at Sittingbourne who pointed out that images still stood in his parish church. Dawby responded by saying 'your curate is more knave'. At this, Plotte put the rhetorical question: 'Why do they stand in Cranebroke then? Seeing that there dwelleth worshipful men, the King's justices, and, as I think, some of them be of your King's council? And by that they are now building of a goodly roodloft'. Why did Plotte choose Cranbrook to make his point if the town was known only as a conservative stronghold? Was it because, as he implied, conservative justices such as Walter Hendley and John Baker, who exemplified the direction in royal policy by 1542 that would wrong-foot the likes of Dawby, wielded considerable influence there despite (and perhaps because of) the presence of dissenters in the town?[30] Of the Kentish Wealden parishes involved in the 1511–12 heresy trials, J.F. Davis sees Cranbrook as having the '… most enduring tradition of dissent …'. The fact that Tyndale's agent Richard Harmon was from Cranbrook and had supporters there in the late 1520s, Cromwell led a commission into sacramentaries there in 1539 and the parish fostered Puritanism later in the century all point, according to Davis, to a dissenting tradition.[31]

As we shall see, conservatism does appear to have been stronger among certain elements of the population at Cranbrook than in Tenterden and the town may have been more deeply divided along religious lines by the early 1540s and perhaps earlier. Cranmer's 1543 dossier finishes with a note stating: 'These towns following are specially to be remembered that in them be placed learned men, with sufficient stipends: Sandwich, Dover, Folkestone, Ashford, Tenterden, Cranbrook, Faversham, Hearne, Whistable, Marden, Maidstone, Wye, Wingham' – all places of strategic importance to the cause of reform and sites of significant religious controversy.[32]

Archdeacon Nicholas Harpsfield's exacting visitation of the diocese of Canterbury in 1557 is generally seen as indicative of the relatively rapid and rigorous enforcement of Henrician and Edwardian reform in Kent and also of the wide extent of Catholic renewal by this date.[33] Cranbrook church appears to have

---

[29] Lutton, *Lollardy*, pp. 202–7; Zell, 'Coming of Religious Reform', pp. 194–5; Collinson, 'Cranbrook and the Fletchers', p. 406.

[30] *LP*, vol. 18/2, 546 (pp. 315–16); Clark, *English Provincial Society*, p. 62; Duffy, *Altars*, p. 436.

[31] Davis, *Heresy and Reformation*, p. 222.

[32] *LP*, vol. 18/2, 546 (p. 378).

[33] Duffy, *Altars*, pp. 555–64; Christopher Haigh, *English Reformations. Religion, Politics, and Society Under the Tudors* (Oxford, 1993), pp. 210–12; Marshall, *Beliefs and*

been relatively well-equipped, but despite this the vicar was commanded, as at Sandhurst, Hawkhurst and Benenden, not to bury anyone who refused to be confessed, receive the Sacrament at Easter or creep to the cross. A regimen of confession, receipt of the Sacrament and procession was imposed on the whole parish. Four men, including James Philpot (who may have been related to the Tenterden martyr John Philpot) were to be apprehended and sent to Canterbury.[34] The impression is of a relatively healthy Catholic devotional life, but also of a significant radical presence.

In contrast, Tenterden seems to have done away with a large part of the physical fabric of Catholic devotion and not replaced it by 1557. It fell within the ten per cent or so of parishes which reported more than one serious deficiency.[35] John Bailie, now of Rye, and George Castlen had pulled down the 'forefronnte' of the Roode loft, presumably removing the carved images of the Rood, Mary and John and other saints. A number of items were not replaced and the Rood loft was not rebuilt by the deadlines set by the visitation.[36] Tenterden appears to have more readily embraced Edwardian reform and resisted attempts to rebuild Catholic devotional life. According to the visitation return, it was not subjected to the same strict policing as Cranbrook, but with four heresy suspects burnt by 1557 and a long history of dissent, the parish was perhaps already under close scrutiny.

Five of the Marian martyrs came from Tenterden and three were from Cranbrook, where Queen Mary's commission into heresy sat. Suspects from seven other Wealden parishes were also burnt for their beliefs. These beliefs were far from uniform and suggest the complex interplay of Lollardy, Protestant evangelicalism and pre-Reformation orthodox pieties. Davis arguably overstates their sacramentarian nature, which he sees as due to the enduring influence of Lollardy, and underestimates the impact of Lutheran-inspired Protestant ideas as well as the transmission of older pieties.[37]

John Philpot of Tenterden's avowal that '... faith doth not justify without works neither do works without faith' appears to rule out Lutheran credentials, but whilst Luther's doctrine of justification by faith may have been understood and

---

the Dead, p. 98. For a less optimistic assessment of the extent of Catholic renewal by 1557 see Zell, 'Establishment of a Protestant Church', pp. 210–13, 224–5.

[34] *Archdeacon Harpsfield's Visitation, 1557*, part I, transcribed by W. Sharp and ed. Rev. L.E. Whatmore (London, Publications of the Catholic Record Society vol. xlv, 1950), pp. 182–3; Duffy, *Altars*, pp. 555–63.

[35] Haigh, *English Reformations*, p. 212.

[36] *Archdeacon Harpsfield's Visitation, 1557*, pp. 134–5. The items that had not been carried out by the time of re-inspection have the word 'non' or 'nihil' in a different hand inserted above them. Compare with similarly slow progress at nearby Bethersden and Hawkhurst: Zell, 'Establishment of a Protestant Church', pp. 227–8.

[37] Davis, *Heresy and Reformation*, pp. 38, 107–29, 149, 222; John Foxe, *Actes and Monuments of these Latter and Perilous Dayes* (London, 1583), vol. 2, pp. 1688, 1858–59, 1954, 1970; *Church Life in Kent being Church Court Records of the Canterbury Diocese, 1559–1565*, ed. Arthur J. Willis (London–Chichester, 1975), p. 61.

seized upon by some, it was the idea of Scripture alone and the assault on the clergy and traditional religion that was so attractive to the majority of early followers of evangelical teaching. Philpot's beliefs were neither unequivocally Lutheran nor restricted to earlier Lollard thought or teaching, but they were certainly evangelical and included, like those of John Lomas another martyr from Tenterden, adherence to the supreme authority of Scripture.[38]

Both Philpot and Adriana Vynall, also from Tenterden, were less sweepingly sacramentarian than earlier Wealden Lollards. Philpot's views that it was unlawful for the sacraments to be administered in any tongue other than English, and that the Eucharist should be administered in both kinds, speak less of a lingering Lollard tradition than experience of evangelical reform. Philpot believed that saints were to be prayed to, contrary to the opinion of most Lollards and the Edwardian reforms, whereas Adriana Vynall saw no value in calling on saints. Both seem to have believed in the value of prayers for the dead. Lollardy was largely silent on the subject of purgatory, whereas English evangelicals had launched a wholesale attack on the doctrine. Their beliefs suggest a selective reception of evangelical teaching and the endurance of deep-seated practices and ideas about the afterlife rather than strict adherence to a Lollard or Protestant programme or creed. Idiosyncratically heterogeneous, they cannot be classified as an identifiable and coherent body of doctrine.[39]

The nature of the contribution of earlier radicalism to Wealden Puritanism remains uncertain. At Cranbrook, the evidence points to there being no more than a Puritan minority by the 1570s and 1580s. However, a wide variety of testamentary charitable giving and bequests for funeral sermons in the late sixteenth and early seventeenth centuries suggests that moderate indigenous pieties were strong enough in their own right to sustain longstanding conventions of commemoration that were slowly moulded into Protestant forms, in ways which may have borne little relation to the attempts of Cranbrook's vicars '… to correct and convert the rest of the community …'. Not everything 'godly' was Puritan at Cranbrook.[40]

---

[38]   Davis, *Heresy and Reformation*, pp. 124–6; Foxe, *Actes and Monuments of these Latter and Perilous Dayes* (London, 1583), vol. 2, p. 1688; Andrew Pettegree, *Reformation and the Culture of Persuasion* (Cambridge, 2005), pp. 25–30, 168–70; Hudson, *Premature Reformation*, pp. 494–507. See also A.G. Dickens, *Lollards and Protestants in the Diocese of York* (London, 1959), pp. 243–5 and other references in Hudson, above, at p. 499 and Zell, 'Coming of Religious Reform', p. 181 and 'Establishment of a Protestant Church', pp. 217, 230.

[39]   Davis, *Heresy and Reformation*, pp. 124–6; Zell, 'Establishment of a Protestant Church', p. 209. *Kent Heresy Proceedings*, p. 46; Hudson, *Premature Reformation*, pp. 289, 302, 309–10, 499, 504; Duffy, *Altars*, pp. 379–477; Marshall, *Beliefs and the Dead*, pp. 47–123.

[40]   Bequests to the poor and for sermons were much more diverse and better resourced at Cranbrook than Collinson suggests: 'Cranbrook and the Fletchers', pp. 413–14.

Giving for sermons – whether of the more radical sort or not – and giving of Bibles or other religious books is even less visible at Tenterden.[41] Testamentary evidence alone is insufficient to identify continuing or emerging strands of radicalism, but there is a relative lack of engagement with charitable giving and preaching in the Tenterden wills. Religious culture at Tenterden was, on the whole, less richly endowed and supported from *c.* 1450 compared to Cranbrook and so the later wills may merely reflect a relatively lower level of long-term investment in institutional religion. Perhaps more radical parishioners deliberately shunned testamentary pious gestures in order to avoid any suggestion of trust in their spiritual merits, but this is an argument wholly from silence. It may be significant that whereas Cranbrook parish maintained relatively moderate incumbents in these decades, parochial religion at Tenterden was shaped from 1571 to 1615 by its Puritan vicar George Ely.[42] His presence in Tenterden for almost 45 years suggests that he may have found and fashioned an environment conducive to his radicalism.

It is clear that Cranbrook, Tenterden and other Wealden parishes were home to Nonconformist activities of a Puritan flavour, including conventicling, in the late sixteenth and early seventeenth centuries. Although this seems to have intensified around 1600, separatism proper – in the sense of withdrawal from parochial church services – did not develop until the 1630s, perhaps at Tenterden before it did at Cranbrook. Cranbrook was one of the few parishes to develop Congregationalism before 1660 outside of Canterbury and, like Tenterden and other Wealden parishes, saw the establishment of a Baptist church and Quakerism. Collinson notes the similarities between the moralistic and socially exclusive ethic of the Wealden Marian martyrs and this new separatist nonconformity, but, as is the case elsewhere, it is treacherously difficult to demonstrate meaningful connections over time between different manifestations of dissent. The ever-suggestive geographic continuities call for new approaches.[43]

---

[41] Collinson's analysis of Cranbrook probate inventories and wills from the late sixteenth and early seventeenth centuries established that only 17 per cent of households appear to have owned Bibles: Ibid., pp. 414, 417.

[42] A.H. Taylor, 'The Rectors and Vicars of St Mildred's, Tenterden. With an Appendix', *AC*, 31 (1915): 207–24, p. 221.

[43] Robert J. Acheson, 'The Development of Religious Separatism in the Diocese of Canterbury, 1590–1660', unpublished Ph.D Thesis, University of Kent at Canterbury (1983), pp. 10–14, 29–30, 34–43, 80–97, 141–271; Collinson, 'Cranbrook and the Fletchers', pp. 410, 418, 424–8; Patrick Collinson, 'Critical Conclusion' in Spufford (ed.), *World of Rural Dissenters*, pp. 393–6 and Margaret Spufford, 'The Importance of Religion in the Sixteenth and Seventeenth Centuries' in ibid., pp. 23–37 and Nesta Evans, 'The Descent of Dissenters in the Chiltern Hundreds', in ibid., pp. 288–308.

Comparing Pre-Reformation Pieties

Comparison of the proportions of lay testators giving to religious institutions and activities in Cranbrook and Tenterden compared to other centres in Kent and elsewhere to *c.* 1535 is shown in Table 1.1. In most categories the proportions of Cranbrook testators who gave matched or exceeded those in other places, including the larger towns. In giving to the religious orders, however, Cranbrook was more similar to other smaller Kent towns. Tenterden's testators, on the other hand, endowed fewer chantries and although they gave quite regularly and generously for funerals and obsequies, bequests to secular clergy were conspicuously low and the religious orders were even more peripheral than at Cranbrook. The most marked contrast was in devotion to saints, reflected in the very different proportions of testators leaving money for votive lights. Seventeen different saints or advocations of a single saint were mentioned at Tenterden, twenty-seven at Cranbrook.[44]

Levels of giving also differed markedly right across the range of religious bequests: on average Cranbrook's testators devoted £6 7s 10d to religious giving in their wills, over twice as much as Tenterden's. There was a general decline in pious giving in the Tenterden wills, 1500–35. In contrast, there was a steady increase at Cranbrook from an average of £4 6s 11d prior to 1470 to £7 17s 7d, 1520–35. Cranbrook's churchwardens' accounts also indicate extensive investment by parishioners in the fabric of the parish church in the early 1520s.[45] Tenterden's rapid decline in testamentary chantry provision together with a marked rise in funerary ritual in the early sixteenth century has been found elsewhere, but not to such a marked degree.[46] By the 1520s, only around a tenth of testators arranged for chantries compared to over a third prior to 1500 and the last endowment before 1535 was in 1527.[47] Arrangements for funerals and subsequent commemorations rose in popularity from about a quarter to almost three-quarters of testators by the 1520s. Belief in purgatory appears to have remained strong, but this trend suggests the financial burden of chantries was becoming less sustainable in the context of early sixteenth–century debates about appropriate forms of intercession for the dead and criticisms of private masses. Obits were cheaper and offered a number of incentives absent from the chantry, including a greater degree of lay control and participation and the integration of a range of good works, including charitable giving.[48]

---

[44]   The number of saints mentioned in the Cranbrook wills is based on a survey of all 231 wills for the parish, 1455–1535 and not just those for selected decades.

[45]   CKS, PRC P100/5/1.

[46]   For example at Sandwich and, to a lesser extent, Bury St Edmunds: Dinn, 'Popular Religion', pp. 539, 714.

[47]   There were only two further endowments: in 1535, by James Ilchynden (PRC 17/20/234) only coming into effect in the event of heirs not inheriting; the second in 1540 by John Austen (PRC 17/22/187).

[48]   Lutton, *Lollardy*, pp. 55–67.

At Cranbrook, the funeral and obsequies also increased in popularity, but, in contrast to Tenterden, although chantries declined in popularity from over 50 per cent prior to the 1470s to a quarter of wills 1500–09, there was resurgence in foundation with over a third of testators making such arrangements 1520–35. These endowments continued right into the early 1540s, some 15 years after they had all but ceased in Tenterden.

Other changes in testamentary giving at Tenterden in the early sixteenth century signal the lack of popularity of some aspects of devotion and point to the emergence of reformist pieties. The last gift to the religious orders was in 1518, and there was no ongoing loyalty to the friars found in other towns up to the Dissolution including, to some degree, Cranbrook.[49] At Tenterden, there was a decline in giving to church fabric from around 1520 to less than a fifth of testators from a fairly steady proportion of around a half during the seventy years prior to this point. At Cranbrook, the proportion making such gifts declined from 61 per cent, 1455 69, to only 22 per cent, 1500–09. However, it rose again, in a similar fashion to chantry foundation, to 46 per cent during the years 1520–35.[50]

Only 8 per cent of the Cranbrook wills from selected decades lack religious bequests (apart from obligatory payments for 'tithes forgotten') compared to 20 per cent at Tenterden, where there were continuities within households and between family generations in frugal testamentary practice and it was a significant element of the parish's piety. At Cranbrook, it was much more marginal and seems to have resulted largely from a lack of cash resources at death.

Saints that were well-established within lay devotion throughout pre-Reformation England by the late fifteenth century such as the Virgin Mary and St Katherine waned in importance at Tenterden by the first decade of the sixteenth century. In Cranbrook, on the other hand, they continued to attract bequests into the early 1530s and new Marian devotions such as Our Lady of Pity incorporating images of the *Pietà* were established earlier and became more popular than at Tenterden.[51]

In the latter parish new saints such as George, Erasmus and Crispin and Crispinianus appeared from 1500–30, suggesting that they might succeed the older figures in the pious preoccupations of parishioners.[52] None of these new images and devotions really caught on however, all but St Erasmus being

---

[49] Lutton, *Lollardy*, pp. 80–82.

[50] This type of giving also fell at Colchester 1500–19 but recovered after 1520: Higgs, 'Lay Piety', pp. 220–23. These gifts increased markedly in the early sixteenth century at Bury St Edmunds: Dinn, 'Popular Religion', pp. 405, 408. At Sandwich giving fell over the period but not as sharply as at Tenterden.

[51] Duffy, *Altars*, pp. 38, 260–62, 332, 382, 419, 436; Marks, *Image and Devotion*, pp. 123–43.

[52] William A. Christian Jr, *Person and God in a Spanish Valley* (1972, this edn Princeton, New Jersey–Guildford, 1989), pp. 64–5, 82–3, at p. 64. See also Marks, *Image and Devotion*, pp. 86–120.

Table 1.1 Percentages of Testators Making Bequests in Cranbrook, Tenterden and Other Centres, c. 1450– c. 1535

	Cranbrook (%)	Tenterden (%)	Sandwich (%)	Canterbury (%)	Dover (%)	Hythe (%)	New Romney (%)	Norwich (%)	Bury St Edmunds (%)	Colchester (%)
Temporary and permanent chantries	36	24	At least 23	–	–	–	–	40	–	–
Funerals and obsequies	61	46	28	47	38	23	15	67	18	–
Church fabric	39	39	39	–	37	52	35	–	19	40 (1518–32)
Religious orders	11	6	30	42	7	6	5	At least 47	–	–
Secular clergy	23	3	14	–	–	–	–	–	–	63 (1485–1529)

Lights	49	15	At least 31	53	76	37	63	33	–	6.5 (1518–32)
Images	5	5	20	–	–	–	–	–	–	–
Jesus Mass	30 (1500–35)	36 (1513–35)	Less than 10	–	–	–	–	12	9	–
The poor	20	21	30	–	–	–	–	–	–	32 (1485–1529)

Sources: Tenterden: 263 Canterbury archdeaconry and consistory court and PCC wills, 1449–1535; Cranbrook: 121 wills 1455–69, 1480–89, 1500–1509 and 1520–35; Sandwich (396 wills), c. 1450–1539, Canterbury (887), Dover (154), Hythe (251) and New Romney (103) all for 1470–1529, figures kindly supplied by Sheila Sweetinburgh and see, also, Sheila Sweetinburgh, *The Role of the Hospital in Medieval England. Gift Giving and the Spiritual Economy* (Dublin, 2004), pp. 169, 221; Norwich, 1440–1532: Tanner, *Church in Norwich*, pp. 220–21; Bury St Edmunds, 1449–1530: Robert B. Dinn, 'Popular Religion in Late Medieval Bury St Edmunds', unpublished Ph.D Thesis, University of Manchester (1990), pp. 195–200, 405, 408, 539; Colchester, 1518–32: Laquita M.A. Higgs, 'Lay Piety in the Borough of Colchester, 1485–1558', unpublished PhD Thesis, University of Michigan (1983), pp. 218–23, 267; Colchester, 1485–1529: Laquita M.A. Higgs, *Godliness and Governance in Tudor Colchester* (Michigan, 1998), p. 89.

mentioned only once or twice. At Cranbrook, succession worked alongside a process of cumulative addition and increasing diversity of images and devotions. Some new saints failed to attract more than one or two bequests but other innovations such as Ss Anthony, Michael and Blaise were more successful and sustained devotion into the 1520s. The years 1490 to 1510 saw the most concentrated innovation with eleven saints attracting testamentary bequests for the first time and giving to lights soaring to a pre-Reformation peak of 75 per cent of wills in the years 1500–09. This decreased to 39 per cent 1520–35, but this was still far higher than the 15 per cent of Tenterden testators who gave to lights during these years. Diversification was less concentrated and came later at Tenterden, suggesting that new fashions in devotion took longer to make an impact. No new saints seem to have been established in either town after the late 1520s, which suggests a reticence to invest, perhaps because attitudes were changing towards devotion to the saints and the place of images in religious practice. The last mention of images in the Tenterden wills was in 1522.[53]

The introduction and reception of the Mass of the Holy Name of Jesus in the two parishes was also different in a number of important ways. The Mass of the Holy Name, or Jesus Mass as it was commonly called, was first mentioned in the Cranbrook wills in 1499 or 1500 having first arrived in Kent in the 1460s.[54] The devotion had an immediate and marked impact, around 50 per cent of testators making bequests from 1500 to 1509, but by 1520–35 this fell to around 15 per cent. Only two testators actually mentioned the Jesus Mass, the rest making small bequests of up to 20d to the Jesus light or the Rood light as it was otherwise sometimes called.[55]

The Jesus Mass was even more successful at Tenterden and attracted very different sorts of bequests. Most were simply 'to the Jesus mass' or 'to the maintenance of the Jesus mass' and only two testators out of the 42 who gave to the devotion mentioned the 'Jesus light' or lights to be set and maintained on the Jesus altar. During its first few years from 1513 to 1519 it attracted bequests from 65 per cent of testators. By 1520–35 this had fallen to 35 per cent but this was still an outstandingly high level of support compared to Cranbrook and other centres (see Table 1.1). Bequests continued right up to 1547 and the Jesus Mass was the most distinctive and pervasive aspect of testamentary piety in the parish before the Reformation. A '... boxe ordenyned to dyverse gatherers in the said parishe for the masse of Jhesu ther to be continued' was mentioned in 1513 and 'the brotherhood

[53]   CKS, PRC 17/15/228.

[54]   Cuthbert F. Atchley, 'Jesus Mass and Anthem', *Transactions of the St Pauls Ecclesiological Society*, 5 (1905): 164 and passim; *Registrum Statutorum et Consuetudinum Ecclesiae Cathedralis Sancti Pauli Londensis*, ed. W. Sparrow Simpson (London, 1873), pp. 435–62, 483–4; *Testamenta Cantiana: East Kent*, ed. A. Hussey (London, 1907), pp. 285, 202, 48, 90, 336, 14, 19, 321, 260; CKS, PRC *Sede Vacante* Reg. F, fol. 46A; PRC 17/7/122.

[55]   CKS, PRC 17/12/142; PRC 32/15/14.

priest' or 'Jesus priest' was supported in a number of wills. In 1526, Thomas Wode left £20 to purchase lands to support the priest to celebrate the Jesus Mass every Friday.[56]

There is evidence that there were Jesus images in other places, distinct from the crucifix, in connection with the Mass of the Holy Name, but at Tenterden no image is mentioned.[57] At Cranbrook, the cult seems to have been focused on a crucifix that was honoured with lights but the monogram of the Holy Name was also employed: sometime before December 1535 the wife of Michael Hellys had left a '… dyapere towhele of yellow silke wythe letters of Jhesus upon yt wythe reded sylke' to the parish church. The Holy monogram may also have featured at Tenterden on the painted altar cloths and curtains for the Jesus altar funded by William Couper. The monogram was particularly malleable to 'moderate Protestant' as well as Catholic reshaping.[58]

The Mass of the Holy Name primarily offered opportunities for the intensification of personal identification with Christ and his saving mercy. The different aspects of the devotion – its focus on the sacrificial mass as well as scripture and preaching – lent it a powerful polyvalency. The radical potential of worship of Christ as supreme if not sole mediator may have struck a chord with those disengaged from or who had doubts about devotion to the saints as suggested by the dynamics of testamentary piety at Tenterden, whilst it also appealed to those with more traditionalist and imagistic pieties as seen in the pattern of its development alongside the continuing strength of the cult of saints at Cranbrook.[59] Its more sustained popularity at Tenterden, however, was just one among a number of changes by the 1520s, including the decline of devotion to saints, the chantry and the religious orders that add up to a significant shift in orthodox piety at least a decade before the years of official reform. Orthodoxy at Tenterden, although far from homogeneous, was drifting towards a particularly English evangelicalism – a moderate Christocentric reformism – in ways that were not experienced ten miles away in Cranbrook where a wider range of traditional religious practices maintained much higher levels of support.[60]

---

[56]   CKS, PRC 17/12/182; PRC 17/17/158.

[57]   For example, in the neighbouring parish of Rolvenden: *Testamenta Cantiana: East Kent*, p. 260.

[58]   Wabuda, *Preaching*, pp. 156–63, 175–6; Hugo Blake, Geoff Egan, John Hurst and Elizabeth New, 'From Popular Devotion to Resistance and Revival in England: the Cult of the Holy Name of Jesus and the Reformation', in David Gaimster and Roberta Gilchrist (eds), *The Archaeology of Reformation, 1480–1580* (London, 2003), pp. 186–93; CKS, P100/5/1, fol. 8r; PRC 32/12/174.

[59]   R.W. Pfaff, *New Liturgical Feasts in Later Medieval England* (Oxford, 1970), 62–83; Atchley, 'Jesus Mass': 163–9; Wabuda, *Preaching*, pp. 147–77; Duffy, *Altars*, pp. 45, 109, 113–16, 120, 224, 370; Peters, *Patterns of Piety*, pp. 98–9, chs 3 and 4; Lutton, *Lollardy*, pp. 69–80. 2; Blake et al., 'Popular Devotion', pp. 175–203. See also Harvey Whitehouse, *Arguments and Icons: Divergent Modes of Religiosity* (Oxford, 2000).

[60]   Lutton, *Lollardy*, ch. 2.

Family Pieties, *c.* 1450–1640

Changing the focus to families as opposed to individual testators provides a means of investigating the comparative heterogeneity of the religious cultures of Tenterden and Cranbrook, continuities over time, and the possible roots of the changes described above.

'Family' is used here in the sense of a multi-generational group of interrelated households and individuals that shared the same surname. The nuclear family, the household and patrilineal descent were all important sites or mechanisms for cultural transmission. Freedom of choice in religious practice was constrained by expectations and conventions defined by family and kinship as much as by parish. In areas such as the Weald of Kent – predominantly wood-pasture economies with weak lordship, scattered settlement, partible inheritance and a diversity of agricultural and industrial activities – the family and household were of greater social and cultural importance than those places where the collectivity of the parish or fraternity may have been more central in shaping pious choices.[61] Affinal collateral kin also played an important part in processes of cultural transmission.[62]

Families were selected on the basis of having left at least three last wills and testaments between 1449 and 1535: twenty-three at Tenterden responsible for 114 wills and twenty-one at Cranbrook leaving eighty-eight wills, in some cases for three or four generations. These prolific will-making families are representative of the most stable and established core of local society beneath the level of the gentry and their pious practices were probably somewhat unusual but disproportionately influential.

There were clear distinctions between the ways in which different families balanced religious preoccupations with other concerns, including family and kin; what might be termed their testamentary strategies. By aggregating the strategies of individual family members, continuities in the testamentary pieties of families can be placed on a spectrum ranging from the relatively sparse or restrained to the elaborately rich (see Tables 1.2 and 1.3).[63]

Although individual strategies varied, families' testamentary pieties were distinctive and family expectations appear to have had a bearing on individual practices. Testamentary and a range of other evidence for Tenterden and the 1524–25 lay subsidy return for Cranbrook hundred indicate that there were families right

---

[61] Lutton, *Lollardy*, pp. 19–26. On individual and family piety see Christian, *Person and God*, pp. 80–88 and Norman Jones, *The English Reformation: Religion and Cultural Adaptation* (Oxford, 2002), pp. 33–57. Zell, *Industry*, p. 75. For an example of a more collective type of parish see Duffy, *Morebath*.

[62] Rob Lutton, 'Godparenthood, Kinship, and Piety in Tenterden, England 1449–1537', in Isabel Davis, Miriam Müller and Sarah Rees Jones (eds), *Love, Marriage and Family Ties in the Later Middle Ages* (Turnhout, 2003), pp. 217–34.

[63] Column 7 of Tables 1.2 and 1.3 shows the % of each family's testators that gave to masses, prayers and religious services, images, lights, cults or fraternities.

across the pious spectrum in both parishes with ample resources at their disposal. If there was any positive relationship between wealth and generosity in pious giving, it was confined to the very top of the pious spectrum. Those who gave least generously were not by any means the least wealthy.[64]

The overall profile of family pieties is quite different between the two centres. Cranbrook families devoted only a moderately larger share of their available resources to religious bequests, but because they had, on average, over twice as much cash at their disposal, they gave between three and five times as much as did Tenterden families to religious ends. Whilst the overall tenor of piety in Tenterden was parsimonious and unelaborate, there was a greater contrast between those families which gave most generously and diversely to religious concerns and those which gave most frugally and narrowly. In particular, there was a strong testamentary tradition which tended to neglect traditional religious elements in favour of frugality and concentration on family and kin. Cranbrook's religious culture was better funded and comprised of a broader range of devotions and, at least among leading stable families, more homogeneous. In both parishes, orthodoxy was neither monolithic nor unchanging, but there were consistent significant differences in commitment to forms of devotion that could not have remained entirely inconspicuous, either within the parish or, in terms of their impact on the material culture of piety, between parishes.

Families that were frugal in their explicitly religious testamentary giving were not necessarily less devout than their more generous counterparts. I have suggested elsewhere that their piety was informed by misgivings about aspects of orthodox practice combined with moral imperatives that contended for resources to the exclusion of religious giving. At Tenterden, differences in pious practices arose, to some extent, out of social and cultural distinctions: in particular, between middling crafts- and tradespeople and truly wealthy yeoman farmers. For example, the moderately well-to-do Castelyn and Pellond families became more generous and diverse as they rose in wealth and status in the early sixteenth century and increased their involvement in parochial and municipal office-holding, but they concentrated on the Jesus Mass, the funeral and anniversary and charitable and civic giving, whilst ignoring devotion to saints and the chantry. The faster a family's upwards social mobility, the less generous and elaborate was its religious giving, possibly because rapid generation of wealth demanded intensive investment in industrial and commercial enterprise and estate building by households linked by kinship. A materialistic and acquisitive mentality, centred on family and kin to the detriment of engagement with the social institution of the parish, may have helped foster what Patrick Collinson terms an '... anti-Catholic and specifically anti-sacramentarian sentiment ...' in the Kentish Weald whose origins may have pre-dated the arrival of Lollardy.[65]

---

[64] Lutton, *Lollardy*, pp. 39–54; NA: PRO, E179, 125/324.

[65] Lutton, *Lollardy*, ch. 4; Collinson, 'Cranbrook and the Fletchers', p. 402.

Table 1.2 The Spectrum of Testamentary Piety across Selected Tenterden Families, 1449–1535

1. Family and number of wills		2. Median amount of all cash left in will in pence	3. Median % of cash left to religious concerns	4. Median of cash to religious concerns in pence	5. Median of cash to religious concerns indexed, where 2867d = 100	6. % of family testators who gave to chantries	7. % who gave to masses, prayers etc.	8. 'Score' (sum of columns 3, 5, 6 and 7)
Foule	4	3,296	81	2,270	79	75	75	310
Strekynbold	3	14,684	34	2,867	100	67	100	301
Stonehouse	4	4,622	71	2,176	76	25	100	272
Carpynter	3	852	67	840	29	67	100	263
Jamyn	3	488	67	488	17	67	100	251
Preston	4	3,542	52	1,174	41	50	100	243
Davy	8	472	94	432	15	37	62	208
Couper	5	604	89	424	15	20	80	204
Donne	6	596	58	354	12.3	17	100	187
Smyth	6	80	61	60	2	17	67	147
Piers	6	1,028	20	184	6.4	33	67	126
Hylles	5	12	54	12	0.4	0	60	114
Pette	5	856	25	80	3	20	60	108
Pellond	7	1,060	22	12	0.4	14	71	107
Brekynden	7	2,216	13	428	15	14	57	99
Gerves	4	1,649	10	356	12.4	25	50	97
Assherynden	5	1,644	28	132	4.6	20	40	93
Bishopynden	5	972	1	18	0.6	20	60	82
Castelyn	7	244	35	26	1	0	43	79
Gibbon	5	44	29	20	0.7	0	40	70
Chapman	4	828	50	11	0.4	0	0	50
Blossom	5	1,000	4	80	2.8	0	40	47
Hoke	3	676	12	64	2	0	33	47

Table 1.3   The Spectrum of Testamentary Piety across Selected Cranbrook Families, 1455–1535

1. Family and number of wills		2. Median amount of all cash left in will in pence	3. Median % of cash left to religious concerns	4. Median of cash to religious concerns in pence	5. Median of cash to religious concerns indexed, where 7872d = 100	6. % of family testators who gave to chantries	7. % who gave to masses, prayers etc.	8. 'Score' (sum of columns 3, 5, 6 and 7)
Hendley	5	20,476	58	7,872	100	80	100	338
Roberts	2	18,391	27	4,810	61.1	100	100	288
Sharpy	3	4,396	78	2,532	32.2	67	100	277
Couchman	4	15,727	53	5,740	72.9	25	75	226
Pynde	4	4,978	83	1,168	14.8	50	100	247
Posse	5	3,316	57	1,328	16.9	60	80	214
Elis	5	1,689	62	1,049	13.3	60	80	215
Hancock	4	2,433	51	1,076	13.7	50	100	214
Portreff	4	2,051	78	1,010	12.8	50	75	215
Taylor	4	6,838	35	1,458	18.5	75	75	203
Cooper	3	1,800	64	1,160	14.7	0	100	179
Everynden	4	1,180	79	600	7.6	50	50	187
Chittenden	13	420	91	166	2.1	15	77	185
Sampson	3	148	60	80	1	0	100	161
Waterman	3	2,110	8	426	5.4	33	100	147
Draner	4	975	64	333	4.2	0	75	143
Lynche	3	266	31	32	0.4	33	67	132
Dowle	4	1,353	9	108	1.4	25	75	110
Beagynden	3	1,646	7	113	1.4	0	100	108
Baker	5	884	13	79	1	20	60	94
Andrewe	3	3,596	1	80	1	33	33	68

This would explain why at Tenterden, Lollardy seems to have been located in the social stratum of middling crafts- and tradespeople that adhered to sparing testamentary strategies. The general tenor of the wills of frugal and socially mobile families and the significant changes in orthodoxy before 1535, including the growth of Christocentricism, accord with sacramentarian, anti-sacerdotal and anti-cultic continuities in Lollard opinions. Two key suspects who abjured heresies in 1511–12, namely Stephen Castelyn and William Pellond, belonged to the aforementioned religiously frugal families, as did the George Castlen, who pulled down the front of the rood loft at Tenterden in Edward's reign. Lollardy may have had a long-term influence on orthodox opinions on the Weald, but there is more evidence for this at Tenterden than at Cranbrook. Nevertheless, even at Tenterden, the reformist Christocentric piety that was informed by humanist vicars and local gentry, and that characterized parochial religion by the mid–1520s, had more in common with moderate Protestant evangelicalism than with Lollardy.[66]

By the late sixteenth century, more than any of its neighbours, Tenterden was increasingly geared to specialized and large-scale commercial livestock farming. The number of small family farms was relatively low and what marks Tenterden out more than anything else is a very high proportion of exceptionally rich inhabitants – greater even than at Cranbrook and other more typical small market towns. These were mainly large-scale graziers and farmers, together with some wealthy shopkeepers and craftspeople.[67]

The generally lower levels of available wealth in the pre-1535 Tenterden wills compared to Cranbrook, and the existence of a few families with much higher amounts of available wealth at their disposal than the rest, suggest that, among the better off, the degree of concentration of wealth may have already been greater at Tenterden than at Cranbrook in the late fifteenth and early sixteenth centuries. The lower distribution of resources across the whole will-making population impacted on levels of religious investment at Tenterden. The accumulation and concentration of resources among fewer families may have accelerated after 1535 but, as we shall see, if Tenterden's leading families had new-found and unparalleled wealth at their disposal by the end of the sixteenth century, they did not expend it in overly impressive pious gestures, but retained a relatively restrained approach to testamentary giving. This enduring mentality appears to have arisen out of the pressures of social survival and advancement in conditions of acute social restructuring; an ethic focused on the family as the paramount social unit and its continuity becoming the chief moral and pious concern at the expense of investment in collective religious institutions.

Cranbrook's seemingly less fragmented pre-Reformation religious culture appears to have grown out of different social and economic developments and have

---

[66]   Lutton, *Lollardy*, chs 4 and 5.

[67]   Zell, *Industry*, pp. 100–103, 106–7, 117–21, 147–50 154–5, 172, 183–4; Zell, 'A Wood–Pasture Agrarian Regime', pp. 72–86; Julian Cornwall, *Wealth and Society in Early Sixteenth-Century England* (London, 1988), pp. 60–61.

led to deeper religious divisions after 1535. The 1524–25 lay subsidy assessments indicate that the distribution of wealth in Cranbrook was very similar to a number of other small country towns as opposed to more rural areas. Sixty-three tax-payers belonged to selected families and it is no surprise that they were disproportionately wealthy with over twice the proportion of tax-payers in the top two bands of assessment compared to Cranbrook hundred as a whole, and slightly more in the lower middling group. The relative homogeneity of the testamentary piety of these selected families may therefore be due in part to their disproportionate wealth. Although the level of bequests in the wills of the parish as a whole suggests that traditionally orthodox practices were strong across a wide social range, it must be remembered that will-makers tended to belong to wealthier groups and that Cranbrook had an exceptionally large proportion of poorer inhabitants – mainly wage labourers employed in the textile industry.[68] It is possible that reformist and more radical pieties, including Lollardy, were more socially and politically marginal at Cranbrook than they were at Tenterden. Nevertheless, judging by what little evidence there is of the social and economic backgrounds of Lollard suspects in Cranbrook, Lollard families such as the Reignolds appear to have been of reasonably high middling status. The fact that the Lollard suspect Agnes Reignold was in service to the wealthy clothier Gerves Hendley in 1511 should not be taken as proof of her low status but rather as an indication of the shared social world of moderately wealthy and higher status families and the close contact of heterodox and traditionally orthodox pieties.[69]

Forty-one wills made by 13 of the 23 selected Tenterden families survive for the years 1535–1640, representing families mainly drawn from the moderate or most frugal groups in the pre-Reformation pious spectrum. Sixty-seven survive for Cranbrook representing 16 of the 21 selected families that tend to be bunched towards the more traditionally generous end of the pre-Reformation testamentary spectrum. The more religiously moderate and parsimonious Tenterden families went on to have more influence and enjoy greater longevity after 1535 than their more traditionally generous counterparts, whereas at Cranbrook the families that sustained their position in the parish into the late sixteenth and early seventeenth centuries tended to be the most lavish pre-Reformation givers.[70]

Apart from the almost complete disappearance of the saints from the wills after 1535, the contrasting pre-Reformation patterns of testamentary piety in the two parishes continued relatively unchanged up to the end of Henry's reign. Traditional orthodox culture remained relatively robust at Cranbrook, particularly in terms of

---

[68] Zell, *Industry*, pp. 144–6.

[69] Lutton, *Lollardy*, pp. 176–8.

[70] In addition to the abovementioned family wills, what follows is based on 438 wills proved in the Canterbury Archdeaconry and Consistory Courts for Cranbrook from 1535 to 1640 and a comprehensive survey of 91 for Tenterden, 1535–*c.* 1560; 27 from the 1580s; 19, *c.* 1600–1610; and 7 from the 1620s.

the place of the mass in the commemoration and salvation of the dead.[71] This was not the case at Tenterden. Traditional forms of devotion to Christ remained relatively strong in both parishes, although the Jesus Mass appears to have retained its relatively greater appeal at Tenterden up to 1547 and may have helped bridge the transition from Catholic to Protestant worship.

With the onslaught against purgatory and the mass as a sacrificial rite heralded by Edward VI's reign, in common with other parts of the country, more marked changes can be seen in the testamentary practices of both parishes, most noticeably a collapse in explicit bequests for masses, which was all the more dramatic at Cranbrook where conservatism was much stronger before 1547.[72] There are no elaborate Protestant preambles in the Tenterden wills in these years, whereas in 1549 James Sharpe of Cranbrook commended his '... soule to Cryst Jesus my maker and my redeemer in whome and by the merytts of whose blessed passion ys all my hole trust of clene remissyon of my synnes ...', and left 46s 8d to John Perynge, curate of Cranbrook, to preach seven sermons.[73]

There was no overt reappearance of pre-Reformation practices and devotions in the wills of Tenterden's parishioners in Mary's reign. The only discernible change occurred in 1557, when some testators began to employ traditionally orthodox preambles. Charitable giving to the poor usually, but not exclusively, linked to commemoration, remained the central pious preoccupation. At Cranbrook some Marian wills contain specific bequests for masses for the soul of the deceased or imply a link between charitable gifts and prayers for the dead that was less apparent in Edward's reign.[74] More striking was the will made by Richard Dence in February 1559, several months into Elizabeth's reign. He gave 12d to each of six priests to say and sing dirges and masses, 26s 8d to the poor of Cranbrook at his burying and instituted a 20-year obit at Cranbrook church for his father's and mother's souls.[75] The late Marian wills suggest that traditional Catholic devotions were beginning to revive at Cranbrook, but not at Tenterden. However, there is no indication that devotion to saints was re-built in either parish. The Cranbrook churchwardens' accounts from 1558 onwards make no mention of the clearing of any images of saints from the church, apart perhaps from in its glass; although they do record the removal of a number of altar stones and the partial dismantling and sealing off of the rood loft as late as 1562.[76]

Between 1558 and 1640, as was the case before 1535, on average Cranbrook families left much larger amounts of money to religious and charitable concerns in their wills than those at Tenterden. On the whole, the moderation and frugality in testamentary giving that characterized practices in Tenterden before the

---

[71] Marshall, *Beliefs and the Dead*, p. 80.

[72] PRC 17/27/112 and PCC PROB 11/34; Marshall, *Beliefs and the Dead*, pp. 93–114.

[73] PCC PROB 11/33/67.

[74] PCC PROB 11/37/31; PRC 17/32/1.

[75] PRC 17/34/217.

[76] CKS P100/5/1, fols 8v–18v.

Reformation was also a feature of the town's wills after 1558. Seventeen of the 30 wills for selected Tenterden families dated 1558 or later failed to make any charitable or religious bequest, whereas only ten out of 44 fall into this category for Cranbrook. As mentioned, charitable giving and bequests for sermons follow the same pattern, as do references to Bibles and other religious books in the wills. Disparities in testamentary piety between the two parishes were continuous throughout the period and must have had a marked affect on the material culture of lived religion.

Conclusions

The consistently different character of testamentary piety in these two Wealden centres over a period of some 200 years raises a number of important issues and questions in relation to the nature and dynamics of piety, continuities of dissent, and the significance and progress of reform.

It is clear that a district such as the Weald of Kent that has traditionally been seen as relatively unified was culturally diverse and probably contained a number of distinct religious cultures. Although similar in terms of geographical size, pattern of settlement and structure of landholding, Tenterden and Cranbrook experienced contrasting economic, social and demographic developments and had different material cultures. I have suggested that these appear to have given rise to distinctive and divergent pieties that shaped responses to devotional innovations before the Reformation and to reformist and radical ideas throughout the period as a whole. It is possible that these distinctive religious cultures influenced religious practices in the town's hinterlands through processes of cultural dissemination and transmission. Investigation of other parishes in the Weald would begin to answer these questions. In addition, detailed reconstruction of family, marriage and migration across a number of parishes alongside examination of continuities and discontinuities in religious practices within and between households, families and kinship networks might provide greater access to the ways in which transitions in piety occurred over time and individual and family pieties interacted with religions of parish and locality.[77]

Although Cranbrook's testamentary giving before the Reformation was much more similar than Tenterden's to other Kent towns such as Dover, Hythe and New Romney, it nevertheless possessed its own distinctive features such as a relatively high level of chantry endowment and commemorative giving more akin to larger centres. This may reflect Cranbrook's extraordinary wealth in this period and status as a town of considerable importance. Tenterden, on the other hand, seems to have been much less similar to other similar sized centres, particularly in terms of the

---

[77] I intend to write a monograph exploring processes of cultural dissemination and transition in relation to Christocentric piety in the Weald as well as other parts of the country *c*. 1400–*c*. 1640.

marginal position of devotion to saints and the secular and regular religious orders in the parish's wills. The implications of these differences for our understanding of piety in Kent as a whole and more widely are profound. They suggest that orthodox religious culture before the Reformation was deeply heterogeneous and that even neighbouring parishes or towns had noticeably divergent levels of commitment to the central elements of traditional devotion. And, continuity in the contrasting patterns of testamentary giving after 1535 implies that different centres developed their own Protestant pieties and their own Puritanisms.

Despite these local contrasts, differences between different parts of the county may have remained significant. Paul Lee's work on the diocese of Rochester suggests that Catholic devotional life on the eve of the Reformation in important centres such as Dartford, Gravesend and Rochester and more rural parishes was thriving in ways quite different from developments in the Weald and perhaps other parts of east Kent. For example, the Mass of the Holy Name of Jesus seems to have made little impact in the west of the county except in Tonbridge and the Medway valley area and the saints and their images appear to have remained central to devotional life into the 1530s.[78]

In what ways do the continuities in piety over the period as whole in these parishes help explain responses to reform and traditions of dissent? In terms of the religious experiences and practices of the majority of inhabitants, it might be argued that the moderate but divergent pieties practised by ordinary, albeit fairly well-to-do, families in these centres were as important, if not more important, than continuities in radical dissent. Also, the enduring differences in testamentary piety over the period as a whole suggest that, although local clergy and leading conservative or radical figures may have played an important role in shaping religious life, underlying long-term mentalities were more important in setting the tone and direction of these parishes' Reformation narratives.

Tenterden's relatively rapid and favourable response to Protestant reform appears to have been due to the strength of reformist elements among its townsfolk in the early sixteenth century that had links to Lollardy. It is difficult to gauge the extent to which Puritanism developed at Tenterden, but the parish seems to have been less religiously divided in the late sixteenth century than Cranbrook. Cranbrook's richer orthodox religious culture took much longer to dismantle and the more traditional pieties of its inhabitants longer to change. It would seem that radical dissenters had little influence in the governance of the town or parish and may have been more socially marginal than at Tenterden but appear to have been of middling status. It is more difficult to identify the types of orthodox pieties that had potential to diverge into heterodoxy at Cranbrook, but dissenters retained a strong minority presence in the parish throughout the sixteenth century. In both places, more than one separatist strand emerged in the 1630s, but new pressures

---

[78] Paul Lee, 'Monastic and Secular Religion and Devotional Reading in Late Medieval Dartford and West Kent', unpublished Ph.D Thesis, University of Kent (1998), pp. 144–97.

were at work by this time and separatism was a phenomenon distinct from earlier dissent.

Due to its size of population, greater degree of urbanization, social complexity and geographic fragmentation, Cranbrook may have been able to sustain greater extremes of piety than Tenterden. Cranbrook seems to have had a more urban corporate identity that strongly expressed itself in religious terms quite different to the dominant townsfolk in sixteenth century Tenterden and which may have been equally distinct from its outlying hamlets such as Sissinghurst and Glassenbury. I have discussed the importance of locality for the fragmented nature of piety within the parish of Tenterden elsewhere and the possible importance of scattered settlement in large Wealden parishes for the development of religious radicalism in this period was raised over thirty years ago.[79]

Was Cranbrook more religious than Tenterden? If we were to judge by outward appearances alone we would have to say yes, but this would be a judgement of style rather than of substance and one with which the pious parishioners of Tenterden are unlikely to have concurred and which Cranbrook's leading families may have welcomed. For obvious reasons, elaborate well-funded parochial religion was a feature of urban culture in Kent as it was elsewhere, but urbanity was expressed in different ways. Neighbouring centres' religious cultures may even have developed in self-consciously oppositional directions, effecting further divergence in their respective predominant orthodoxies.

Cutting across such differences in corporate piety were the networks and affiliations of household and family piety. Lollardy, radical Protestant dissent and Puritan conventicling, whatever their precise doctrinal content, were all dependent on the types of social bonds and networks that were more important in the Weald than the corporate life of the parish. These household-centred religious practices were more in tune with Wealden patterns of life and went hand-in-hand with family-centred pieties. Despite repeated attempts to annihilate them they coexisted with, and did not entail complete withdrawal from, corporate religion until the 1630s.[80] Separatism may have grown out of household religion and the affiliations of the dissenting network, but, instead of championing the piety of the family and the household, it replaced one type of corporate religious life with another.

---

[79] Lutton, *Lollardy*, ch. 3; Everitt, 'Nonconformity in Country Parishes', passim. See also Collinson, 'Cranbrook and the Fletchers', p. 425.

[80] David Aers, *Sanctifying Signs. Making Christian Tradition in Late Medieval England* (Notre Dame, Indiana, 2004), pp. 157–65.

Chapter 2

Martyrs of the Marsh

Elizabeth Barton, Joan Bocher and Trajectories of Martyrdom in Reformation Kent

Andrew Hope

Kent's two most famous Reformation martyrs – if one discounts episcopal incomers – were women. Elizabeth Barton, variously The Nun of Kent or The Holy Maid of Kent, denied Henry VIII's headship of the church and was executed for treason in 1534. Joan Bocher, variously Joan of Kent or Joan Knell, denied the physicality of Christ's incarnation, and was burnt for heresy in 1550.[1] Although their causes had little in common, their worlds were very similar, and, it will be argued here, even linked.

Neither Elizabeth Barton nor Joan Bocher has been regarded unambiguously, either by those who might have been considered well disposed toward them at the time, or by posterity. Elizabeth Barton was eclipsed by those who followed her in martyrdom the following year, especially Sir Thomas More and Bishop John Fisher. In addition, More was cool toward her, and she undermined her own case by her retractions.[2] Thus even those sympathetic to her cause have often been dismissive. For Philip Hughes in 1950 she was '… a more or less conscious imposter, a poor thing with a disturbed brain, foolishly encouraged by the superstitiously inclined and by the less discerning of the clergy'.[3] In this time almost her lone champion has been Alan

---

[1]   The new *ODNB* has entries for both: see vol. 4, pp. 201–4 for 'Barton, Elizabeth (*c*.1506–1534)' by Diane Watt, and vol. 6, pp. 387–8 for 'Bocher, Joan (d.1550)' by Andrew Hope. I wish to thank the editors of the *Dictionary* for inviting me to contribute the entry on Joan Bocher, which was the starting point for this article.

[2]   Peter Burke, 'How to be a Counter-Reformation Saint', in Kaspar von Greyerz (ed.), *Religion and Society in Early Modern Europe 1500–1800* (London, 1984), pp. 45–6; David Knowles, *The Religious Orders in England* (3 vols, Cambridge, 1959), vol. 3, *The Tudor Age*, pp. 190–91.

[3]   Philip Hughes, *The Reformation in England* (3 vols, London, 1950, 5th edition, 1963), vol. 1, *The King's Proceedings*, pp. 276–7. See G. Constant, *The Reformation in England* (2 vols, London, 1934), vol. 1, *The English Schism. Henry VIII. (1509–1547)*, p. 209, for a very similar estimate. See also J.D.M. Derrett, 'Sir Thomas More and the Nun of Kent', *Moreana*, 15 and 16 (1967): 277, 279. Knowles, *The Religious Orders in England*, vol. 3, pp. 182–91, is more considered. She is absent from J.J. Scarisbrick, *The Reformation and the English People*

Neame in a full-length and avowedly Catholic biography of 1971, *The Holy Maid of Kent*.[4] Historians from other traditions have in some ways been less judgmental but often just as dismissive, the subject of interest being less her personal psyche than the nature and extent of the manipulation and misrepresentation to which she was subject.[5]

In recent years, however, Elizabeth Barton has been rescued, not so much as a Catholic voice as a female one. She has been taken as one of the few audible female voices of the early Reformation. Although much of the direct evidence of her words has been lost, the sources for her life are relatively full.[6] In the vanguard of this reappraisal has been Diane Watt.[7] Watt drew attention to the action of her confessor Dr Edward Bocking in introducing her to the lives of Saints Catherine of Siena and Bridget of Sweden.[8] They provided role models for Elizabeth's censure of the secular powers of her time.[9] Both Elizabeth and her supporters saw her activities in terms of those of Catherine of Siena.[10] One difficulty here is that this kind of female assertiveness is even rather commonplace in medieval lives of the saints. Particularly those set in antiquity often feature young females countermanding in some way rich and powerful males. A recent study of the popular lives of Katherine of Alexandria described how the Katherine there depicted could function as a model of domesticity.

(Oxford, 1984) and Eamon Duffy, *The Stripping of the Altars: Traditional Religion in England c.1400–c.1580* (London, New Haven, 1992).

[4] Alan Neame, *The Holy Maid of Kent: The Life of Elizabeth Barton, 1506–1543* (London, 1971).

[5] G.R. Elton, *Policy and Police: The Enforcement of the Reformation in the Age of Thomas Cromwell* (Cambridge, 1972); Peter Clark, *English Provincial Society from the Reformation to the Revolution: Religion, Politics and Society in Kent, 1500–1640* (Hassocks, 1977), pp. 32–8, 53–5. See Christopher Haigh, *English Reformations: Religion, Politics, and Society under the Tudors* (Oxford, 1993), pp. 137–9, for a good recent summary.

[6] E.J. Devereux, 'Elizabeth Barton and Tudor Censorship', *Bulletin of the John Rylands Library*, 49 (1966): 91–106.

[7] Diane Watt, 'The Prophet at Home: Elizabeth Barton and the Influence of Bridget of Sweden and Catherine of Siena', in Rosalynn Voaden (ed.), *Prophets Abroad: the Reception of Continental Holy Women in Late-Medieval England* (Woodbridge, 1996), pp. 161–76; Watt, 'Reconstructing the Word: the Political Prophecies of Elizabeth Barton (1506–1534)', *Renaissance Quarterly*, 50 (1997): 136–63; and Watt, *Secretaries of God: Women Prophets in Late Medieval and Early Modern England* (Cambridge, 1997). See also Sharon L. Jansen, *Dangerous Talk and Strange Behaviour: Women and Popular Resistance to the Reforms of Henry VIII* (Basingstoke, 1996); and Denise L. Despres, 'Ecstatic Reading and Missionary Mysticism: *The Orchard* of Syon', in Voaden (ed.), *Prophets Abroad*, pp. 157–9.

[8] L.E. Whatmore, 'The Sermon Against the Holy Maid of Kent and her Adherents, Delivered at Paul's Cross, November the 23rd, 1533, and at Canterbury, December the 7th', *English Historical Review*, 58 (1943): 263–75; Neame, *The Holy Maid of Kent*, pp. 151, 190; Watt, 'The Prophet at Home'.

[9] Watt, 'The Prophet at Home'.

[10] Hughes, *The Reformation in England*, vol.1, pp. 276–7, thought her 'no Catherine of Siena'; *The Correspondence of Sir Thomas More*, ed. Elizabeth Frances Rogers (Princeton, 1947), letter 197, pp. 480–88; Neame, *The Holy Maid of Kent*, p. 148.

Nevertheless, she also upbraids an emperor, very much in the fashion of Elizabeth Barton and the newly imperial Henry VIII.[11] The most appropriate model for Elizabeth Barton, however, lay even closer to hand. *The Golden Legend* tells how after the resurrection, Mary Magdalene travelled to Marseilles. There she preached before the governor of the province. Initially he was hostile, but eventually she won him round. Then this exchange took place:

> The governor and his wife then said to her: 'See here, we are prepared to do whatever you tell us to if you can obtain a son for us from the God whom you preach.'

> 'In this he will not fail you,' said Magdalene. Then the blessed Mary prayed the Lord to deign to grant them a son. The Lord heard her prayers and the woman conceived.[12]

As the political and religious crisis over the King's marriage deepened, Elizabeth Barton's visions changed from being centred on the Virgin Mary, to being communications with Mary Magdalene. The culmination of these contacts was a 'golden letter' which she received from the saint. Its text is largely unknown. If, however, Elizabeth Barton was adapting this material from *The Golden Legend*, it is easy to see why the government decided she should be silenced.[13]

Joan Bocher was, of course, martyred by the Edwardian Protestant establishment. Magisterial Protestantism had always two fronts to defend. On one side were Papalists recognizing the authority of Rome, and on the other were sacramentarians of various hues. Thomas Cranmer in his preface to the Great Bible famously sought to correct the errors of 'two sundry sorts of people', those '… that be too slow, and need the spur; [and] some other seem too quick, and need more of the bridle'.[14] Joan Bocher was in the latter category and at the end of her life turned the analogy back on Cranmer: one day he would catch up with her. On the issue at stake, that day never came. She did, however, subsequently come to be celebrated in a modest way by Whig-inclined historians, either as a victim of intolerance or as a rationalist, though it became increasingly difficult to see her as either.[15]

A problem is that the sources for the life of Joan Bocher are more meagre, late, and problematic than they are for Elizabeth Barton. The 1982 interpretation of John Davis

---

[11] Katherine J. Lewis, 'Model Girls? Virgin-Martyrs and the Training of Young Women in Late Medieval England', in Katherine J. Lewis, Noël James Menuge, and Kim M. Phillips (eds), *Young Medieval Women* (Stroud, 1999), pp. 25–46.

[12] Jacobus de Voragine, *The Golden Legend: Readings on the Saints*, trans. William Granger Ryan (2 vols, Princeton, 1993), vol. 1, p. 377.

[13] See Peter Marshall, *Reformation England, 1480–1642* (London, 2003), pp. 49–50, for an assessment of Elizabeth Barton as a more substantial and formidable opponent of Henry VIII.

[14] *Documents of the English Reformation*, ed. Gerald Bray (Cambridge, 1994), p. 234.

[15] Echoes of a rationalist Joan can still occur, for example in Norman Jones, *The English Reformation: Religion and Cultural Adaptation* (Oxford, 2002), p. 102, she is burned for refusing 'to recant her denial of the virgin birth of Christ'.

that Joan Bocher is to be identified with a Lollard of that name has met wide acceptance.[16] Around this identification Davis went on to build a considerable scholarly edifice about the continuity of radical dissent in the period. A Lollard ancestry, Davis argued, lay behind radical opposition to magisterial Protestantism.

There was a Lollard named Joan Bocher living in the Essex village of Steeple Bumpstead in 1528.[17] She is assumed to be the same person as a 'Mother Bocher' who was the host of a Lollard conventicle which probably met in the same place, and to be connected with William Bocher, ploughwright, of Steeple Bumpstead, a heretic whose great-grandfather was burnt for heresy.[18] The Bochers were therefore heretics of long-standing. Davis identifies this Joan Bocher with the martyr of 1550, partly on the basis of evidence which emerged during the Prebendaries' Plot against Cranmer. The plotters claimed Joan Bocher, the future martyr, had been released at the instance of Cranmer's Commissary, Christopher Nevinson, even though she was an abjured heretic. Robert Serles claimed that he had been told of her previous abjuration by John Myllys, who had been told of it by the parson of Westbere, a village four miles northeast of Canterbury. The parson, along with two other 'honest men' had heard Joan Bocher's husband say that she had abjured at Colchester in 1538.[19] Nevinson was dismissive of their evidence. He had, of course, his own reasons, but there is no evidence of any abjuration by a Joan Bocher in Colchester in 1538, nor is the Joan Bocher mentioned in the depositions of 1528 known either to have abjured or to have lived in Colchester.[20] If Nevinson was right then there is no reason to suppose that Joan Bocher's ideas are derived from Lollardy.

Despite the uncertainties, recent studies have gone some way to contextualizing how it was that these two women came to defy and offend the establishments of their day. However, these are still very much what Patrick Collinson calls analyses of vertical structures, an understanding of tunnels through time.[21] A more rounded

---

[16] J.F. Davis, 'Joan of Kent, Lollardy, and the English Reformation', *Journal of Ecclesiastical History*, 32(2) (1982): 225–33. Davis is followed by, for example, Anne Hudson, *The Premature Reformation: Wycliffite Texts and Lollard History* (Oxford, 1988), p. 479, and Christopher Marsh, *Popular Religion in Sixteenth-Century England: Holding Their Peace* (Basingstoke–London, 1998), p. 180. Dissenting is A.G. Dickens, *The English Reformation* (2nd edition, London, 1989), p. 263.

[17] John Strype, *Ecclesiastical Memorials* (3 vols, Oxford, 1822, Records and Originals, no. 21), vol. 1, part 2, pp. 61–2.

[18] Ibid., pp. 59–60 (Records and Originals, no. 19).

[19] *LP*, vol. 18(2)/546, part 20(1) (pp. 331–2); and part 7 (pp. 313–14). Joan Bocher's husband is remarkable by his absence in accounts of her, leading to the suspicion that Joan Bocher was, like Anne Askew, living apart from her husband.

[20] Steeple Bumpstead was in the Archdeaconry of Middlesex and not either the Archdeaconry of Colchester or the Archdeaconry of Essex.

[21] Patrick Collinson, 'Towards a Broader Understanding of the Early Dissenting Tradition', in C. Robert Cole and Michael E. Moody (eds.), *The Dissenting Tradition: Essays for Leland H. Carlson* (Athens, Ohio, 1975), pp. 3–38, reprinted in his *Godly People: Essays on English Protestantism and Puritanism* (London, 1983), pp. 527–62.

historical picture may be generated by looking at their more immediate contexts. This may be, as Patricia Crawford suggests, through the mobilization of sociological concepts such as functionalism or various forms of symbolic interactionism, or by attending to how religious convictions worked themselves out in the particular circumstances of networks of social or family ties.[22] It is to these networks of relationships within which Elizabeth Barton and Joan Bocher found themselves that we now turn.

Elizabeth Barton enters history as the teenage servant girl of Thomas Cobb, a member of the Kentish gentry, living in the village of Aldington on the edge of Romney Marsh (see Map 1.1). He managed the Aldington manor estates of the Archbishopric of Canterbury. Erasmus briefly held the rectory and had his scholarship financed by Cobb's labours. Cobb and his wife Joan had at least six children, including four boys and a girl. Elizabeth's parentage is unknown. She is usually assumed to have been of lower social status than her employer. This can by no means be assumed in the sixteenth century, but the absence of any known Barton family of social significance in the area, suggests the assumption is correct.

In 1525, when she was in her late teens, she fell ill with some disorder which apparently affected her stomach, throat and breathing. Whilst subject to these attacks she had visions and was able to prophesy. Her fame spread after she foresaw the death of a sick child who shared her room. She began to talk of wider religious issues revealed to her when in a trance state. Her parish priest Richard Master brought her to the attention of her ordinary, Archbishop William Warham. Warham established an episcopal commission under Dr Edward Bocking, a Benedictine of Christ Church, Canterbury, to enquire into her case. Meanwhile, the small chapel of St Mary the Virgin at Court-at-Street, about three miles from the Cobbs' house, had been adopted by Elizabeth as the very public site of her trances and visions. Pilgrims flocked to see her and the image of the Virgin to which she attributed her revelations. She impressed Warham's commission and became a nun at St Sepulchre's in Canterbury.

In Canterbury, Elizabeth Barton began to attract a following, both lay and clerical. She had a correspondence with John Fisher, the bishop of Rochester. The relationship between Elizabeth and her supporters was a symmetrical one of mutual reinforcement. They were attracted to her because they were sympathetic to the sentiments she expressed: she confirmed and articulated their convictions. There is no need to suppose, as her critics have done, that there was anything especially sinister about this, or to suppose, as have some supporters, that her visions were unaffected by the expectations of those about her. Theirs was a mutually supportive (or mutually exploitative) relationship.[23] Her visions do seem to have become more specific after she became a nun.[24] There were reasons why this may have been so.

---

[22]   Patricia Crawford, *Women and Religion in England, 1500–1720* (London, 1993), p. 3; Collinson, 'Towards a Broader Understanding', pp. 548–9.

[23]   Patrick Collinson, ''Not Sexual in the Ordinary Sense': Women, Men and Religious Transactions', in his *Elizabethan Essays* (London, 1994), pp. 142–3.

[24]   Noted by Jansen, *Dangerous Talk and Strange Behaviour*, p. 45. It is difficult to see

Dr Edward Bocking became her spiritual director. As we have seen, he had his own notions of what a visionary nun should be, and put before Elizabeth his favoured models of Catherine of Siena and Bridget of Sweden. However, there is a sense in which to focus on Elizabeth Barton's textual inheritance and her part of and in a textual community misses the point of why Fisher, Bocking, and others, became so taken up with her. Elizabeth's visions held out the prospect of access to authoritative truths which were not textual but personal. Since Erasmus's Greek New Testament with its Latin translation of 1516 and especially since the controversies begun the following year by Luther, Christendom had been beset by unresolved textual questions.

Elizabeth presented the possibilities of a way out, and they were seized on by Fisher. Fisher was open to the idea that there could be streams of authoritative utterances which Christendom had not fully appreciated. Thus he was interested in Florentine Neo-Platonism and the Cabbala.[25] Fisher had become embroiled in a controversy over the number of Marys in the New Testament. Traditional exegesis (and *The Golden Legend*) held that Mary Magdalen, and the woman 'which was a synner' (Tyndale) of Luke 7, and Mary of Bethany, were one person. In 1517, Lefèvre d'Etaples had argued on scholarly grounds that the Marys were three different people. Fisher replied with *De unica Magdalena*, upholding the traditional position. There were replies from Lefèvre and Josse Clichtove and further rejoinders from Fisher.[26] Elizabeth Barton offered a way out of this cycle of refutations. She was in touch with St Mary Magdalen and could report back.[27]

---

how she can be described as part of the *devotio moderna*, as in Mary Polito, *Governmental Arts in Early Tudor England* (Aldershot, 2005), p. 117.

[25]   H.C. Porter, 'Fisher and Erasmus', in Brendan Bradshaw and Eamon Duffy (eds), *Humanism, Reform and the Reformation: The Career of Bishop John Fisher* (Cambridge, 1989), p. 89. See also Eamon Duffy, 'The Spirituality of John Fisher', ibid., on Fisher's 'ready acceptance of the thought-world of late medieval popular Catholicism' (p. 210).

[26]   James K. McConica, 'John Fisher of Beverley, 1469–22 June 1535', in Peter G. Bietenholz (ed.), *Contemporaries of Erasmus: A Biographical Register of the Renaissance and Reformation*, (3 vols, Toronto, 1986), vol. 2, pp. 36–9; Desiderius Erasmus, *Collected Works of Erasmus* (86 vols, Toronto, 1974–), vol. 5, *The Correspondence of Erasmus, Letters 594 to 841, 1517 to 1518* (Toronto, 1979), trans. R.A.B. Mynors and D.F.S. Thomson, annotated by Peter G. Bietenholz, letter 766, pp. 282–4; and vol. 6, *The Correspondence of Erasmus, Letters 842 to 992, 1518 to 1519* (Toronto, 1982), trans. R.A.B. Mynors and D.F.S. Thomson, annotated by Peter G. Bietenholz, letter 936, pp. 288–92.

[27]   Neame, *The Holy Maid of Kent*, p.189. Richard Rex, 'The Polemical Theologian', in Bradshaw and Duffy (eds) *Humanism, Reform and the Reformation*, p.110, and (more tentatively) Maria Dowling, *Fisher of Men: a Life of John Fisher, 1469–1535* (Basingstoke, 1999), pp. 95–7, propose that Fisher was putting the question to Elizabeth as a test. This is also the implication of Cromwell's letter to Fisher of February 1534 (*The Life and Letters of Thomas Cromwell*, ed. Roger Bigelow Merriman (2 vols, Cambridge, 1902), vol. 1, letter 68, p. 375). However, since the issue was a matter of debate among humanists whom Fisher respected the question could not function in this way.

Henry Gold is another example of a supporter's particular concerns.[28] He was a graduate of Fisher's St John's College, Cambridge. He took some interest – as did a number of colleagues with similar backgrounds – in the possible uses of the study of Greek for combatting heresy.[29] Notwithstanding this humanist interest, his was a very clerical churchmanship. He became caught up in a famously unpleasant tithe dispute with his parishioners in Hayes in Middlesex.[30] He arrived in Kent when his college presented him to the living of Ospringe near Faversham in 1525. He became a chaplain to Warham. He was suspicious of Wolsey and of Wolsey's schemes, such as the suppression of religious houses to endow Cardinal's College in Oxford.[31]

By the late 1520s, however, the scheme, often thought to be Wolsey's, which was dominating all other was the annulment of the King's marriage. Elizabeth predicted Wolsey's fall and destruction if he did not do as she laid down. She showed Wolsey '... of iij. swordes that he had in his hand, one of the spirytuallty, another of the temperallty, and the other of the kynges maryage'.[32]

Elizabeth Barton is here adapting the traditional idea of the two swords of spiritual and temporal power, and the claim of the church to the direction of both, to the exigencies of the royal divorce. The suggestion that a cardinal wielded both swords would have been alarming to any English monarch, let alone a Tudor.[33] It would seem likely that the idea of the two swords was fed to Elizabeth by Bocking or Gold, and was then applied by Elizabeth, somewhat clumsily perhaps, to the question of the divorce.

A number of Elizabeth's prophecies or visions have this character. They depend on information for which she would have had to rely on others and to which she then gives what seems to be her own twist.[34] Thus, for example, she saw how her prayers had prevented a ship leaving harbour which was carrying two monks from England to

---

[28]   On Gold see Richard Rex, 'Gold, Henry (d.1534)', *ODNB*, vol. 22, p. 645.

[29]   Richard Rex, 'The English Campaign against Luther in the 1520s', *Transactions of the Royal Historical Society*, 5th series, vol. 39 (1989): 85–106.

[30]   G.R. Elton, *Star Chamber Stories* (London, 1958), ch. 6.

[31]   'For trewly theis men that thus destroye religiouse places, they sey they do it to this entent, that the possessions & londes of them myghth be applyd to better usys', in 'A Sermon of Henry Gold, Vicar of Ospringe, 1525–27, Preached Before Archbishop Warham', by L.E. Whatmore, *AC*, 57 (1944): 37–8.

[32]   *Three Chapters of Letters Relating to the Suppression of Monasteries*, ed. Thomas Wright (London, 1843), p. 15. Thomas More is an independent witness: *Correspondence of Sir Thomas More*, letter 197, pp. 482, 483.

[33]   J.A. Watt, 'Spiritual and Temporal Powers', in J.H. Burns (ed.) *The Cambridge History of Medieval Political Thought, c. 350 – c.1450* (Cambridge, 1988), pp. 367–423, esp. 387–8. See Luke 22:38.

[34]   On the relations between written and oral culture see Adam Fox, *Oral and Literate Culture in England, 1500–1700* (Oxford, 2000). It seems to be this dependancy which her hostile interrogators expose in 1533. See Neame, *The Holy Maid of Kent*, p. 241; Diarmaid MacCulloch, *Thomas Cranmer, A Life* (New Haven, 1996), pp. 104–5.

visit William Tyndale in the Low Countries.[35] One of the best attested of her visions was that when the King was at mass in Calais in October 1532, the host became invisible to him and was delivered instead from the hands of the priest to Elizabeth who had been transported there. It would be difficult to imagine a more vivid demonstration of the withdrawal of God's favour from the king and his endorsement of the nun.[36] These stories depend on outside knowledge for their circumstances, but their denouements seem much more likely to be the product of Elizabeth's mind than Bocking's or Gold's. The kind of trickery they feature now reads remarkably like the trickery of Marlowe's Faustus: tragedy indeed replayed as farce. Sometimes there are hints of Elizabeth's mobilization of her own experience. She is much taken in a number of her visions with the geography of hell. Her 'place of punishment – a place of no salvation as they call it – which is neither hell nor purgatory' was suggested by Whatmore to be the *Limbus Infantium*.[37] In the light of the circumstance of her very first prophecy – the death of an infant – this may have been something about which she had often thought.

There can be no doubt that it is necessary to understand Elizabeth Barton to some extent in the context of the literary and intellectual traditions with which she came into contact when she entered St Sepulchre's. Nor can there be any doubt that she was befriended and lauded by those who were convinced of the religious necessity of resisting Henry VIII's schemes. She was, for example, visited incognito by conservative members of the aristocracy, some of whom had Yorkist blood in their veins. Nevertheless, prior logically and chronologically to this network and these supporters were her own visions and dreams, themselves not untouched by such magical fantasies of what the world might be like as were current in sixteenth century Kent.

As has been seen, there are problems identifying the life history of Joan Bocher. However, one aspect has never been properly explored. In the records, Joan Bocher almost always appears with a further alias, Joan Knell. Knell was an unusual name in Tudor England. Beyond a few scattered examples the name is overwhelmingly Kentish, and highly localized even within Kent. It is found on the rim of Romney Marsh, not far from where Elizabeth Barton had been active.

It has been possible so far to identify only one Joan Knell. She was the wife of William Knell the younger. Her husband died in 1526 leaving her with a life interest in

---

[35]   *Three Chapters of Letters relating to the Suppression of Monasteries*, p. 16.

[36]   Neame, *The Holy Maid of Kent*, pp. 175–6.

[37]   L.E. Whatmore, 'The Sermon', 471. The issue was also a matter of some topical interest. The doctrine of the immortality of the soul was officially promulgated for the first time at the Fifth Lateran Council in 1513, and went on to split the reformers. See Brian P. Copenhaver and Charles B. Schmitt, *Renaissance Philosophy* (Oxford, 1992), pp. 103–11; Andrew Hope, 'Plagiarising the Word of God: Tyndale between More and Joye', in Paulina Kewes (ed.), *Plagiarism in Early Modern England* (Basingstoke, 2003), pp. 93–105.

his lands in Wittersham and Appledore and with a daughter Anne, a minor.[38] There is no reason to identify this Joan Knell with Joan Bocher the martyr, who was possibly a generation younger. However, there is every reason for supposing that this is the Knell family of which Joan was a member either by birth or by marriage.

William Knell the younger was survived by two of his brothers, William Knell the elder and Thomas Knell. William Knell the elder seems to have been the head of the family. He had in the region of 450 acres scattered through the Marshland parishes of Brookland, Ivychurch, Snargate, Snave, Stone-in-Oxney, Appledore and Kenardington. In all these parishes except Snargate he also held at least one messuage and at least one barn. At Appledore he also held a mill-house and stables. In addition, he acquired and rented out ten messuages in the parish of St Mary Axe in London, which had been part of the estate of Holy Trinity Priory, dissolved in 1532.[39] His Brookland holding included the manor of Court at Wake rented from St Augustine's Abbey in Canterbury from 1520.[40] These lands amounted to a very considerable estate and would have made Knell a significant figure on the Marsh.

William Knell's principal residence was in Brookland where his house, barn and some of his lands were held of the Archbishop of Canterbury as of his manor of Aldington, as were some of his Ivychurch holdings.[41] The steward of the manor was, of course, Thomas Cobb, the master of Elizabeth Barton. Knell therefore would have had occasion regularly to visit Cobb and have the opportunity to meet Elizabeth. There were other links between the Cobbs and Knell. After his death in 1528, the payment of some of Cobb's legacies to his children proved problematic, especially after the death of his executor Nicholas Harte. The result was a suit in Chancery between Cobb's daughter Elizabeth and Harte's executors and assigns. Sorting out Cobb's estate then fell partly to another member of the local gentry, Stephen Thornhurst. Thornhurst was closely associated with Knell. They were both feoffees of Edmund Robin of Appledore and both witnesses to his will, proved in May 1533.[42] Under the provisions of the will they were jointly responsible for the maintenance of a chantry in Appledore church.[43]

On 13 September 1537, William Knell spoke words in support of the papacy in contravention of the Treason Act of 1534.[44] For some months they went unreported, but then word of them leaked out over the Christmas season. Thomas Joyce of Brookland and Edward Godfrey of Appledore reported the words to Stephen Thornhurst. Thornhurst, his long association with Knell notwithstanding, wrote to the

---

[38]   CKS, PRC17/17, fol. 207v.– 208. The will is unusually generous to Joan. There is no provision for her forfeiting her life interest in favour of Anne if she remarries.

[39]   *LP*, vol. 13(2)/491.

[40]   NA: PRO, C1/532/8.

[41]   *LP*, vol. 13(2)/491.

[42]   NA: PRO, PCC 3 Hogan 1532.

[43]   *Kent Chantries*, ed. Arthur Hussey (Kent Archaeological Society, 1936), pp. 1–2. It may be in relation to this chantry that Knell and Thornhurst are defendants in a case in King's Bench reported by Spelman: *The Reports of Sir John Spelman*, ed. J.H. Baker, 2 vols (London, 1977–78), vol. 1, pp. 139–40.

[44]   *LP*, vol. 13(2)/491.

oleaginous attorney-general John Baker, who lived not far away in the Weald at Sissinghurst near Cranbrook. Baker examined the witnesses on 2 January 1538, and then arrested Knell. Knell was sent up to Cromwell to be examined. A commission of Oyer and Determiner was appointed at the beginning of April. Knell was convicted at Maidstone on 16 April, and was executed by the beginning of May.[45] It was almost exactly four years since the execution of Elizabeth Barton.

It seems probable that Knell was one of those deeply affected by Barton's career. Memories of England's greatest martyr, Becket, were also strong on the Marsh where tradition had it he owned land. Knell's church at Brookland had a vivid wall painting of the Archbishop's murder. There was a weight of history, recent and not so recent, pressing for resistance to a King Henry invasive of the liberties of the church.

Where then does this leave Joan Bocher, alias Knell? On any estimate she was probably an approximate contemporary of Elizabeth Barton.[46] It would have been impossible for her to be unaffected in some way by the great surge of public interest in the maid and her visions which swept east Kent in the mid 1520s, and which probably embraced at least one older kinsman. Joan Bocher's was not a Lollard background, remaining faithful to some ancient tradition of dissent; rather it seems she had turned her back on her own family, and was now faced with the terrible problem of how to validate her existence in the shadow of William Knell's martyrdom. Each generation, in Alan Garner's phrase, has to 'get aback' of its predecessor.[47] Her answer seems to have been to become the Protestant Elizabeth Barton.

Joan Bocher's heretical career may have begun with smuggling William Tyndale's New Testament into England.[48] Thus, at a time when Elizabeth Barton was delivering her visions, Joan Bocher was probably delivering Tyndale's New Testaments. The worlds of Tyndale and the nun were not far apart. He first attacked her in print in 1528 in his *Obedience of a Christian Man*, written whilst living in the Antwerp house of a Cranbrook merchant, Richard Harman. Harman was almost certainly exporting books to the Weald, probably through the Cinque Ports.[49] Elizabeth Barton retaliated with

---

[45]   NA: PRO, SP 1/128, fol. 12–13, 55–6, 94–5; SP 1/131, fol. 142–3; *LP*, vol. 13(1)/12, 48, 79, 680, 783, 877; vol. 13(2)/491; vol. 14(1)/867; vol. 14(2)/782 (pp. 323, 334); *Life and Letters of Thomas Cromwell*, vol. 2, letter 251, pp. 133–4.

[46]   Elizabeth Barton was born about 1506. Joan Bocher was an active heretic in the 1530s and by some accounts the 1520s. No one commented that she was old at the time of her execution in 1550.

[47]   Alan Garner, *Granny Reardun* (London, 1983), p. 50.

[48]   Robert Parsons, *A Temperate Ward-Word, to the Turbulent and Seditious Wach-Word of Sir Francis Hastinges Knight, Who Indevoreth to Slaunder the Whole Catholique Cause, & All Professors Therof, Both at Home and Abrode* (1599), p. 16. Parsons's evidence is late, but it is credible and he claimed to have spoken to someone who was present at Bocher's trial.

[49]   P. Genard, 'Personen te Antwerpen in de XVIe eeuw, voor het "feit van religie" Gerechtelijk Vervolgd', *Antwerpsch Archievenblad*, 7 (n.d.): 176; *The Letters of Sir John Hackett, 1526–1534*, ed. Elizabeth Frances Rogers (Morgantown, 1971), no. 79, p. 175–7; William Tyndale, *The Obedience of a Christian Man*, reprinted in *Doctrinal Treatises*, ed. Henry Walter (Cambridge, 1848), p. 327. See also *An Answer to Sir Thomas More's Dialogue*,

visions denouncing him and his work. Similarly, just as members of the court made their surreptitious way to Elizabeth's cell in Canterbury, so Joan Bocher made her way to court, surreptitiously carrying, as one report has it, outlawed books under her skirts. Her companion in this was the future Protestant martyr Anne Askew.[50]

Joan Bocher settled in Canterbury, where, from the late 1530s, she was increasingly found in the company of the Canterbury Protestant élite. They, in their turn, protected her when she was denounced for heresy and imprisoned. Christopher Nevinson eventually secured her release on the grounds of the gentility of her birth, highly suggestive again that her origins are the landed Knells of Kent rather than the ploughwright Bochers of Essex.[51] As well as being protected by Nevinson, Joan Bocher lived for a while in the house of John Toftes in Canterbury. Among Toftes's other guests were two outspoken radical priests, John Bland and Richard Turner, and a monk from Dover who claimed to be ordained but was not.[52]

John Bland had, like Henry Gold before him, been presented to the living of Ospringe by St John's College, Cambridge (and was also, like him, to die for his faith). Bland was as outspoken in his attacks on some aspects of traditional religion as Gold had been outspoken in their defence. Bland touched on the highly sensitive area of the Trinity. Erasmus' New Testament corrections called up a storm of protest when they seemed to undermine traditional arguments for the Trinity, which far exceeded anything Lefèvre's three Marys had stirred up.[53] Bland was reported as saying that images of the Trinity were not to be tolerated, and that the term 'Trinitas' originated with Athanasius and was not scriptural.[54] Margaret Toftes the younger observed that it could not be proved from scripture that the Virgin Mary was in heaven.[55]

The questioning of the Trinity and of the status of the Virgin Mary may have made Joan receptive to the startling doctrine which was to place her beyond the pale of even Edwardian Protestantism. She held the idea of the celestial flesh, that is, that Christ's physical body was not derived from his mother but was in some way a divine distillation. Given Aristotelian views of the process of conception, the idea had a certain persuasiveness. Aristotle held that generation was the male role and receptivity the female role. This was, however, an area where there were alternatives. Galen believed that in conception the female contributed her own seed, though his interpreters disagreed whether this imparted matter or form or both.[56]

---

ed. Walter (Cambridge, 1850), pp. 91–2, where Tyndale, writing two years later, is more detailed.

[50] Robert Parsons, *A Temperate Ward-Word*, p. 16.
[51] *LP*, vol. 18(2)/546, part 7 (pp. 313–14).
[52] *LP*, vol. 18(2)/546, part 22(10) (p. 358), and part 7 (p. 312).
[53] Jerry H. Bentley, *Humanists and Holy Writ: New Testament Scholarship in the Renaissance* (Princeton, 1983), pp. 44–5, 151–5; Robert Coogan, *Erasmus, Lee and the Correction of the Vulgate: The Shaking of the Foundations* (Geneva, 1992), chs 2 and 3.
[54] *LP*, vol. 18(2)/546, part 7 (p. 311–12).
[55] *LP*, vol. 18(2)/546, part 7 (p. 307).
[56] The complexity of these issues is greater than can be entered into here. See Ian Maclean, *The Renaissance Notion of Woman: A Study in the Fortunes of Scholasticism and Medical Science in European Intellectual Life* (Cambridge, 1980), pp. 30–37.

According to the historic creeds of the Church, Christ 'was incarnate by the Holy Spirit of the virgin Mary'. The two prepositions in the clause were needle points on which danced many doctrinal angels. Aristotle and Galen provided different tunes. What came from fathers and what from mothers? Did the body of Christ originate in heaven or on earth? These things mattered: if the Church was the body of Christ did it have earthly or spiritual authority? How was the kingship of Christ constituted?[57] We are back with Elizabeth and her three swords, except Joan's position was implicitly diametrically the opposite.

Joan Bocher was arrested and convicted of heresy in 1549, and so began a year in which a succession of Protestant luminaries attempted to wean her back to orthodoxy, including Thomas Cranmer, Nicholas Ridley, Thomas Lever and Roger Hutchinson. She even ended up lodged in the house of Lord Chancellor Richard Rich. The Archbishop of Canterbury, the Bishop of Rochester, the Lord Chancellor, the vicar of Ospringe: she had put together the same cast list as Elizabeth Barton. If the crowds were missing, they were there in her mind. There were a thousand in London of her opinion she said, and the church leadership was genuinely alarmed about the spread of radical ideas in Kent and Sussex in 1549–50.

As yet it has not been possible to trace her highly developed ideas on the celestial flesh to a particular source. They seem to have owed little or nothing to an English tradition in which Mary was dismissed as no more than a vessel which had contained Christ. It may be doubted whether these were celestial flesh ideas at all. They were, rather, a means of denying Mary any peculiar role in the divine economy of salvation. The first known reformation appearance of these ideas in England was in 1535 when they were among the 'damnable opinions' held by a number of Flemings.[58] The clearest printed statement of celestial flesh ideas would seem to be in the Dutch anabaptist Menno Simons's *Brief and Clear Confession*, published in 1544.[59] Christ was 'nourished and fed in Mary', but '[h]e was not divided nor separated as being half heavenly and half earthly, half the seed of man and half of God, as some express it'.[60] Simons did not set out his most developed arguments until after Joan's death, in his *The Incarnation of our Lord* of 1554. Here Simons confounded his opponents with a mixture of Genesis and Aristotle: 'it is quite evident that the birth of man, according to the ordinance of God, cannot be without father and mother; ... it is also evident that the child does not proceed from the mother, but from the father'.[61] His opponents, he said,

---

[57] Diarmaid MacCulloch, *Reformation: Europe's House Divided, 1490–1700* (London, 2003), pp. 186–7.

[58] *The Lisle Letters*, ed. Muriel St Clare Byrne (6 vols, Chicago, 1981), vol. 2, pp. 492–5, esp. no. 396; John Foxe, *Acts and Monuments of these Latter and Perilous Dayes* (London 1583), vol. 2, p. 1049; D. Andrew Penny, *Freewill or Predestination: The Battle Over Saving Grace in Mid-Tudor England* (Woodbridge, 1990), p. 30.

[59] *The Complete Writings of Menno Simons, c.1496–1561*, trans. Leonard Verduin, ed. John Christian Wenger (Scottdale, Penn., 1956), pp. 419–54.

[60] Ibid., p. 428.

[61] Ibid, p. 807; see also p. 826.

make the same assumptions: 'Micron himself acknowledges that a woman has no procreative seed, but only a menstrual flux.'[62]

However, both Joan Bocher and her opponents based their arguments on Galenist, not Aristotelian, ideas about conception. Thus Joan's reasons for denying that Christ took flesh of Mary are theological not physiological. She told Roger Hutchinson:

> I deny not that Christ is Mary's seed, or the woman's seed; nor I deny him not to be a man; but Mary had two seeds, one seed of her faith, and another seed of her flesh and in her body. There is a natural and a corporal seed, and there is a spiritual and an heavenly seed, as we may gather of St John, where he saith, 'The seed of God remaineth in him, and he cannot sin.' [1 John 3]. And Christ is her seed; but he is become man of the seed of her faith and belief; of spiritual seed, not of natural seed; for her seed and flesh was sinful, as the flesh and seed of others.[63]

Hutchinson was also a Galenist:

> The seed which is promised unto Adam is named to be 'semen mulieris', the seed of a woman: the same is the seed of Eve; the selfsame afterward is called the seed of Abraham, of Jacob, the seed of David, and of the blessed virgin. But the seed that St John speaketh of is 'semen Dei', the seed of God; that is, the Holy Spirit; not Abraham's seed, David's seed, or Mary's seed.[64]

It may be that there are unrecognized sources, written or oral, for Joan's views. Alternatively, Joan herself may have developed them in her protracted arguments after her arrest. Many people were having to think quickly in unfamiliar areas.[65] As with Elizabeth Barton, it here is possible to see the ways in which Joan Bocher may have been reworking her textual inheritance. She differed, however, in her perseverance. She would have seen how the reputation of Elizabeth had been destroyed by her failure to hold to her vision. Hence, perhaps, her long frustration of the Edwardian authorities who were doing everything they could to bring her back to orthodoxy. It was to no avail. At her execution Joan insulted John Scory, the priest assigned to accompany her. It made an impression. Edward VI noted it in his diary.[66]

---

[62] Ibid., p. 874.

[63] Roger Hutchinson, *The Image of God or Layman's Book*, in *The Works of Roger Hutchinson*, ed. John Bruce (Cambridge, 1842), p. 146.

[64] Ibid.

[65] Cranmer had a number of editions of Galen. See David G. Selwyn, *The Library of Thomas Cranmer* (Oxford, 1996), nos 567–71. In an extraordinary move, the conservative Robert Serles, who had supplied the Prebendaries' Plot with the information that Joan Bocher had previously abjured, seems to have combined celestial flesh notions with the extreme Aristotelian position that lactation as well as conception was due to male initiative to make exaggerated claims for the Virgin's milk. See *LP*, vol. 18(2)/546, part 7 (pp. 303–4); part 8 (2) (p. 317); part 25(2) (p. 372–3).

[66] *The Chronicle and Political Papers of King Edward VI*, ed. W.K. Jordan (London, 1966), p. 28.

Brad S. Gregory in his survey of martyrdom in early modern Europe postulated that there were models of martyrdom current in the later middle ages which proved normative during the reformation period. Susannah Brietz Monta has looked at convergence during the reformation.[67] Although she mentions Anne Askew, Diane Watt seems reluctant to pursue the influences of her saints' lives beyond the death of Elizabeth Barton, and into the lives and deaths of those who did not share Elizabeth's particular faith.[68] The cases, however, of Elizabeth Barton and Joan Bocher show that the patterns are not merely literary, but may operate at a very personal level. The historian's universe contains much such dark matter of individual psychologies and family dynamics of which it is almost impossible to speak. But it is possible to note the more visible landmarks, and to suggest that martyrs did not die by texts alone.

There was however one major difference in the way in which Elizabeth and Joan operated. Elizabeth Barton's voice was a ventriloquized voice. It was not her voice but a voice within her. At a time when the female voice carried little or no authority in matters of religion, it was, unconsciously or not, a way to be heard.[69] Thomas Cranmer described it:

> Then was there heard a voice speaking within her belly, as it had been in a tun; her lips not greatly moving; ... the which voice, when it told any thing of the joys of heaven, it spake so sweetly and so heavenly, that everyman was ravaged with the hearing thereof; and the contrary, when it told any thing of hell, it spake so horribly and terribly, that it put the hearers in a great fear.[70]

On the other hand, Joan Bocher's voice was her own because she laid claim not to words but to the Word, whose authority, self-sufficiency, and transparency was recognized both by her and by her opponents. However, as Protestantism fractured and authority faltered, the voices were to come back.[71] But not for the Knells. They too had to get aback of Joan and before them lay four generations of Anglican clergy, often beneficed in and around the Marsh. Thomas Knell the elder was rector of Warehorne and Snave and vicar of Lyminge (d.1576–67); Thomas Knell the younger (1543–44–c.1592) lived in Kenardington; Barnabas Knell was beneficed in north Kent; and Paul

---

[67]   Brad S. Gregory, *Salvation at Stake: Christian Martyrdom in Early Modern Europe* (Cambridge, Mass., 1999); Susannah Brietz Monta, *Martyrdom and Literature in Early Modern England* (Cambridge, 2005). See also the review by Thomas S. Freeman, 'Early Modern Martyrs', *Journal of Ecclesiastical History*, 52/4 (2001): 696–701.

[68]   Watt, 'The Prophet at Home', pp. 175–6.

[69]   Mary Polito, *Governmental Arts*, p.127. Patricia Crawford is cautious: Crawford, *Women and Religion in England*, p. 112.

[70]   Thomas Cranmer, *Miscellaneous Writings and Letters of Thomas Cranmer*, ed. John Edmund Cox (Cambridge, 1846), pp. 272–3.

[71]   Alexandra Walsham, '"Frantick Hacket": Prophecy, Sorcery, Insanity and the Elizabethan Puritan Movement', *The Historical Journal*, 41/1 (1998): 27–66.

Knell was vicar of Newchurch. Paul Knell endured his own bloodless martyrdom as a royalist propagandist in the 1650s, and a vindication of sorts before his death in 1666.[72]

They all would have known the chapel where the Virgin came to Elizabeth Barton. It still stands on the slope which was the shoreline of Roman times, deserted and crumbling, alone in a field, visited mostly by sheep. Only the remains of a simple Tudor doorway locate the walls in time. The sea is now beyond the horizon, and the crowds which once pressed around the chapel are gone. Matthew Arnold's poem 'Dover Beach' of the mid-nineteenth century envisioned just such a retreat of sea and of faith. Its final stanza contrasts a world 'where ignorant armies clash by night' with one of personal fidelity in an impersonal world. The sixteenth century was not an impersonal world but a personal one of voices within and voices without, and the faithfulness and the conflict could be within the same family and under the same roof.

---

[72] See the respective entries 'Knell, Thomas the elder', 'Knell, Thomas the younger', and 'Knell, Paul', by David J. Crankshaw, Brett Usher, and J. T. Peacey, *ODNB*, vol. 31, pp. 874–5, 875–6, 873–4.

PART II
Institutions as Evidence for Transitions in Piety

Chapter 3

The Poor, Hospitals and Charity in Sixteenth-century Canterbury[*]

Sheila Sweetinburgh

To give to the poor was a pious act. Christ's commandment, 'You shall love the Lord your God ... and your neighbour as yourself', was echoed in the Pauline notion of the dual nature of charity. This duality encompasses the 'vertical links' associated with love of God and the 'horizontal links' associated with love of neighbours.[1] Thus charity might be said to encompass the medieval Christian's relationship with God, with his or her every spiritual act being a demonstration of this bond. While not discounting this holistic biblical concept of charity and its centrality in the Church's teachings during the Middle Ages and beyond, this chapter will focus on the second aspect – the love of neighbours – and, in particular, how benefactors and beneficiaries may have regarded the bonds produced through love of one's fellow man.

For those seeking to lead good Christian lives, the scriptural view of everyman as neighbour had important implications, which affected who should be helped, and how, because few were prepared to follow completely the example of men like St Francis. Thus charitable giving involved choices, and whomever the fifteenth- or sixteenth-century individual considered to be a neighbour may now provide valuable insights concerning the practice of piety and religious belief. During times of religious change and dislocation, this may be especially true, though doctrinal issues were not the only factors affecting charitable provision; potential benefactors also responded to ideological, economic and social considerations. In addition, the processes of almsgiving and associated attitudes to the poor were neither homogeneous nor unchanging in medieval England and, even though the religious changes of the sixteenth century – especially the denigration of purgatory – had fundamental implications for the role of the poor, heterogeneity remained the norm.

In general terms, the religious changes of the sixteenth century altered the

[*]   I should like to thank Dr Graham Durkin for permission to use his unpublished doctoral thesis on Elizabethan Canterbury and Dr Claire Bartram for providing a transcription of Sir Roger Manwood's last will and testament. The Canterbury Archaeological Society kindly provided a grant towards the cost of research.
[1]   John Henderson, *Piety and Charity in Late Medieval Florence* (Chicago and London, 1997), p. 9.

relationship between benefactors and beneficiaries. No longer was purgatory and the need for intercessory prayers uppermost in people's minds, nor could good works bring salvation, rather it was faith in the passion, death and resurrection of Christ that was considered sufficient. In essence, the will of John Mayor, a London scrivener, written in the 1540s, sums up this difference: his gift of a 20s portion of an outstanding 40s loan was to be given to the poor but he directed that those who were aided by this bounty should not pray for his soul, but were instead to '… be thankful unto God and to pray for the king'.[2] In some ways, divisions drawn between Catholics and Protestants on the basis of motivation are illusionary because Protestants also perceived the value of good works as demonstrations of 'the faith that brought salvation'.[3] Nonetheless, though they continued to use good works, their meanings were open to new interpretations.[4]

Charitable giving was complex in the sixteenth century. Potential benefactors were never exclusively motivated by religious considerations, and they might also employ different strategies, which could be used for various political reasons.[5] A wide diversity of benefactors was responsible for the sophisticated deployment of various forms of almsgiving to achieve a range of goals.[6]

Although doubts have been cast over the usefulness of wills in the study of piety during the Reformation, they often provide the main documentary source for these investigations.[7] Their widespread survival from the late medieval period has allowed them to be used to analyse communal and, more occasionally, familial

---

[2]   Guildhall Library, MS. 9172/1b, fol. 153 quoted in C. Daly, 'The Hospitals of London: Administration, Reformation and Benefaction, *c.* 1500–1572', unpublished D.Phil. Thesis, University of Oxford (1993), p. 97, n. 108.

[3]   Ibid., p. 96.

[4]   For a demonstration of this in relation to the wills of London's Elizabethan mercantile élite see David Hickman, 'From Catholic to Protestant: The Changing Meaning of Testamentary Religious Provisions in Elizabethan London', in Nicholas Tyacke (ed.), *England's Long Reformation, 1500–1800* (London, 1998), pp. 119–20.

[5]   Daly, 'Hospitals of London', pp. 75–111; Sandra Cavello, 'The Motivations of Benefactors: an Overview of Approaches to the Study of Charity', in Jonathan Barry and Colin Jones (eds), *Medicine and Charity Before the Welfare State* (London and New York, 1991), pp. 54–60.

[6]   Colin Jones, 'Some Recent Trends in the History of Charity', in Martin Daunton (ed.), *Charity, Self-interest and Welfare in the English Past* (London, 1996), pp. 56–60. Peregrine Horden, 'A Discipline of Relevance: The Historiography of the Later Medieval Hospital', *Social History of Medicine*, 1 (1988): 359–74.

[7]   Eamon Duffy, *The Stripping of the Altars: Traditional Religion in England c. 1400–c. 1580* (London, New Haven,1992), pp. 504–23. See also Clive Burgess, 'London Parishioners in Times of Change: St Andrew Hubbard, Eastcheap, c. 1450–1570', *Journal of Ecclesiastical History*, 53/1 (2002): 38–63.

charitable practices based on the parish or town.[8] For the sixteenth century there have been numerous studies of will preambles as a mark of the testator's religious beliefs.[9] Some of the more recent investigations have employed sophisticated preamble categories and have examined the will in its entirety to try to uncover shades of belief and apparent contradictions.[10] Their findings suggest that wills are useful as a means of elucidating how people from different areas, social groups and families used and appropriated conventional pious forms while remaining within the boundaries of ecclesiastical acceptability.

Canterbury in the Sixteenth Century

As a case study of charitable provision during the sixteenth century, Canterbury has certain advantages. Over 1,400 people from the city and its suburban parishes had wills proved in either the archdeaconry or consistory court between 1500 and 1600. Like the vast majority of will collections, lay male testators form by far the largest group, though Canterbury's extensive clerical population is an important sub-group and women are more common during the later decades. There is a fairly even spread of wills by decade across the century, and most decades produced a hundred wills or more, though this constituted only a small proportion of the adult population. The city's population has been estimated at about 3,700 in the 1560s following a forty year decline or stasis, but thereafter it rose rapidly reaching 6,000 in the 1590s.[11]

At various times during the sixteenth century, and especially during the middle decades, the polarization of religious views resulted in public and sometimes violent outbursts and disputes among Canterbury's citizens.[12] These highlight the actions of a vocal minority, and amongst the city's population as a whole there was apparently considerable religious diversity. This diversity was fuelled in a range of ways during different periods but preaching may have been especially significant. Among those likely to be influential in the early part of the century were friars and evangelical clerics, while in later decades, members of the re-founded cathedral clergy

---

[8]   For example: Andrew Brown, *Popular Piety in Late Medieval England: The Diocese of Salisbury 1250–1550* (Oxford 1995). Robert Lutton, *Lollardy and Orthodox Religion in Pre-Reformation England: Reconstructing Piety* (Woodbridge, 2006).

[9]   Of special reference to Kent: Peter Clark, *English Provincial Society from the Reformation to the Revolution: Religion, Politics and Society in Kent 1500–1640* (Hassocks, 1977), pp. 58–9, 74–6.

[10]   Claire Cross, 'The Development of Protestantism in Leeds and Hull, 1520–1640: The Evidence from Wills', *Northern History*, 18 (1982): 230–38. Graham Mayhew, 'The Progress of the English Reformation in East Sussex 1530–1559: The Evidence from Wills', *Southern History*, 5 (1983): 38–67; Hickman, 'From Catholic to Protestant', pp. 117–35.

[11]   Graham Durkin, 'The Civic Government and Economy of Elizabethan Canterbury', unpublished Ph.D Thesis, University of Kent (2001), p. 4.

[12]   Clark, *English Provincial Society*, pp. 29, 38–44, 59–61, 73–7, 98–102, 154, 163, 169, 174, 176.

proclaimed their views through sermons in the chapter house and, throughout the century, parishioners were probably affected by their local parson. For example, John Clerke, the incumbent at St Paul's until his death in 1555 was, like his curate, a strong believer in the Protestant cause, and several of his parishioners, including John Lamberhurst and Hugh Downey, seemingly followed his Calvinistic lead.[13] A decade later John Stone, the cleric at St Alphege, was equally committed to the cause, whereas two years earlier Rafe Prescott and at least one of his parishioners at St Mildred's, Agnes Benchkyn, wished to retain the 'old religion'.[14]

Canterbury was a regional market centre for a wide range of products. Victualling, inn-keeping and allied trades had been important for centuries but the loss of Becket's shrine in 1538 and the dissolution of the local monasteries had a serious impact on the city's provisioning industry. A certain amount of manufacturing continued to take place and the cloth industry did receive a considerable boost from religious refugees from continental Europe, who brought new skills. This was short lived, however, and during the later decades of Elizabeth's reign the civic authorities adopted a range of protectionist policies.[15] Nevertheless, the city's generally broad manufacturing base may have saved it from many of the economic and social problems faced by towns reliant on a single industry, but its population was adversely affected by such factors as inflation and prolonged harvest failure. Moreover, as a group the poor were the most vulnerable and cases of acute hardship were probably commonplace during years of crisis.

Like many civic authorities facing what appeared to be an ever-growing problem, the corporation tried to minimize the number of poor people entering the city, to aid those considered to be deserving, to provide work for the unemployed poor who were willing to do so, and to punish and, if possible, expel those who refused. This last group was seen as a moral blight on society, and, as part of its policy of social control to maintain public order, the corporation passed a number of ordinances to try to regulate their behaviour.[16] In this the leading citizens were supported by the ecclesiastical authorities: the church courts, like their secular counterparts, were used to punish those seen as transgressors.[17] Although the corporation does not seem to have been innovative in its policies, it was prepared to address the problems posed by the poor though, as elsewhere, not the root causes.[18] For example, its provision of hemp for unemployed workers preceded national legislation in Elizabeth's reign, and it similarly saw the value of certain hospitals as houses of correction.[19] The deserving poor were also aided through the parish, the overseers using the poor rate to relieve those under their jurisdiction.

---

[13] CKS, PRC 17/30/153; 17/27/127; 17/29/97; 17/26/295.
[14] CKS, PRC 32/29/65; 17/33/119v; 17/34/253.
[15] Durkin, 'Elizabethan Canterbury', p. 7.
[16] Ibid., p. 205.
[17] Ibid., pp. 188–91.
[18] Ibid., pp. 202–3, 205.
[19] Ibid., pp. 206–7.

The city had a number of medieval hospitals. Three survived the religious and political changes: the archiepiscopal hospitals of St John and St Nicholas, and also Maynard's spittle. This last foundation was brought under the corporation's jurisdiction in the mid-sixteenth century. One leading member of the judiciary, Leonard Cotton, seems to have taken a special interest in its welfare, building extra accommodation for named persons and making further provisions for the house in his will of 1605.[20] The Poor Priests' hospital became a municipal bridewell and a blue-coat school, while the third archiepiscopal foundation, the pilgrim hospital of St Thomas, went through several changes before finally becoming an almshouse and school. Under monastic patronage, the leper hospitals of St James and St Lawrence did survive the dissolution of their respective mother houses but not the envious eyes of certain Canterbury citizens, and both became private houses. In the 1590s, Sir Roger Manwood and Sir John Boys founded two well-endowed almshouses.

The Poor, Hospitals and Charitable Provision

During the first three decades of the sixteenth century, about a third of Canterbury's testators included the poor among their beneficiaries. Thereafter the proportion increased to over a half during Edward VI's reign. The poor were similarly remembered by just over half of Canterbury's Marian testators, but under Elizabeth the proportion dropped, though it was still higher than the early years of the century. However, even if in general terms these figures suggest continuity rather than change, the form of the bequest does appear to have altered. Between the reigns of Henry VIII and Elizabeth there was a shift in practice. Instead of leaving the choice of recipients to executors or to chance, testators chose to select paupers who were members of their current parish or from their home parish or other designated parishes. Throughout the century, alms were distributed on the day of burial or at the discretion or convenience of the executors, which may have placed severe geographical restrictions on potential recipients. Yet this was not seen as sufficiently limiting during the later decades and, instead, testators often provided precise instructions, possibly in response to the growing numbers of locally resident poor people who might otherwise expect to share in such bounty.

Nonetheless, even though these charitable acts were increasingly focused on the local, some later sixteenth-century Canterbury testators still wished to retain elements within the gift-giving process employed by their predecessors. Cash doles had always been used but a widely chosen alternative was bread, occasionally with beer, cheese, beef or pottage. Its distribution was overwhelmingly tied to the burial day, and sometimes to the other funeral services, and this form continued to be used by mid-century testators, though its popularity had severely declined by 1580. Some Puritan preachers considered this might be construed as linking charity to prayers for

---

[20] Ibid., pp. 208–9. W.K. Jordan, 'Social Institutions in Kent 1480–1660: A Study of the Changing Patterns of Social Aspiration', *AC*, 75 (1961): 46–7.

the dead.[21] However, a few testators in the later decades of the century continued the practice of 'feeding the hungry' on special days such as certain Fridays, Christmas, Good Friday or Easter, and on their obits; an approach that their ancestors would have understood with regard to its religious symbolism. Echoes of the seven corporal works of mercy can also be found in the distribution of clothing to the poor (or of fuel), especially when linked to the day of burial or to feast days. For example, John Lewis of St Paul's parish seemingly adapted these traditional pious forms. As well as leaving various sums of money for the poor of Canterbury, he stipulated that whosoever had his house in St Paul's parish would every year on Christmas Eve give a gown, a pair of shoes and 6d to the poorest man or woman in the parish.[22] Even though this too would have been well understood by his forebears as likely to produce intercessional prayers by a series of grateful recipients, for Lewis his beneficence may have been seen in other ways. In itself it would make little difference to the local poor but this ongoing gift may have been influenced by ideas about community, belonging, commemoration and remembrance. Though belonging to one of a number of Welsh families in St Paul's parish, Lewis seems to have been childless at his death, and he might, therefore, have wished to be remembered by his kinsmen and fellow parishioners through his charitable actions.

In contrast, a single cash bequest to the poor of a specific parish or to the poor box probably indicates different ideas. The poor box was most popular in Edward's reign, regaining some of its popularity during the first years of Elizabeth but thereafter testators primarily returned to employing their executors to distribute their gifts. Paul Rychmonde of St Andrew's parish held several properties in Canterbury and in east Kent when he made his will in 1551. He left the arrangements for his burial to his executors, his pious bequests comprising 6s 8d for tithes unpaid, 3s 4d to the poor folk's box and £6 13s 4d to be distributed to the poor in their houses within fifteen days, the task to be carried out by his executors.[23] His gift to the parish poor box would be used to supplement the sums collected by the overseers of the poor, thereby aiding both the poor and possibly his fellow parishioners. The overseers would be expected to know the most deserving cases and, like his bequest to the poor householders, such people would not be itinerants. Instead, his beneficiaries might include those who had temporarily fallen on hard times through no fault of their own, as well as the sick and old. Thus his charitable giving might imply that he was a supporter of the Edwardian commonwealth ethos which criticized the whole notion of salvation by works, viewing it as detrimental to society through its waste of precious material resources on religious houses, saints' relics and other dead sticks and stones.[24]

---

[21] Peter Marshall, *Beliefs and the Dead in Reformation England* (Oxford, 2002), pp. 167–8.

[22] CKS, PRC 17/51/375.

[23] CKS, PRC 17/27/248.

[24] Diarmaid MacCulloch, *Tudor Church Militant: Edward VI and the Protestant Reformation* (London, 1999), p. 125.

For men such as Rychmonde, the socio-economic and life-cycle status of the poor was crucial. Executors, churchwardens and parish overseers might be expected to identify suitable recipients but some testators left nothing to chance. Concern for particular groups in society had been a feature of some early sixteenth-century Canterbury wills, and among those mentioned were the infirm, imbeciles, bedridden, poor married couples who were householders, poor scholars and poor neighbours. In part, these groups were selected because they were needy through no fault of their own and such gifts might at least temporarily improve their living conditions. Others were targeted because they had the potential to become useful members of society and to rise above their current circumstances. This could be achieved through the provision of education, an apprenticeship or, particularly for young women, through marriage. Even though the proportion of testators who made bequests for the marriages of young maidens was never large, as a category of poor person they were the most popular during the early decades of the century but their favoured status declined after 1560. It is not clear why this should be, because the patriarchal family was seen as the bedrock of the Protestant Church and of society, and sermons reinforced this view of the naturalness of the married state for women.[25]

In addition to their life-cycle status, it seems likely some testators were concerned about the moral wellbeing of their poor beneficiaries. Selecting those of good fame and knowledge was frequently the task of executors, but Sir William Bull's desire in 1529 that his poor recipients should say a psalter of Our Lady for the benefit of his soul suggests that he was looking for something more.[26] It is worth noting that certain almshouse statutes made provision for inmates to be instructed in these basic prayers. By the last years of Henry VIII's reign, the reasons for helping such people had seemingly changed. In 1544, Robert Browne still intended that his poor beneficiaries should be honest and good-living poor people and householders, yet his wife was to distribute the money for his soul and those of his friends in honour of Jesus Christ, which may indicate that the perils of purgatory had not totally disappeared from his thoughts.[27] This apparently hybrid position is interesting, though how far this focus on Christ is suggestive of a new type of attitude to charity is difficult to determine; it may have its roots in the early sixteenth-century interest in devotions associated with the Jesus Mass. Five years later John Mylles wished the poor to be helped 'for God's sake' and, in 1551, William Wellys stipulated that his executors should exercise their duty for '... fear of God and in tender care of poor widows and fatherless children', a paternalistic attitude that was adopted by some

---

[25] Anthony Fletcher, 'The Protestant Idea of Marriage in Early Modern England', in Anthony Fletcher and Peter Roberts (eds), *Religion, Culture and Society in Early Modern Britain. Essays in Honour of Patrick Collinson* (Cambridge, 1994), pp. 162–3. Such charitable bequests had a long history in England: Diana O'Hara, *Courtship and Constraint. Rethinking the Making of Marriage in Tudor England* (Manchester, 2000), p. 197.

[26] CKS, PRC 17/18/240.

[27] CKS, PRC 17/23/213.

late sixteenth-century testators.[28] Under Mary's rule John Codyngton and Richard Crosse were able to express their wishes to receive prayers from the poor, indicating a return to the traditional pre-Reformation reciprocal arrangement between the rich and the poor.[29] In the 1580s, however, James Benchkyn's and Stephen Vincent's desire to aid the 'godly poor' and the 'God-fearing poor', respectively, presumably denotes a very different relationship and a total rejection of the link between good works and salvation.[30] Instead, their beneficiaries were expected to express their Protestant (possibly Puritan) credentials whereby, in a sense, they reflected the piety and social reputation of their benefactors. Thus reciprocity was not dead, but was adapted to meet the expectations of those who saw 'their poor' as fulfilling the counter-gift through religious observances, gratitude and sober behaviour.[31]

It may also be possible to chart such shifts in the ideas of benefactors with regard to their charitable giving to the city's hospitals. During the first three decades of the sixteenth century, all the hospitals, except the Poor Priests', were mentioned in at least one Canterbury will. Support for St Thomas' and the two leper hospitals of St Lawrence and St James was extremely muted, but Maynard's, St John's and St Nicholas' were more popular; and in total about 15 per cent of the Canterbury testators made at least one hospital bequest. The differing level of support enjoyed by the various hospitals was a product of several factors: type of inmate accommodated, type of patron, topographical position, its reputation and status and possibly its financial position. For example, the apparent indifference to the plight of St Lawrence's and St James' (few sisters were living in either hospital during Henry VIII's reign) may be linked to their extra-mural position to the south of the city because their benefactors came exclusively from the city's southern parishes.[32] Neighbourliness may have been important for William Laurence of St Paul's parish. In 1506, he made bequests to three named sisters and the prioress at the nearby hospital of St Lawrence.

For many of these early sixteenth-century Canterbury benefactors the hospital formed one element in their gift-giving strategy, cash bequests to these hospitals complementing alms given to some or all of the city's friaries and religious houses. Yet in most cases the primary recipient of these pious bequests was the testator's parish church. For example, in 1509, Margaret Chestefeld bequeathed 3s 4d to the brothers and sisters at the nearby hospital of St John. She also gave 6s 8d towards the steeple at the neighbouring priory of St Gregory and wished to be buried in its churchyard. Her other pious bequests were directed towards her parish church and a

---

[28]   CKS, PRC 17/26/222; 17/27/126.

[29]   CKS, PRC 17/32/214; 17/32/186.

[30]   CKS, PRC 17/44/36; 32/35/138v.

[31]   Hickman, 'From Catholic to Protestant', pp. 126–30.

[32]   The presence of a beer stall run by Richard Welles's wife in the precincts of St James' hospital may also have deterred potential benefactors: *Kentish Visitations of Archbishop William Wareham and his Deputies, 1511–12*, ed. K.L Wood-Leigh (Kent Records, vol. 24, 1984), p. 12.

parish church in Thanet, and her funeral days and temporary chantry were placed under the care of her parish priest.[33]

Some donors, however, were apparently prepared to develop their relationship with the hospital beyond a simple cash gift which was made with or without the explicit request for intercessory prayers for their souls. Such donors established links with their chosen institution by seeking a range of counter gifts that were important in terms of the living and the dead. Intercessory services were one vital part of this gift-exchange process but benefactors were similarly concerned about matters of commemoration and remembrance. By inclusion in the house's bede roll or by receiving the services reserved for departed inmates, benefactors became part of the hospital community at death. In 1503, John Whytlok, for example, wished to be remembered in the bede rolls at both St Nicholas' and St John's hospitals. Joane Bakke, in 1500, intended that the brothers and sisters of St John's, Canterbury, would receive 3s 4d annually for three years in order to celebrate her obit as they would for a brother or sister who had died there.[34]

Benefactors seem to have shown almost no interest in the poor pilgrims at St Thomas' hospital. Instead, the few testators who remembered this place focused their gift giving on the Corpus Christi fraternity that met there. In 1521, John Williamson, the parson at St George's parish, left small sums of money to the prioresses, brothers and sisters at four Canterbury hospitals but neither the staff nor the pilgrims at St Thomas' were mentioned, his gift of 26s 8d being directed towards the fraternity. This may reflect his unwillingness to aid the itinerant poor, because his will contains several charitable bequests, including the stipulation that there was to be no common dole; instead, within five days of his burial, his executors were to visit every Canterbury parish and, with the help of the various curates, give at least 1d to each needy and deserving poor man and woman.[35]

During Edward's reign, interest in the hospitals fell considerably and the city suffered its first casualty when St James' was surrendered to the crown in 1551.[36] It is not clear what was happening at St Lawrence's but it survived the destruction of St Augustine's abbey, its mother house, and may have become a hospital for the poor.[37] Yet, there is nothing to suggest that the leading citizens had followed their counterparts in London where hospitals were re-established as part of the Edwardian commonwealth enterprise.[38] Though holding considerable capital assets, the

---

[33] CKS, PRC 17/11/91.

[34] CKS, PRC 32/7/70; 17/7/213.

[35] CKS, PRC 17/15/101.

[36] *CPR* 1550–53, p. 181.

[37] In 1552, it was called the 'spytall of St Lawrence': CKS, PRC 17/27/127.

[38] Susan Brigden, *London and the Reformation* (Oxford, 1989), pp. 477–80. Daly, 'Hospitals of London'. MacCulloch, *Tudor Church Militant*, p. 23.

absence of a strong patron may have left St Lawrence's in a weak position and, in 1557, it too was dissolved.[39]

This seeming indifference to the fate of these two ancient houses is reflected in the marked drop in the proportion of Canterbury testators who made hospital bequests, a decline that had its beginnings in the mid-1530s. However, in Elizabeth's reign, especially during the middle years, the hospitals of St John, St Nicholas and Maynard received slightly more bequests. It is not clear if this was in any way linked to the corporation's use of St Thomas' hospital, and then the Poor Priests', to house the poor, but it does suggest that the leading citizens saw the value of the ancient hospitals, especially when they could be used as part of the corporation's strategy for dealing with the poor. Yet both St Thomas' and the Poor Priests' hospitals had fallen into decay by the early years of Elizabeth. Archbishop Parker 'rescued' St Thomas' in 1569, but within a few years it was again said to be ruinous and let out as tenements; and the master at the Poor Priests' had apparently abandoned his dilapidated house at about the same time.[40] Such structural problems were insufficient to stop the corporation from using the buildings: both St Thomas' and the Poor Priests' were employed as municipal houses of correction by 1572 and 1575 respectively.[41] Probably as a consequence of these developments, in 1586, Archbishop Whitgift re-established St Thomas' hospital as an almshouse, drawing up detailed ordinances for the selection and conduct of the inmates.[42]

It is possible to detect in the hospital bequests from the 1570s and 1580s what might be described as something akin to the corporation's paternalistic attitude towards the various groups of poor people it dealt with. A few testators continued to establish simple almshouses, donors apparently seeing their charity in terms of the recipients' material welfare rather than that of their own souls. Moreover, by providing shelter, benefactors may have believed that their beneficiaries would be seen and see themselves as householders, and by extension upright members of the community. Similarly, by providing a succession of poorer people with the means of earning their own living through the lending of stock – a method Elizabeth Bassocke wished her executors to adopt in 1583 – testators might see themselves as aiding the community, as well as certain poor individuals.[43] Yet her other charitable bequests, which included various sums of money to be given to the poor and needy by ward, with a further 20s to be given to the poor at Maynard's spittle, seem highly reminiscent of earlier charitable forms, though without the intercessional clause.

Nevertheless, even if at times there are problems in trying to uncover evidence about belief and motivation from the testamentary evidence alone, the foundation documents for Manwood's almshouses, the Jesus hospital and the re-founded St

---

[39]   In 1557, the only people said to be present were the prioress, a sister and a young woman: W. Page (ed.), *Victoria County History, Kent* (London, 1926), vol. 2, p. 212.

[40]   Ibid., p. 213.

[41]   Durkin, 'Elizabethan Canterbury', pp. 205–6, n. 699.

[42]   CCAL, U24/1.

[43]   CKS, PRC 17/45/226.

Thomas' hospital under Whitgift may provide clues for the late Elizabethan period. Manwood records that he founded his almshouse for the 'comon welthe', the six inmates to be aged, poor and honest.[44] Such people might equally have found a place at Boys's hospital assuming they had been living in certain local parishes for at least seven years, and the disabled unemployed were also received into the Jesus hospital.[45] Similarly, the brothers and sisters at St Thomas' were to be aged and impotent but, most important of all, they had to be local residents. The stipulation that they should have dwelt in Canterbury or its suburbs for at least seven years was very different from Archbishop Parker's intention that twelve beds should be kept for the itinerant poor, which was in itself a reflection of the hospital's original function.[46] These criteria are not unlike those applied by some medieval hospital patrons, but there is a greater stress on the benefit to the local community in caring for those no longer able to be productive members of society. In this way, Boys and Manwood, in particular, emphasized their weighty response to the ills of late Elizabethan England.

Having assigned places to those who had been contributors to Canterbury society, whether as poor artisans, servants or the recipients of parish or municipal hemp, these hospital founders also considered the young.[47] The founding of almshouse schools was a second feature of many well-endowed fifteenth-century houses, and the provision of education continued to be seen as important in Edwardian and Elizabethan England. For late sixteenth-century Canterbury, even though Manwood's grammar school was at Sandwich, his will indicates that his almshouse and school were components of his holistic strategy to provide for the poor and the local communities of which he and his ancestors had been a part. The third institutional component was a house of correction to be sited next to the 'comen jayle howse'. Here the middle-aged poor who refused to work at home could be 'honestly' employed. At the Jesus hospital and St Thomas' the scholars were to be members of the institution. Their education provided useful skills allowing them to become assets to the local community, while a favoured few were helped to attend certain colleges at Oxford and Cambridge, possibly to become ministers and preachers. Consequently, these founders were in many ways emulating the earlier chantry foundations, where the production of an educated clergy from the sons of the laity in order to counter problems of heresy had been an important function.

Also like their predecessors, religious observance was a vital part of almshouse routine. Boys built a chapel at his hospital, there was already a chapel at St Thomas', and Manwood's almsfolk lived next to the parish church. At all three establishments, the almspeople were expected to attend morning and evening prayer most days, to be joined by the poor scholars at St Thomas' and at the Jesus hospital. For Boys, such

---

[44] CCAL, CC/S7.
[45] CCAL, U38/1; U38/3.
[46] CCAL, U24/1.
[47] Hemp, flax or wool was provided by the corporation or parish overseers for the poor to work in their own homes to counter idleness and to make them productive.

attendance was a significant act of piety, and whereas their early sixteenth century counterparts had said the *Ave Maria* and *Pater Noster* daily for the soul of the hospital's patron and benefactors, his almsfolk followed the Book of Common Prayer. They were also expected to take communion at least twice a year and, possibly just as importantly, they were to attend sermons in the cathedral chapterhouse on Sundays and holy days. Manwood's grateful recipients were to follow a slightly different routine: attending morning service they were to sit together in their own pew, their behaviour watched over by the effigy of Manwood which had been set up according to his wishes in the south aisle (see Plate 7.1). Manwood also seems to have adapted traditional aspects of the patron/recipient relationship. His almspeople collected their 1d loaves from a board set up by his tomb, allowing him to appropriate the religious symbolism of his forefathers to which he could attach new meanings where he considered it fitting. For example, the loaves offered the enduring symbolism of the Eucharist and its focus on Christ as the 'bread of life', yet not in pre-Reformation terms. Manwood's bread, like the communion bread, remained just that, providing the means to demonstrate his paternalism through the giving of 'daily bread'.

It is difficult to gauge how recipients of institutional charitable provision responded to the changing circumstances of the sixteenth century, but the surviving 37 wills made by inmates at St John's hospital may produce some clues. Almost half of these were made by inmates living at the hospital before 1545, four date from Mary's reign and the remainder from the Elizabethan period. Those belonging to the first group almost invariably included bequests to the hospital and/or to the brothers and sisters, but only a small minority also intended the unnamed poor should be helped. Gift giving to the hospital covered a number of different areas including bequests for burial, to the hospital chapel for specific items, for improvements to the inmates' living quarters, for funeral services, to priests (sometimes for conducting the services) and to the brothers and sisters collectively and as individuals. John Rooper was exceptional in the level of his bequests to the hospital chapel, seeking to provide a new window in the Lady Chapel and a chantry chapel for the benefit of his soul and those of several others.[48] Instead, most inmates preferred to give to their fellows at the hospital. The provision of bread, possibly also ale and cheese, at burial (and at the other funeral services) was apparently customary, but its inclusion in wills may indicate feelings of regard that transcended custom. A few testators expected their largesse to extend to the poor. Exceptionally, Johanna Harder also provided small cash doles for the brothers and sisters with the specific intention that they should pray for her soul.[49] Personal regard was presumably an important factor and many included other members of the hospital by name among their beneficiaries. Such practices may have been especially valued by those without close kin, but for several inmates they were able to give numerous items to their relatives and to those seen as part of the 'family' at the hospital.

---

[48]   CKS, PRC 32/15/8.
[49]   CKS, PRC 32/10/144.

Though willing to help their own institution, the pre-1545 group of will-makers at St John's showed relatively little interest in other religious houses, especially after *c.* 1520. This is reflected throughout the bequests of east Kent testators.[50] For example, in 1501, Richard Mildnale of St John's had left most of the money from the sale of his property to St Augustine's abbey and in 1520, Thomas Bencher wished someone to go to the Rood of Grace at Boxley, Kent, on his behalf but bequests of this sort disappear thereafter.[51] This is perhaps an indication of changing doctrinal ideas. At least some, although not all, members of the hospital were sympathetic to Protestant ideas in the early 1540s, but social and moral issues were probably also significant.[52] Yet it is difficult to discern any clear differences in the wills up to the mid-1540s and the absence of any Edwardian wills is disappointing, especially since the few that survive from Mary's reign demonstrate traditional charitable provision. In 1555, John Corneforde bequeathed money for altar cloths and he also gave money for marriages of poor maids and poor young men. His fellow brothers and sisters were to receive bread and wax for tapers, possibly to be used at his burial.[53] For Nicholas Scott in 1556, however, his family were the principal beneficiaries, receiving cash, goods and his property; while St John's received 6s 8d if he died there and the poor gained alms at his burial.[54]

Those making wills at St John's during Elizabeth's reign left no specific bequests to the poor and far fewer gifts to either the chapel or inmates of the hospital. Instead, family was seemingly the first and sometimes only concern. In 1578, Jane Grene was the sole testator who named the hospital's chapel among her beneficiaries, though in 1598, George Keies did leave money for general repairs.[55] Gifts to other brothers and sisters were slightly more common, either to named individuals: Jane Grene gave Sister Fourd a smock; or to the inmates: in 1585, Alexander Smith intended 5s should be given for customary drinking, presumably as a mark of commemoration, and a further 3s 4d to the poor of the hospital, though whether he meant the brothers and sisters or those renting tenements within the hospital precincts is not clear.[56] Anthony Allen wished, in 1560, that most of his livestock would pass to his wife and son.[57] His wife may have left the family home to move into his house at St John's after his death, possibly bringing with her the poultry he had bequeathed to her. She certainly inherited all his household goods at the hospital and one of the swarms of bees, which were to be installed there in their hive. The other two swarms and their hives were to become the property of St John's for the

---

[50]   Sheila Sweetinburgh, *The Role of the Hospital in Medieval England. Gift-giving and the Spiritual Economy* (Dublin, 2004), p. 118.

[51]   CKS, PRC 32/7/27; 17/14/309.

[52]   *LP*, vol. 18, pp. 291, 312, 345, 366.

[53]   CKS, PRC 32/26/126.

[54]   CKS, PRC 32/26/141.

[55]   CKS, PRC 32/34/4; 32/38/211.

[56]   CKS, PRC 32/35/184.

[57]   CKS, PRC 32/38/228.

benefit of the hospital community. In contrast, Richard Russell (1596), Margaret Hilles (1597) and Magdalene Colbrand (1579) bequeathed all their property to their kinsfolk.[58] Some of these items may have been at the family house outside the hospital and would not have been seen as belonging to St John's, whereas others may have been in the brother's or sister's dwelling within the precincts. For example, Colbrand gave a joined cupboard 'standing in my chamber' to her son Nicholas. Some medieval hospital ordinances stipulated that the goods of a deceased inmate became the house's property. However, at St John's it is not certain if such goods were ever envisaged as belonging to the hospital as a type of mortuary gift. The inmates seem to have considered their goods as private property to be bequeathed as they saw fit.

For many at St John's in the late sixteenth century, the hospital seemingly offered a place of shelter in old age where the demands of communal living were relatively minor, amounting to daily prayers in the chapel and some meals in the refectory. As almsfolk of the archbishop, and therefore members of the institutional poor, they were presumably expected to be respectable and God-fearing Protestants. Additionally, it is possible that the Protestant Church's stress on the value of the family may have meant that those in authority encouraged the inmates to maintain familial and other contacts outside the hospital, a practice that carried over into testamentary provision. Yet how far this differed from the experiences of those living at St John's in the first decades of the century is difficult to ascertain. The revised hospital ordinances of 1299 had stressed the inmates' spiritual duties and for some this involved at least a partial withdrawal from secular society. In contrast, by the mid-sixteenth century, the hospital gate was no longer a barrier to the outside world and instead of praying for the souls of their benefactors the inmates were expected to follow the Book of Common Prayer.

Conclusions

The Christian duty to help one's neighbour was adopted by some testators throughout the sixteenth century. Whereas it had been linked to the doing of good works, to the reciprocal response of the poor to provide intercessory prayers and to the perils of purgatory, the abandonment of such doctrinal ideas did not lead to a decline in testamentary charitable provision in Canterbury. Instead, concern for the poor seems to have increased, at least in terms of the proportion of testators giving to the unnamed poor, though whether this was a result of the loss of other avenues of pious giving or a response to the growing numbers of paupers is unclear. Certainly the city's testators remained committed to family and community, though concern for the latter seems to have produced a narrowing of the categories of poor person who should be helped. This narrowing was typological and topographical, leading in broad terms to a concentration on local poor householders who had been resident for

---

[58]   CKS, PRC 17/51/310; 32/38/58; 32/34/83v.

several years in the benefactor's parish. If unemployed, the recipient should be willing to work if able, and the provision of wool, hemp or some other commodity that could be worked was seen by a few testators, and the municipal and parish authorities, as part of their charitable strategy. Consequently, the poor were divided into three groups: those incapable of work, those willing to work if employment could be provided, and the idle (and often itinerant). Such ideas seem to have become increasingly important in Canterbury from the middle years of Henry VIII's reign and continued to take shape during the rest of the century. This was a product of crown legislation and the national and local situation, as well as the developing perceptions of the city's leading citizens and the middling sort. In addition to these and other ideological and cultural factors, religion played a part in the shaping of these perceptions and responses to the poor.

Throughout the century, there were those whose charitable provision consisted of a simple bequest to the generic poor or to designated groups, but there was a minority who employed a symbolic vocabulary in their gift giving. For example, during the sixteenth century, some testators gave gifts that suggest the corporal works of mercy, used symbolic numbers such as four or 12, and distributed gifts on saints' feast days or the principal Christian festivals. The religious changes under Edward and Elizabeth did not result in a total rejection of the employment of such elements, even among those holding apparently Calvinistic views. Their willingness to deploy charitable forms that would have been understood by their ancestors in spiritually symbolic terms is extremely interesting, suggesting a desire to adapt forms which contained within them special qualities. Thus, on one level the enduring nature of these charitable expressions was seen as valuable but, even more significant, such expressions could be given new meanings. The vocabulary of charitable provision concerning the poor employed by some late sixteenth-century Canterbury testators differs little from that used at the beginning of the century. However, the meanings of that vocabulary were now understood in Protestant terms. The appropriation of an apparently ancient vocabulary of charitable provision in the late sixteenth century enabled contemporaries to highlight the advancement of the new faith.

Chapter 4

'There hath not bene any gramar scole kepte, preacher maytened or pore people releved, other then … by the same chauntreye'

Educational Provision and Piety in Kent, c. 1400 – 1640[*]

G.M. Draper

Introduction

This chapter explores the funding of educational provision by laypeople. It examines how personal and communal devotion acted as a motive for providing this funding either directly or indirectly. It is only through texts that we can begin to reach the personal sanctity of heartfelt beliefs, hopes or fears, or practices of individual prayer which lay behind the outward expressions. Education provided the basis by which people read and interpreted texts, and must therefore be considered as part of religious practice and of literate culture as a whole.

The chapter places piety within the specifics of region and locality. Kent is a county whose society, economy and culture before the modern period must be analysed with respect to its natural *pays* such as marshland.[1] Romney Marsh is one of the few areas to have received a detailed consideration of literacy and schooling in the medieval period.[2] Together with the adjacent Cinque Ports of New Romney

---

[*] At the request of the author, initials instead of the forenames of cited authors are supplied in the footnotes.

[1] A. Everitt, *Continuity and Colonization: The Evolution of Kentish Settlement*, (Leicester, 1986), p. 43.

[2] On this and for what follows see G.M. Draper, 'Literacy and its Transmission in the Romney Marsh Area *c*. 1150–1550', unpublished Ph.D. Thesis, University of Kent (2003); G.M. Draper and F. Meddens, *The Sea and the Marsh; the Medieval Cinque Port of New Romney* (Pre-Construct Archaeology monograph, forthcoming).

and Hythe, Romney Marsh had a highly developed and early literate culture.[3] (See Map 1.1) For example, Romney Marsh had a peasant landmarket which was recorded in writing by local scribes from the 1220s. Religious, liturgical and legal texts were possessed by both rural and urban parishes there from *c.* 1200.[4] From the late fourteenth century there were developments in education and in literate practice, particularly the greater involvement of laypeople in writing for so-called pragmatic purposes. In the later fifteenth century, the use of writing in either Latin or English by local inhabitants for routine accounting was encouraged. The question of whether such developments influenced pious practice or *vice versa* is explored in this chapter by reference to a range of subjects: the foundation of chantries which funded a building or a priest; colleges of priests; the educational functions of hospitals; book ownership and university attendance; the endowment of an exceptionally early Kentish school; and a specific example of pious personal self-expression embedded in the material and written culture of Kent.

This chapter addresses a set of questions concerning the transitions in education and devotion between the medieval and early modern periods. How did expressions of piety change in the foundation and endowment of schooling? How did the tensions within local communities between old and new practices of religion relate to the uses of writing? What were the changing roles of individual and communal ways of providing education?

The Provision of Schooling in Kent

Piety and education in later medieval Kent were fundamentally tied together within four different spheres: schools in the old established monastic houses; teaching provided locally in parishes by priests and chaplains; instruction which was part of the life of chantries, hospitals, colleges of priests and collegiate churches; and grammar schooling at Sevenoaks which was supported financially by a London merchant in the early fifteenth century. Schooling in monastic houses across Kent was significant but lies outside the scope of this study. Examining the other spheres raises particular questions about the changing role of piety in educational provision between the late medieval and early modern periods: how did piety and education relate to the Dissolution and Reformation in terms of events and chronology? Can and should school foundations and a literate revolution, or at least a strong growth of literacy, be seen indisputably as early-modern events and part of the Protestant

---

[3]   A.F. Butcher, 'The Functions of Script in a Speech Community of a Late Medieval Town, c.1300–1550', in A. Walsham and J. Crick (eds), *The Uses of Script And Print 1300-1700* (Cambridge, 2004), pp. 157–70.

[4]   G.M. Draper, 'Small Fields and Wet Land: Inheritance Practices and the Transmission of Real Property in the Romney Marshes c.1150–1390', *Landscapes*, 6 (Spring 2005): 18–45.

Reformation, as Clark suggested?[5] Did the endowed grammar school in the county at Sevenoaks represent a new form of both education and commemoration, and did this very early school, as has been suggested, embody a rejection by a new generation of individualistic founders of the role of chantries in education? Moreover, was it a development foreshadowed by changes in the curriculum and purposes of a late medieval college in Kent? These questions pose a challenge to the historiography of the last century which ignored both the nature and extent of medieval education in Kent.

Chantries and Hospitals as Places for Learning and Teaching

A number of chantries were established in Kent in the high Middle Ages, probably 300 chantries and chapels before 1350.[6] They included, for example, the ones in Sevenoaks and Ashford parish churches where education took place by, and most likely before, the fifteenth century. After the Black Death and the subsequent epidemics of the later fourteenth century, there was a renewed stimulus to found or re-found chantries. Excessive deaths focussed the minds of those near the end of life on prayer for the health of their own souls, of their parents and all the faithful deceased.

Chantry foundations can be analysed in three categories: small and localized ones supporting a chaplain, larger ones typically involving a building such as a chantry chapel in a parish church, and very significant ones outside the county but supported by lands in Kent acquired for the purpose. All types, however, supported education. The duty of education was sometimes specified in documents concerning chantry foundation from the late fourteenth century but many chantry priests, both rural and urban, offered education.[7] It may have been so commonly viewed as part of their duties as to be only mentioned in passing. This proposition contrasts with an earlier view in which the *Maison Dieu* at Ospringe near Faversham, and Higham and Tenterden chantries were described as '... the only Chantries in Kent where the priest was to teach scholars'.[8] Evidence for education in the context of chantries in Kent is rather random and patchy and could suggest

---

[5]   See P. Clark, *English Provincial Society from the Reformation to the Revolution: Religion, Politics and Society in Kent 1500–1640* (Hassocks, 1977), pp. 185, 189–190. Clark based his analysis on Stone's evidence mainly from 1640 onwards.

[6]   S. Sweetinburgh, 'The Territorial Organisation of the Church', in T. Lawson and D. Killingray (eds), *An Historical Atlas of Kent* (Chichester, 2004), p. 40.

[7]   M. Bennett, 'Education and Advancement', in R. Horrox (ed.), *Fifteenth-Century Attitudes: Perceptions of Society in Late Medieval England* (Cambridge 1994), p. 84; M. Clanchy, *From Memory to Written Record: England 1066-1377* (2nd edition, Oxford–Cambridge, Mass., 1993), p. 241.

[8]   *Kent Chantries*, ed. A. Hussey (Kent Records, vol. 12, Ashford, 1936), p. 305.

that such education was too: rather it seems to have been an accepted function of chantries and of the chaplains based there. Where chantries were small and local, typically funding a chantry priest, the provision sometimes continued only for a limited period after the founder's death, with a perception that this was the crucial period for prayers and reflecting a founder's realistic hopes of remembrance by family and friends.[9] This may have contributed to apparent discontinuities of education at a period when it was often based around individuals such as chantry priests rather than buildings. A good example is the chantry which John Lynot endowed in the later fourteenth century at Ivychurch on Romney Marsh. John left some land to provide for a priest and it seems a relative, Elias Lynot, was to be the chantry priest. Lynot's chantry was no longer operating by the 1420s, and in fact Canterbury Cathedral Priory had acquired the land.

A notable clergy-list of 1374 demonstrates the role of parochial and chantry chaplains in education. It shows that there were two chaplains in Ivychurch parish in addition to the parish priest, one probably standing in for the non-resident rector and the other, presumably Lynot's chantry priest, teaching. This clergy-list covered Lympne deanery, encompassing churches on Romney Marsh and north and east towards Ashford and Folkestone.[10] In some parishes, chaplains were performing priestly functions in the absence of a rector or vicar. However, in others the chaplains were additional to the rector or vicar and here education was apparently among their functions.[11] This was certainly the case in the wealthier churches of Romney Marsh, which had a greater proportion of such chaplains than parishes elsewhere in the deanery. The education provided by clerics was used for pragmatic as well as liturgical purposes: legal, estate, administrative and urban record keeping. In 1374, the vicar of New Romney Robert de Bregges and/or one of the four chaplains in the town were teaching reading and writing. These skills were employed locally in manorial administration by a member of the next generation, Thomas de Bregges, perhaps Robert's nephew.

A chantry at Sandwich is a good example of a larger foundation and its educational functions. Thomas Elys, a prosperous merchant, founded and endowed a chantry in the parish church in 1392, apparently based on a priest house of the thirteenth century or earlier in the church.[12] One of the three priests was specified to give instruction to the youth of the town in Elys's will. This was therefore another chantry whose priest was required to teach. Testamentary evidence indicates the continued activity of this school at the end of the fifteenth century, when education in Kent was in some interpretations supposed to be at a very low

---

[9]   S. Sweetinburgh, 'Joining the Sisters: Female Inmates of the Late Medieval Hospitals in East Kent', *AC*, 123 (2003): 27, 29, 31, 33.
[10]   CCAL, Chartae Antiquae DCc S425.
[11]   G.M. Draper, 'Church, Chapel and Clergy on Romney Marsh after the Black Death', *Romney Marsh Irregular*, 16 (October 2000): 6–8.
[12]   E. Parkin, 'The Ancient Cinque Port of Sandwich', *AC*, 100 (1984): 189–216.

ebb. In 1497, Henry Pyham of St Clement's parish, Sandwich, intended that five shillings' rent which he had given to the St George's mass in St Clement's church should be allocated to the parish clerk, so that he might teach the children pricksong each week and keep the mass with them at the appointed time.[13]

Education in the fifteenth century was focussed around individual chaplains or priests rather than in dedicated school buildings. This was partly because the parish church itself or a chantry chapel within it provided the teaching space. The chantry priest of Higham who taught '… the children of thenhabitants there frelye …' had a '… chamber over the Chapell and the little gardeyn adjoyning'.[14] In Sevenoaks parish church, the room used was over the church porch, as the provision of a chimney and window there indicate. In the early sixteenth century, pious gifts in wills still tended to support not educational buildings, but rather the schooling of an individual child or the teaching of individual priests, for example that of Master John Fyshare of Lydd. However, the example of Tenterden in the 1520s suggests that this was an important time of change when testamentary or charitable gifts began to be directed towards funding not a teacher, but a dedicated school building. At Tenterden testamentary bequests indicate that a chantry was established, or perhaps re-established, here between 1494 and 1512 by Peter Marshall, vicar of Tenterden. The chantry priest acted as teacher from some time during these years. In 1524, there was a move towards '… buying, building or making a suitable house for the priest in which he could lodge and teach his scholars'. Not until 1524 did schooling become focussed on a building instead of, or as well as, the teacher.[15]

Not all the small or even the larger chantries like Sandwich survived to be formally dissolved in 1548.[16] This was partly because small chantries did not last long in their original form. Nevertheless, where such chantries provided education, local communities, led by an individual, might wish to continue that provision by re-founding the chantry. At Ivychurch, where John Lynot's chantry had existed until the 1420s, one Robert Stonestrete re-established a chantry in 1449, perhaps because the chaplain's teaching as much as his prayers were valued in a locality with a strongly established and popular literate culture.[17]

This kind of episodic re-foundation is also clear at hospitals with distinctive chantry functions. In some cases medieval hospitals were almost indistinguishable

---

[13] CKS, PRC 17/6/291. I owe this reference to Dr S. Sweetinburgh.

[14] *Kent Chantries*, pp. 150–51.

[15] *Kent Chantries*, pp. 304–5; extract from the will of William Marshall, in A.H. Taylor, 'The Rectors and Vicars of St Mildred's Tenterden. With an Appendix.' *AC*, 31 (1915): 239.

[16] Those which did were mapped in M. Reynolds, 'Reformation and Reaction, 1534–69', in Lawson and Killingray, *Historical Atlas*, p. 81.

[17] *Kent Chantries*, p. 169.

from chantries.[18] At the leper hospital or Hospital of Stephen and Thomas, New Romney, commemoration of benefactors continued from the early thirteenth to the late fifteenth century as a series of foundations and re-foundations transformed it into a merchant family chantry.[19] Hospitals were involved in both local literate activity and education from the thirteenth and fourteenth centuries. This included the storage and creation of records as at the *Domus Dei* in Dover. Hospitals between London and north Kent were staging-posts for those carrying letters; for example, the *Maison Dieu*, Ospringe, was *en route* from Lambeth to Canterbury and here there was a school at the hospital or chapel and '... the priest was to teach scholars'.[20] In 1511, the *Maison Dieu* had a master, '... priests, clerks, boys and other servants', and so still apparently functioned as a school then.[21]

A network of men centred on the Hospital of Stephen and Thomas, New Romney, in the first half of the fifteenth century facilitated land-acquisitions on Romney Marsh by Archbishop Chichele for the endowment of his new College of All Souls, Oxford. These men made and kept extensive legal and administrative writings at the hospital. This hospital with its master and chaplains was a focus of literate activity and probably also education, since training in writing and numeracy were integrated with administration in the fifteenth century. In 1451, it was noted that this 'hospital or chantry' had been given books for divine service.[22] An early- to mid- fifteenth-century base metal counter bearing the sacred trigram *ihs*, a cross and two pious Latin legends, was excavated there.[23] Such counters were used with an abacus for accounting and/or instruction in numerate skills, notably as part of archiepiscopal accounting systems.[24] The sacred trigram formed part of the contemporary cult of the Holy Name of Jesus and between 1450 and 1550 appeared often on objects and documents, including wills, accounts and correspondence. The cult was widespread in the Midlands, southern and eastern England, notably Kent, and was particularly popular in the parish of Tenterden, just to the north-west of Romney Marsh.[25] At New Romney the sacred trigram was

---

[18]   Sweetinburgh, 'Joining the Sisters': 27, 29, 31, 33.

[19]   A.F. Butcher, 'The Hospital of St Stephen and St Thomas, New Romney: the Documentary Evidence', *AC*, 96 (1980): 21.

[20]   *Kent Chantries*, pp. 127, 305.

[21]   *Kentish Visitations of Archbishop William Warham and his Deputies, 1511–1512*, ed. K.L Wood-Leigh (Kent Records, vol. 24, Maidstone, 1984), p. 32.

[22]   MCM (Magdalen College Muniments Oxford) Romney deed 1 (1451).

[23]   S. Rigold, 'Two Kentish Hospitals Re-examined', *AC*, 79 (1964): 47–69.

[24]   F. Du Boulay, *The Lordship of Canterbury: An Essay on Medieval Society* (London, 1966), p. 274.

[25]   H. Blake, G. Egan, J. Hurst and E. New, 'From Popular Devotion to Resistance and Revival in England: the Cult of the Holy Name of Jesus and the Reformation', in D. Gaimster and R. Gilchrist (eds), *The Archaeology of Reformation, 1480–1580* (London, 2003), pp. 177, 179, 182, 184–6, 188; R. Lutton, *Lollardy and Orthodox Religion in Pre-Reformation England: Reconstructing Piety* (Woodbridge, 2006), pp. 69–80.

also used on pragmatic records, for instance in an early example on one of three leases (1378) concerning this hospital's property, two of which were written in its chapel. It was used too on the seal of Master Andrew Aylwyn, priest of Lydd and master of the Hospital (1428).[26] The trigram also appeared on an acquittance of the Hospital rents (1508), the last surviving local document concerning this Hospital.[27] Devotion to this cult was expressed in the area around New Romney, with the hospital of the Blessed Stephen and Thomas as its focus. Initial memoranda on the first Lydd town account book are also headed 'Jesu', as are several town accounts of 1428–84.[28] Marshland inhabitants leased the land on Romney Marsh which Archbishop Chichele had given to All Souls. They wrote or had written bills of expense related to their farms, and between 1460 and 1482 a few headed them with the letters 'Jhu C'. This suggests that they understood these writings as a moral or spiritual act with their claim to veracity being made in the name of faith, specifically of this cult of Jesus' name.[29] In this period, the cult was an integral part of literacy and its teaching in this locality. The widespread appearance of the sacred trigram was arguably not mere fashion but a '… true expression of devotion to the Holy Name'.[30] The examples of its use around New Romney similarly suggest that it was not a conventional gesture, but an individual and pious choice. However, the use of a written *ihs*, or similar, is not obvious after the very early sixteenth century and so provides no evidence of the 'resistance' to reformation suggested for other parts of the country.[31] Furthermore, the suggestion that Protestant reformers were concerned that the Bible should be '… conveyed verbally and not emblematically', as in the sacred trigram, is problematic, since references to the Holy Name were in several cases actually in word form; even *ihc* or *ihs* can hardly be considered an emblem when found in a locality with a popular literate culture of two centuries' duration.[32]

In the mid- to late fifteenth century, Oxbridge colleges such as Magdalen, Oxford, and St John's, Cambridge, absorbed the property of some chantries such as the Hospital of Stephen and Thomas, New Romney, Higham chantry and the *Maison Dieu* at Ospringe. The Master, fellows and scholars of St John's College, Cambridge, provided the stipend of the chantry-priest of Ospringe in the mid-sixteenth century because they had received its land and income.[33] Where the local

---

[26] The charter of 1428 was between a lay couple and Aylwyn, with two seals, of which the one bearing *ihc* is more likely to have belonged to the priest. MCM Romney deeds 7, 33, 48, 52.

[27] MCM Romney deed 51.

[28] East Kent Archives Office, Ly/FAc 1.

[29] Bodl. Mss. dd All Souls c321.6, c322.2. c324.

[30] Blake and others, 'From Popular Devotion to Resistance', p. 186.

[31] Ibid., pp. 188-90.

[32] Ibid., pp. 176–87, 192.

[33] *Kent Chantries*, pp. 127, 305.

evidence has been examined, it demonstrates that such absorption by an Oxbridge college meant that a hospital's property was all leased out, and increasingly to non-local people. In the late fifteenth century (1485), the Hospital of Stephen and Thomas, New Romney continued to attract at least one bequest, despite its property being absorbed by Magdalen College, which provided a chaplain.[34] The rents of the hospital's property were collected by a man of the town who could keep and write simple accounts in English.[35] However, in the early sixteenth century, such property on Romney Marsh was rented by men from farther away, such as the Weald of Kent or Canterbury. Rents were sometimes paid in London and it is unlikely that any spiritual provision was made by Magdalen College for a chaplain at the Hospital of Stephen and Thomas in the sixteenth century; the chapel building of the hospital fell into complete disrepair before 1683.

These Oxbridge colleges were themselves partly chantries for the bishops or archbishops who founded them, and part of the developments in university education. This transfer of endowment away from Kent to Oxford and Cambridge did not benefit the education of local children, for the evidence from Romney Marsh is that few if any attended a university, nor owned books as individuals, in the late fifteenth or sixteenth centuries. Rather those who did so were the sons of Wealden and Canterbury gentry or near-gentry families, holding land profitably as lessees on Romney Marsh from the early sixteenth century. A number of such families prospered as absentee lessees of land on and around Romney Marsh. The Knatchbulls were an early example and, being exceptionally wealthy, funded the education of their sons equally, not just that of the eldest. Some of their riches were directed towards conventional devotional objects of the pre-Reformation period while acknowledging the move from script to print. In 1522, Richard Knatchbull provided new printed missals for three parish churches in south-east Kent where the family's landed interests lay, as well as contributing to a new steeple at Aldington, giving a new chalice to Mersham church and making routine bequests to the high altars of four other parish churches.[36]

Wealth extended the educational and career opportunities of male children of such Wealden and Canterbury families, and also opened up possibilities of pious devotion through individual book-ownership for women which are not evident earlier among Marshland lessees. By the late sixteenth century, after a generation or two of university education, some men of these prosperous families personally used extensive estate, administrative, legal, testamentary and historical documentation of greater length and complexity than had previously been the case among Marshland lessees. For example, written bonds comprising both Latin and English replaced personal pledges as security for leases. The sixteenth-century lessees' university education enabled them to read, and sometimes write, Latin, not

[34]   Butcher, 'The Hospital of St. Stephen and St. Thomas', p. 24.
[35]   Bodl. MS dd All Souls c321.4, 321.6, 321.12, 321.13, 322.2, 322.15, 325.
[36]   Du Boulay, *Lordship of Canterbury*, pp. 127, n. 5, 236.

simply basic pragmatic Latin but on occasion '... humanistic Latin ... in a fine Italic hand'.[37] Their own records, such as testaments, seals and letters, expressed a self-confidence based on wealth.[38] It stands in contrast to the unassuming devotion which seems to be expressed in the previous century by local inhabitants in the inscription of the name of Jesus or the sacred trigram on their writings.

The greater number and sophistication of documents surviving from a locality over the course of the sixteenth century at first sight suggests a more extensive literate culture and therefore a growth in education. However, the study of Romney Marsh raises serious questions about identifying rising literacy in the early-modern period without taking account of the detailed local socio-economic phenomena. Between the fifteenth and the mid-sixteenth centuries not only did religious practices change, but also the characteristics of the social groups that made the writings from which piety and literacy are examined in this chapter.

Colleges of Priests in Kent[39]

Colleges of priests in Kent, like chantries, entered the historiography of the Dissolution and Reformation as 'decayed' institutions of the late Middle Ages. They were said to be few in number, offering little in the way of pious activity or education.[40] The dominant historiography presented their functions of education and support for the poor or elderly as new early-modern developments in the places where colleges or chantries had in fact already existed and operated. These 'new' developments were frequently linked by Clark to the activity of strongly Protestant gentry and lawyers in Kent.[41] The evidence from Kent was fitted into wider debates on late medieval education in England. Simon, for example, denied earlier suggestions by Leach, Power and Tate of the widespread availability of medieval education, although such schooling was demonstrated, for example in the West of England and the diocese of York, by Orme in 1976 and Moran in 1985.[42]

---

[37] J.K. McConica, 'Warden Hovenden', *Unarmed Soldiery: Studies in the Early History of All Souls College Oxford*, The Chichele Lectures, 1993–4, (Oxford, 1996), p. 94.

[38] G. Draper, 'The Farmers of Canterbury Cathedral Priory and All Souls College Oxford on Romney Marsh c.1443–1545', in J. Eddison, M. Gardiner and A. Long (eds), *Romney Marsh: Environmental Change and Human Occupation in a Coastal Lowland* (Oxford, 1998), pp. 121–2.

[39] The evidence about education in colleges of priests in Kent is examined in detail in a forthcoming publication.

[40] For example W.K Jordan, 'Social Institutions in Kent, 1480–1660: A Study of the Changing Patterns of Social Aspiration', *AC*, 75 (1961).

[41] Clark, *English Provincial Society*, pp. 287–8.

[42] J. Simon, *Education and Society in Tudor England* (Cambridge, 1979); N. Orme, *Education in the West of England, 1066–1548: Cornwall, Devon, Dorset, Gloucestershire,*

The negative view of medieval education focussed instead on post-Reformation growth in grammar schools. It helped set the scene for surveys such as Houston's *Early Modern Literacy*, which suggested low levels of medieval literacy and rapid literate development in the early-modern period, a model certainly inapplicable to the Romney Marsh area.[43]

Recent research on medieval literacy and education in Kent demonstrates that there were several colleges which, while sometimes small, were active and vital in providing education in the late Middle Ages, including for boys of Romney Marsh. Several colleges of priests or collegiate churches in Kent were founded or re-founded mainly between the later fourteenth and mid-fifteenth centuries, either by archbishops or by laymen. In some cases, they were really re-foundations, reviving earlier chantries. Ashford collegiate church, for example, incorporated an earlier chantry with two chaplains which had been founded by a woman in 1344. It was re-built and 're-founded' by a layman, John Fogge, in the later fifteenth century. Fogge had the support of other local people, and Ashford church was in part both a Fogge and a parochial chantry. One of the most distinctive features of Ashford wills is the leaving of books to this collegiate church.

The collegiate churches were groups, small or larger, of priests with nearby accommodation. The intention of founders of medieval colleges in Kent was that they should be active communities of priests who would 'eat and live together'.[44] The best-known colleges were at Ashford, Wye, Wingham, Maidstone, Cobham and Bredgar. The activity at these colleges included commemoration; pensions and opportunities to study for men of the Archbishop of Canterbury's *familia*; the strengthening of orthodox education for priests as at Wye and Wingham, and if necessary a place of confinement for unorthodox ones, as at Maidstone.[45] A notable possibility is that the foundation and development of Bredgar college may have been responding to demand for a new kind of curriculum in the fifteenth century, which would teach the skills of estate-management as well as fitting some boys to become priests.[46] When a collegiate foundation was by a layman, an important intention was to provide a new or grander family mausoleum within a parish church; this was pre-eminently the case at Ashford. Less immediately obvious, but clearer on investigation, are the educational and literate activities at

---

Somerset, Wiltshire (Exeter, 1976); J. Moran, *Education and Learning in the City of York, 1300–1560* (York, 1979).

[43] R. Houston, *Literacy in Early Modern Europe: Culture and Education 1500–1800* (London 1998, this edition 2002) cf. H Neveux and E. Osterburg, 'Norms and Values of the Peasantry in the Period of State Formation: a Comparative Interpretation', in P. Blickle (ed.), *Resistance, Representation and Community* (Oxford, 1997), pp. 152–67.

[44] *Kent Chantries*, p. 22.

[45] *Register of Henry Chichele*, ed. E.F. Jacob (Canterbury and York Series, xlvii, 1947), vol. 1, pp. 175–6; vol. 4, p. 203.

[46] Bennett, 'Education and Advancement', p. 91.

these colleges. At Cobham, Wye, Bredgar, Maidstone and probably Ashford colleges of priests, there was continuity of formal schooling or educational provision into the sixteenth century. The colleges had extensive collections of books. At Wye and Ashford colleges, this included texts bequeathed around 1489 by a notable proponent of the new learning, Master John Morer, vicar of Tenterden, through which students had contact with humanism. Also clear is the subsequent continuation or replacement of schooling after the Dissolution in the same places where a college had existed or in its immediate vicinity. There may, for example, have been a school at the chantry or college of priests at Maidstone from as early as 1395 until 1549, at which time Clark noted what he called the 'founding' of the town grammar school.[47] At Ashford, the late medieval clergy house or college of priests was in the close or 'churchyard' where the seventeenth-century buildings of the grammar school, said to have been founded in the 1630s by Sir Norton Knatchbull, also lie.[48] This proximity suggests a continuity of education based in these places which is masked by an historiographical concentration on post-Reformation founders and (re)builds. Education, provided by the vicar, continued in Bredgar where it had been established in the Middle Ages even though the college as an institution was lost in the religious changes of the sixteenth century.

Clark insisted that colleges such as Cobham were not providing active education at least by 1500, whereas Orme argued that they were doing so. Clark asserted that Orme painted '… a rather optimistic view of education at the end of the Middle Ages', and that 'Orme's check-list of schools included a number of educational establishments (e.g. Cobham college) which had almost certainly ceased to have any educational function by 1500'.[49] Clark was then able to draw a contrast between what he saw as the educationally moribund medieval Cobham college and a 'new' hospital foundation there in the late sixteenth century, without any acknowledgement that the latter was based on the medieval institution and buildings. Clark stressed the role of strongly Protestant or Puritan lawyers such as William Lambarde, Henry Halle, Sir John Boys and Sir Roger Manwood as 'notable benefactors of the poor' in such foundations, with little or no acknowledgement of the medieval antecedents, sometimes direct, of their foundations.[50]

---

[47] *Kent Chantries*, pp. 193, 193; U. Eveleigh Woodruff, 'Inventory of the Church Goods of Maidstone', *AC*, 22 (1897): 29–33; Clark, *English Provincial Society*, p. 75. Clark's suggestion was accepted by Zell, 'The Establishment of a Protestant Church', in M. Zell, (ed.), *Early Modern Kent 1540–1640* (London, 2000), p. 208, and J. Bower, 'Kent Towns, 1540–1640', in Zell, *Early Modern Kent*, p. 145.

[48] Clark, *English Provincial Society*, p. 193.

[49] Ibid., p. 443, n. 14.

[50] Clark, *English Provincial Society*, p. 288.

Founders and Piety: Hospitals and Education at New Romney and Sevenoaks

A concentration on founders and re-foundations is part of the historiography of institutions which provided education as part of their pious functions. A major interpretative contrast has traditionally existed between medieval communal religious practices and early-modern individual devout activity. This was underpinned by a view of medieval piety, at least for the masses, as non-literate, performative and ritualistic, and led by clerics such as chantry priests. In Kent, there was no such definitive contrast; it is an interpretation based on an inadequate understanding of the nature and extent of medieval schooling as part of the pious, literate and communal culture in the county. This is argued firstly from the example of a hospital, later an almshouse, in New Romney, and secondly from the medieval grammar school at Sevenoaks and the interpretation of its origins by the early Kentish historian William Lambarde.

At New Romney, there was a second hospital, St John's, a thirteenth-century establishment strongly linked to the town's jurats (ruling council) and their corporate activities. St John's appears to have been the focus of educational activity in the town after the mid-fifteenth century when the network based at the Hospital of Stephen and Thomas ceased to have that function.[51] The location of St John's Hospital points up its connections with traditional corporate and communal religious activity. It lay in the west of the town close to the place where New Romney's passion play was performed. St John's Hospital stopped carrying out conventional hospital activities between 1498 and 1509 when its property was leased out. However, a local man, William Southland, acquired the hospital site in 1584. In 1610, John Southland by his will provided an almshouse there. He also provided for the schooling of children in his will, to be under the control of the town government (the jurats), and this education probably took place at Southland's Hospital from the sixteenth until the nineteenth century.[52] Charitable and educational functions were thus continued on this site and in this quarter of the town in the early seventeenth century and probably more informally during the sixteenth century. This kind of continuity between hospital and almshouse was typical of the Cinque Ports of Sandwich and Hythe and, temporarily, New Winchelsea (Sussex), as well as Canterbury, Rochester, Faversham and possibly Lewisham and Deptford.[53]

---

[51] The town council and townsfolk were expressing great concern about schooling in the 1560s to 1580s: H.T. Riley, 'The Manuscripts of New Romney Corporation', in *Fifth Report of the Royal Commission on Historical Manuscripts* (London, 1876), p. 553; CKS PRC 32/34/53; PRC 32/35/87.

[52] East Kent Archives Office, NR/Z/8, dated 1611.

[53] S. Sweetinburgh, 'Medieval Hospitals and Almshouses', in Lawson and Killingray, *Historical Atlas*, p. 44; D. Martin and B. Martin, *New Winchelsea, Sussex: A Medieval Port Town* (London 2004), p. 91.

John Southland's almshouse, the former St John's Hospital, was described as 'Southland's Hospital' in a plaque which honoured the individualism of the 'founder' rather than the corporate memorialization which had been a function of the medieval hospital. Southland's plaque incorporated changing understandings of pious or other motives lying behind hospital and school foundations. This applies also to Sir Norton Knatchbull's grammar school in the close at Ashford, whose buildings are also marked by a plaque, and behind which lay a long history of learning at the collegiate church. This celebration of individuals is also particularly clear from the example of Sevenoaks School.

Sevenoaks was a medieval market town in west Kent, about 24 miles from London. Sevenoaks School is sometimes described as an early endowed grammar school and equated with part of a growth of such schools. But in fact Sevenoaks was exceptional both in Kent and nationally. Its 'foundation' occurred several decades earlier than that of comparable schools.[54] William Sevenoke of Kent is usually said to have been the founder of Sevenoaks School, and this origin myth is reinforced by a statue in this case, rather than a plaque, on the main school building. However, Sevenoaks School is adjacent to the parish church and to the mid-thirteenth century chantry established there by the rector, Henry of Ghent, for his parents' souls. Henry's chantry is likely to have offered education by the chaplain well before the so-called foundation of schooling at Sevenoaks.[55]

In his will of 1432, William Sevenoke left money to fund a teacher of poor children in Sevenoaks 'in some convenient House' and notably money for the support of 'twenty poor Men or Women'. By 1438, a '... messuage with its appurtenances which late was the said William Sevenoke's' was being used for the school, and 'cottages with appurtenances' for supporting the poor.[56] But it was the Protestant county historian of Kent, William Lambarde, who in 1576 attributed the erection of buildings to Sevenoke: 'therefore of his own charge, [William Sevenoke] built both an Hospitall for the reliefe of the poore, and a free schoole for the education of youthe within this Towne'.[57] Lambarde thus put the focus strongly on the school building, and indeed on the erection of a 'hospital', as he himself had done at Greenwich. William Sevenoke was also said by Lambarde to have been an orphan, found in the streets of Sevenoaks, and brought up by a local lord of the manor.[58] Sevenoke in adult life was a London merchant, member of the Grocers' Company, and city administrator with royal connections. Lambarde's story placed him firmly within a later sixteenth-century ethic of the benefit of hard work in amassing wealth and then dispensing it for charitable good.

---

[54]   Bennett, 'Education and Advancement', p. 91.
[55]   D. Killingray (ed.), *Sevenoaks People and Faith: Two Thousand Years of Religious Belief and Practice* (Chichester, 2004), p. 69.
[56]   B. Scragg, *Sevenoaks School: A History* (Bath, 1993), p. 24.
[57]   Quoted in ibid., p. 24.
[58]   Ibid., p. 12.

Lambarde set the tone for subsequent interpretations of Sevenoke's actions. The historiography of education has until very recently followed the Protestant interpretation of change between medieval and early-modern periods, and in some cases still does so. Leach, for example, suggested, in an interpretation of Sevenoke's will which itself is not absolutely clear, that Sevenoke did not want a man in holy orders, a chantry-priest, as master of the school, because he wanted to avoid '… the appointment of a schoolmaster wasting his time and performing masses for the dead'.[59] Sevenoaks school is also presented by its own historian as one of a new breed of early fifteenth-century free grammar schools which, in contrast to 'church schools', was '… committed … to the idea of learning as an end in itself, and as a preparation for professional and vocational activities'.[60]

William Sevenoke's foundation was crucial to Bennett's model of a movement to endow schools in the fifteenth century, and part of a chronology of schooling which sees a growth in the availability of schooling in the later Middle Ages and Tudor period, some of which was not church based.[61] Bennett argued that the 'emergence' of endowed grammar schools was 'a development of prime significance'.[62] Sevenoke was Bennett's premier and earliest example of a London merchant founding a grammar school intended to provide for secular commercial concerns as well as educating some young men for the priesthood.[63] The argument partly depends on the suggestion of the popularity of a new 'business' or 'commercial' curriculum from the late fourteenth century, self-evidently prompted by financial rather than pious concerns. This kind of curriculum has been argued to have existed at the private grammar schools of Oxford such as Thomas Sampson's, and it can be noted that Robertsbridge Abbey, an important landowner on Romney Marsh, possessed a copy of Sampson's formulary at this time, which dealt with such matters as writing charters, conveyancing and bills. Nevertheless, the kind of skills of estate management which are suggested as being taught at Sevenoaks and Bredgar College, as well as in Oxford, were present among certain local men of Romney Marsh such as reeves, serjeants and bailiffs as early as the thirteenth century. They learnt these skills through the interaction between centre and periphery in the direct management of ecclesiastical estates. It may be that Romney Marsh had an early literate culture which was exceptional, and that more generally there was in fact a growing demand from the late fourteenth century for more formal provision of non religious or commercial schooling. Sevenoaks School should nevertheless not be assumed to be just an early example of widespread endowed grammar schooling in the fifteenth century. The local factors need to be

---

[59]   Quoted in ibid., p. 21.
[60]   Ibid., p. 20.
[61]   Cf. the list of reading concerning 'education and advancement' in Bennett, 'Education and Advancement', p. 231.
[62]   Ibid., pp. 83–4.
[63]   Ibid., p. 91.

taken into account, in particular the proximity of London and William Sevenoke's strong connections there. Nor should Lambarde's suggestion that the foundation of Sevenoaks School specifically rejected pious provision of education be taken at face value. The evidence that Sevenoke spurned the educational services of chantry priests is thin, and the so called school foundation of 1432 may well have been based on earlier teaching at the chantry within the parish church. William Sevenoke's role as 'founder' was largely the construct of the early Protestant historian Lambarde, followed by a focus on buildings and origins by subsequent historians.

Conclusions

'There hath not bene any gramar scole kepte, preacher maytened or pore people releved, other then … by the same chauntreye'.[64] In this comment from a rural parish in east Kent, the churchwardens of Ickham made clear that the chantry priest provided education in their parish. It was made in 1548 at a pivotal period in the pious transitions of the sixteenth century. The churchwardens' comment sets a challenge to two models of education: one which, especially for Kent, dismisses the extent and achievements of medieval education; the other which, again especially for Kent, associates the teaching of 'grammar' with endowed schools in towns from the late sixteenth or early seventeenth centuries. The churchwardens' remark also sought to defend the chantry on the grounds that it supported preaching and relieved the poor. This placed its functions, and the pious motives of those who supported it, firmly within the religious ethos and social priorities of the period: preaching and poor relief as well as schooling.

This chapter has suggested that supporting schooling was a widespread activity in late medieval Kent because education was set within various objects of pious devotion. Support for chantries apparently peaked for about a century after the Black Death and then ebbed, perhaps as smaller chantries, which were not always long-lived institutions, ceased to receive ongoing local support or re-foundation. However, the record of chantries formally dissolved in 1546–48 probably underestimates their numbers, especially those of small endowments without written records, given the number there were in 1350.[65] The supporters of chantries were able to incorporate religious changes into old forms of devotion as at Ickham, and at Tenterden where the important move towards funding of (chantry) school buildings, as opposed to teaching by chantry priests, was discernible in the 1520s.

During the late fifteenth and early sixteenth centuries, the mopping up of small hospitals and chantries by archbishops and Oxbridge colleges tended to remove the benefits of pious provision of education from local inhabitants to wealthier

---

[64] *Kent Chantries*, p. 168.
[65] *Kent Chantries*, pp. vi–vii, xi–xiv.

individuals often living at a distance. On Romney Marsh, from where detailed evidence comes, this coincided with significant demographic decline. However, individuals and local communities actively continued or revived long-term provision of schooling and poor relief, as at Southland's Hospital, New Romney.

Late medieval support for chantries and colleges of priests appears to have been prompted very strongly by the need for commemoration, whether for the post-Black Death period or for family status, as notably at Cobham and Ashford. However, it was more complex than the crude equivalence of remembrance prayers with the desire to be speeded through purgatory, by which even in 2004 some historians can characterize the Middle Ages. This view argues for 'the works-based nature of medieval Catholicism', meaning primarily the prayers of the living and the institutions which offered them, and sees it undermined by 'a series of challenges' of the 'European Reformation'.[66] Instead, medieval commemoration should be seen as deeply rooted in the lives and social aspirations of individuals, but expressed corporately and extending beyond personal and family benefit. For benefactors of chantries and colleges it was expressed in their support of institutions which linked ongoing remembrance and worship with pious provision including education and poor relief. In the transitions of the sixteenth century, the variations between different social groups in religious opinion and enthusiasm for the new was important. Local communities, including townsfolk and urban leaders, could mould traditional institutions, particularly hospitals, to accommodate the priorities and practices of the Reformation. The early but influential Protestant county gentry in Kent, whose views were epitomized in Lambarde's work, in contrast saw their devotional and educational activities as a break with past piety and a fresh start.

The evidence of a prevalent literate culture from Romney Marsh and the adjacent Cinque Ports makes clear that medieval schooling, at least in this part of Kent, was to be found widely. As well as being based in institutions such as chantries or hospitals, it was clustered around priests and chaplains. However, the demographic and relative poverty of the Marshland *pays* in the late fifteenth and sixteenth centuries meant that university education and individual book ownership was outside the experience of local inhabitants, apart from a few clerics based nearby such as Master Morer of Tenterden. Instead, educational opportunities were available to members of families who began to hold land profitably in the locality from the 1530s but did not live there. It was such social change, not a plethora of new school foundations based on commercial or individualistic charity, which largely produced the apparent 'rising literacy' of the period.

The most recent comment on schooling and literacy in Kent between 1500 and 1700 is based largely on Clark and accepts the focus on school buildings and founders so often presented as a feature of post-medieval financial support of

---

[66]   Reynolds, 'Reformation and Reaction', in Lawson and Killingray, *Historical Atlas*, p. 80.

education. However, it is modulated to acknowledge '… the growth of literacy arising from the intellectual revolutions of the fifteenth century', and this would have included the contact with humanism which clergy such as Master Morer provided. Nonetheless, the comment also assumes that a growth of literacy resulting from the 'upheavals of the Reformation' encouraged more parents to seek the education of their children.[67] It does not accord well with the widespread evidence of literacy and schooling in Kent in the medieval period, nor take into account the extent to which education at an earlier period was provided in small institutions lost at or before the Dissolution, and in 'schools' which were focused around teachers rather than buildings.

---

[67]   E. Edwards, 'Education 1500–1700', in Lawson and Killingray, *Historical Atlas*, pp. 94–5.

Chapter 5

The Continuum of Resistance to Tithe, *c*. 1400–1600[*]

Paula Simpson

This chapter examines conflict over tithe payment in the diocese of Canterbury during the sixteenth century. It reveals strong continuities against a background of many different transitions. Grievance over tithe payment was influenced by economic pressures and agricultural change. It was also a reflection of the unresolved nature of the Protestant Reformation in many communities. This chapter will make observations in two sections concerning the significance of tithe extraction as a long-term structuring force for the determination of social relations, firstly, by describing the increase in dispute and the geographical continuities identified and, secondly, by describing some of the enduring forms of resistance to tithe. The analysis is based on a study of material from the Canterbury ecclesiastical courts. The reasons lying behind disputes pursued in the courtroom were very complex. Suits were informed by traditions of dispute, local politics, collective concerns and interpersonal rivalries. The particular social, economic, political and religious circumstances of the sixteenth century may have encouraged a less tolerant attitude toward strategies of evasion and opposition. Even so, the continuity of dispute within a period of profound religious dislocation and adjustment is marked. Study of tithe payment and its related issues – including customary practice and lay-clerical relations – therefore offers important insights into the nature of piety. The enduring forms of resistance to tithe may have important implications for continuities of pious practice. Detailed community study suggests much about the routine, everyday behaviour of parishioners, but also sheds important light on issues of national significance.

The Numerical and Geographical Incidence of Tithe Suits

In the period 1501–1600, 6,304 tithe disputes were instigated in the ecclesiastical courts of the diocese of Canterbury.[1] This figure is, moreover, certainly an

---

[*] This chapter is dedicated to the memory of my mother, Margaret Simpson.
[1] Material in this chapter is drawn from Paula Simpson, 'Custom and Conflict:

underestimate because of the partial survival of Act Books in certain years.[2] Figure 5.1 shows the total number of suits entered in both the Archdeaconry and the Consistory courts. In the first 25 years of the century, the number of suits instigated was relatively high, with a noticeable peak of activity in the years 1517–22. After this date, there was a considerable drop in the number of suits and this low level of dispute continued until the year 1548. The reduction in the number of suits recorded after 1525 can, to some extent, be explained by a paucity of record from the Archdeacon's Court. From 1548 until the end of the century, the number of disputes varied from year to year, in contrast to the more sustained levels of the first half of the century. Finally, there was a continuous period of high levels of dispute in the years 1595–1600. It is possible, then, to point to three distinct periods of litigation: a sustained term of relatively high dispute until the mid-1520s; then a period of low level activity until 1548; followed finally, by years of fluctuating incidence, but during which the overall trend was upwards. It might be noted, moreover, that had the evidence survived in full for the period 1525–40, the overall trend upwards might have been much clearer.

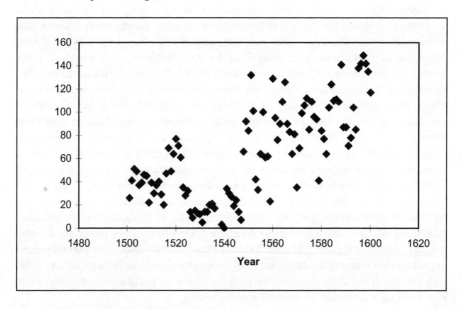

Figure 5.1   Numerical Incidence of Tithe Suits, 1501–1600

It is apparent therefore that use of the courtroom to resolve dispute over tithe increased steadily during the sixteenth century. The indications are that tithe

Disputes over Tithe in the Diocese of Canterbury, 1501–1600', unpublished Ph.D Thesis, University of Kent (1997).
    [2]   For a list of the volumes consulted see Simpson, 'Custom and Conflict', Manuscript Bibliography.

litigation accounted for a significant and increasing proportion of court business in a period when the overall volume of instance (suits between parties) business was falling. The 135 disputes recorded for both 1551 and 1601 represented 49 per cent and 61 per cent of the total volume of business respectively.[3] This again suggests that this period saw an increasing determination by litigants to pursue tithe suits in the courtroom.

During the sixteenth century, prices rose steadily and it has been proposed that the pressures of inflation may have prompted an upward trend in litigation over tithe.[4] An examination of the average price of all agricultural products together with the number of tithe suits entered into the ecclesiastical courts at Canterbury reveals that there is a positive link between average prices and the number of suits entered in the courts in any one year.[5] Even so, it would be unwise to designate this as a relationship of cause and effect. It can, however, be demonstrated that both prices and disputes increased over time and a broad conclusion is that there was a positive relationship between the two which implies that rising prices may have induced conditions in which dispute over tithe was more likely.

Tithe collectors who would have been most immune to the effect of rising prices would have been those who farmed their own glebe or who collected their tithes in kind. For rectors (clerical and lay) the great tithe (on direct products of the soil) was the most important source of income and this was more likely to have remained a payment in kind. Vicars, in contrast, rarely received any great tithe and were more dependent on small tithes (on livestock and products such as milk). Often these small tithes had been commuted (a money payment was made in lieu of the tithes formerly paid in kind). The value of commuted tithe would have fallen in a period of rising prices. Likewise, the vicar's dependence on income from offerings and fees would also have rendered him more susceptible to the effects of high prices. The holders of urban benefices were probably among those most affected by rising inflation and also the decreasing value of commuted personal tithe (on income, after expenses, from trades and crafts). After 1540, the number of disputes initiated by vicars from the diocese of Canterbury was substantially higher than those instigated by rectors and of particular significance are the very high levels of dispute in the 1590s undertaken by vicars.[6]

An analysis of the number of disputes in terms of the status of plaintiffs (clerical

---

[3]   Simpson, 'Custom and Conflict', pp. 129–33.

[4]   Christopher Haigh, *Reformation and Resistance in Tudor Lancashire* (London, 1975), p. 26.

[5]   This analysis is based on Bowden's figures for the annual average price of all agricultural products in Joan Thirsk (ed.), *The Agrarian History of England and Wales 1500–1640* (Cambridge, 1967), pp. 846–50. For detailed discussion see Simpson, 'Custom and Conflict', pp.135–7.

[6]   With regard to the effect of rising prices on income from tithe, it should be noted that, in theory, the laity would have been as susceptible as the clergy, although it might be presumed that they had alternative sources of income.

or lay) also provides distinctive results. One of the major truisms concerning tithe disputes is the claim that they greatly increased in number in the years following the official Reformation. These claims are usually adduced by reference to the increase in the number of disputes brought by lay plaintiffs.[7] A statute in 1540 legislated to allow the laity to sue for tithes,[8] and the upsurge in lay litigation is often explained by reference to the transfer of monastic lands to the laity after the dissolution of the monasteries and the contention that parishioners would have been markedly more reluctant to pay tithe to a lay owner. For the diocese of Canterbury, the issue is far less clear-cut. As shown, the number of disputes certainly increased as the century progressed. Figure 5.2 shows that the number of cases brought by clerical plaintiffs prior to 1537 constituted the major proportion of tithe disputes and clerical cases exceeded lay cases in every year until 1553. From 1546 onwards, however, it is apparent that not only did the total number of tithe cases begin to rise, but also that an increasing number of these cases were brought by members of the laity. Lay-inspired cases consistently exceeded clerical ones in the 1560s and the number of cases initiated by lay plaintiffs also peaked at 77 in 1565. Despite this observation, lay plaintiffs outnumbered clerical plaintiffs in only 18 of the years after 1540, usually by a fairly narrow margin (as already noted, the exceptions being 1560–62 and 1565–67). In fact, the 1560s was the only decade in which lay cases consistently outnumbered clerical cases, while from 1581 until the end of the century the reverse was true. Most significant is the apparent decline in the number of lay-inspired cases in the last two decades of the century, in tandem with an especially high incidence of clerical disputes. This was specifically so in 1595, 1596 and 1598.

These findings are in direct contrast with the data from York where it was found that lay plaintiffs were always in the majority after 1541 and that this majority was often a substantial one.[9] The dominance of clerical cases in the diocese of Canterbury is striking. It should also be remembered that the influence of the Church was implicit in many of the lay cases, since the rectories and vicarages might be leased directly from an ecclesiastical proprietor. The high incidence of clerically inspired suits and the inferred assumption of opposition towards payment to the clergy may be attributed to the predominance of the Church in Kent, especially as landowner. It suggests the likelihood of traditions of resistance to all forms of ecclesiastical dues.

An examination of deposition material for both courts demonstrates that the number of cases that reached the stage where depositions were heard constituted a low percentage of the total number of cases for which an initial citation was

[7]　　See, for example, John Stanley Purvis, *Select 16th Century Causes in Tithe* (London, 1949), Introduction, p. 7.

[8]　　*The Statutes of the Realm*, 32 Henry VIII, c. 7.

[9]　　William J. Sheils, 'The Right of the Church: The Clergy, Tithe and the Courts at York 1540–1640', in William J. Sheils, and Diana Wood (eds), *The Church and Wealth* (Oxford, 1987), p. 325.

made.[10] Several reasons for this might be suggested, including the cost and time involved in pursuing a suit. Probably the most persuasive reason, however, was the extent of extra-courtroom negotiation, arbitration and conciliation.[11] Discussion later will show that matters of tithe were fundamentally matters for negotiation and agreement within local communities. When suits were initiated in the ecclesiastical courts, this was usually because these relatively informal and local means of negotiation had broken down. The implication is that the threat of prolonged litigation occasioned by the issuing of a citation or the production of a libel was sufficient to bring the parties involved back to face-to-face discussion and that the disputes would often be resolved in this way. This does, nonetheless, have to be balanced by the recognition, particularly in relation to tithe, that some cases were entered into the courts by way of being test cases which might establish a precedent.

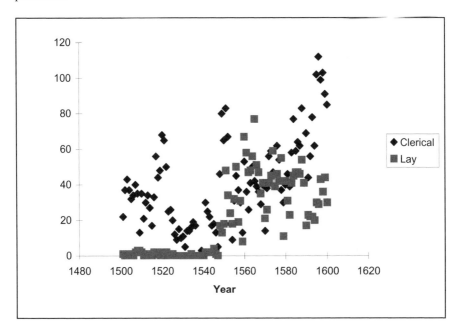

Figure 5.2   Status of Plaintiffs Instigating Tithe Suits, 1501–1600

Analysis of the geographical incidence of dispute is based on the parish of residence of plaintiffs in tithe cases. This derives from the assumption that the

---

[10]   Between 8 and 10 per cent of cases. See Simpson, 'Custom and Conflict', pp. 149–52.

[11]   James A. Sharpe, '"Such Disagreement betwyx Neighbours": Litigation and Human Relations in Early Modern England', in John Bossy (ed.), *Disputes and Settlements: Law and Human Relations in the West* (Cambridge, 1983), especially pp. 173–7.

contested tithes would invariably have pertained to this parish. When the period
1501–1600 is considered as a whole, a wide variance in the incidence of dispute in
individual parishes is discernible. This ranges from those parishes that experienced
no disputes at all to Ivychurch on the Romney Marsh that experienced a total of
110 disputes.[12] The majority of parishes experienced between one and 20 disputes
during the period considered and those parishes exhibiting a relatively high
numerical incidence of disputes (over 60) constitute less than 10 per cent of the
total number of parishes.

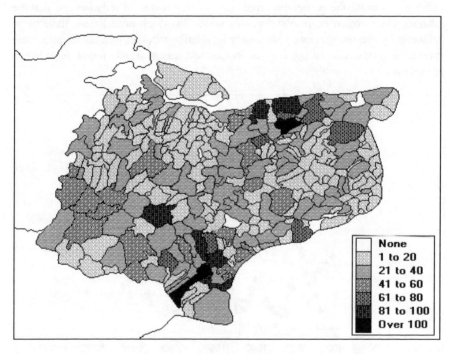

Figure 5.3   Geographical Distribution of Tithe Suits, 1501–1600

This high incidence of dispute in certain parishes is especially significant, since
these parishes also exhibit a geographical concentration (see Figure 5.3). This is
particularly evident on the Romney Marsh (Ivychurch, Ruckinge, New Romney,
Newchurch, Bilsington and Appledore). It is also apparent in a group of parishes to
the west of the Isle of Thanet (Sturry, Herne, Whitstable, Chislet and, arguably,
also including Ash). Bethersden in the Weald also exhibits a high incidence, along
with a significant Wealden cluster to the west of this parish (Marden, Staplehurst,
Frittenden, Headcorn and Cranbrook). In these Wealden parishes, the combined

---

[12]   The parish in which the plaintiff resided was recorded in 94 per cent of cases.

total of disputes exceeds 100.[13] This evidence points to conflict of a peculiar kind that should be viewed as part of a continuum of activity, located within traditions of resistance and dispute.

The following paragraphs broaden the analysis of conflict to examine features – structural and cultural – that may inform the identification of geographical clustering of parishes that experienced a high incidence of dispute. Examining factors such as population levels, traditions of heresy, of radical Protestantism, and the value of benefices did not reveal any significant correlation between those parishes experiencing a high number of disputes and any of these circumstances. By parish the experience was very varied.[14] This suggests, therefore, that the clustering of incidence is derived from regional and not parochial factors. The Kentish landscape is distinctive in its diversity and consequently permits the identification of regions or *pays*.[15] While precision is difficult since boundaries were very fluid and subject to change, as a broad generalization, it is possible to draw attention to marshland and woodland regions as particular foci for dispute. For the purposes of this chapter, the following discussion will centre on the Romney Marsh.[16]

Romney Marsh is located in the south of the diocese and its singular nature has long been noted. It is characterized by a continually changing coastline and was susceptible to both fresh and salt-water flooding. The widest application of the name Romney Marsh encompasses all of the marshland between Winchelsea and Hythe and northwards towards Bodiam. In reality, Romney Marsh is divided into a number of distinct marshes that reflect the different chronologies and strategies of reclamation. Those with which this section will be most directly concerned are Romney Marsh proper, Walland Marsh and Denge Marsh, an area roughly twelve miles from east to west and from north to south. Proximity to the continent ensured that the Marsh was an early and important centre for trade, commerce and defence systems. At various stages in its history there have been four important ports: Hythe, Romney, Winchelsea and Rye. Until the early fourteenth century, the area had been densely populated, but by 1600 population levels were in significant decline. The ports of Romney and nearby Hythe had silted up, Winchelsea had been partly washed away, and only Rye remained a town of any commercial significance. By now the area was characterized by fertile pasture (for both sheep

---

[13] It should be noted that there are three other parishes exhibiting a high incidence (more than 60 disputes) not associated with the identified geographical clustering: Harbledown, St Dunstan's (Canterbury) and Folkestone.

[14] For further discussion see Simpson, 'Custom and Conflict', pp. 154–60.

[15] Alan M. Everitt, 'The Making of the Agrarian Landscape of Kent', *AC*, 92 (1976): 1–31.

[16] The following paragraphs are based on Jill Eddison, *The World of the Changing Coastline* (London, 1979) and particularly Jill Eddison, 'The Making of Romney Marsh' (unpublished paper: 1995). I am grateful for permission to consult the latter work.

and cattle), a limited amount of arable farming, seasonal salt-making on the tidal reaches and small fishing settlements.

It has been argued that the population decline reflected a discernible shift during the sixteenth century from mixed farming to pastoral. The practice of transhumance in all likelihood had pre-Conquest origins. Herds were driven in the summer from settlements north of the downs to the detached pasture lands in the Weald and on the Romney Marsh, but by the sixteenth century the Weald had ceased to be used for pasture, intensifying pressure on pastoral resources on the Marsh.[17] While many of the resident farmers were graziers, wealthier farmers from the uplands were both hiring and buying pasture on the Marsh. Bailiffs and 'lookers' would oversee these pastures. Tithe disputes instigated by Ivychurch plaintiffs, for example, especially in the latter half of the century, were often against men styled 'gentleman' and usually resident in relatively distant parishes. Furthermore, many of the defendants were of Wealden origin. The implication is that there was valuable land to be farmed in Ivychurch (and on the Marsh as a whole) and that these disputes may have reflected the seasonal use of marshland pasture.[18]

This suggests that shifts in agricultural practice and land use, as well as short-term influences such as the weather, were reflected in the tithe disputes and that the agrarian changes, which occasioned an increased pressure on resources at a time of rising prices, may have also have stimulated tithe litigation in this area. As already noted, tithes that had been commuted to a fixed payment, for example, on pasturage would have decreased significantly in value as the century progressed. In an area in which there was very little arable, the economic effect of this would have been considerable. Many disputes focused on attempts to collect a commuted tithe on barren cattle, that is, on working beasts. In 1587, cases were brought by three different plaintiffs seeking to claim the tithe in the parishes of Ivychurch, Brenzett and Lympne.[19] Another highly significant case, which also addressed the issue of the tithe of barren cattle in the parish of Burmarsh, was that of Lane *contra* Cheeseman in 1598. Much later the decision pertaining to this case appears to have constituted a precedent in the negotiations following the petition of the poor clergy beneficed in the Romney Marsh presented in 1636. By this date the value of commuted tithe had depreciated to levels that the clergy maintained would not support them.[20] The generation of the petition reveals the long-term and corrosive nature of many of these problems.

Finally, the prevalence of ecclesiastical lordship – in particular through the estates of the Archbishop of Canterbury and the priories of Christchurch and St Augustine's – on the Romney Marsh is also noteworthy. In this light, it is

---

[17]   Everitt, 'Agrarian Landscape of Kent', p. 20.

[18]   CCAL, X.10.11, fol. 101.

[19]   Peerson *contra* Swaynslands, Borne *contra* Thirbarne and Merricke *contra* White. For full references see Simpson, 'Custom and Conflict', Manuscript Bibliography.

[20] For a transcription of the petition see Simpson, 'Custom and Conflict', Appendix 4.8.

interesting to observe the preponderance of clerically inspired disputes in these areas. This was especially marked in the high incidence parishes of Appledore and New Romney. The long experience of ecclesiastical lordship and histories of exacting financial dues and work obligations may have predisposed people in these areas towards an opposition to tithe, another financial obligation to the Church.

Resistance to Tithe Payment

Against the background of the continuum of dispute – both numerical and geographical – identified in the previous section, the second half of this chapter will highlight some of the enduring forms dispute over tithe took in the period 1500–1600. Direct confrontation over tithe normally took place outside the courtroom and was preliminary to the instigation of a suit (though of course the detail pertaining to the confrontation was revealed in the course of examination in court). These encounters may have been verbal clashes, some of which included a threat of physical aggression, or they may have arisen from more indirect methods of opposing tithe. Conflict in terms of petty disputation and minor expressions of opposition was a pervasive aspect of everyday relationships. Court cases were very often the result of the culmination of a series of small-scale actions and confrontations. Whether the confrontations were direct or indirect, spontaneous or planned, at all levels the encounters seem to have been informed by a strong symbolic element.

In describing encounters to the courts, deponents were typically sensitive to matters such as where the exchanges had occurred, the language employed, those who participated and those who observed. Confrontation took place in houses, shops, streets and fields, but more often in churches or their immediate vicinity. Disputations over tithe in churches were characterized by the general willingness of both appointed witnesses and bystanders to become involved. Thus, although arguments may have originated with seemingly individual acts of defiance, they inevitably developed to involve a larger number of people. Typically, the exchange took place after a service. This ensured the presence, as witnesses, of a number of the parishioners. At a time when it is thought that relatively few attended church, these parishioners probably constituted a particular aspirant group within local society.

The confrontations usually addressed matters of common concern and often drew on a history of dispute. A controversy described in a defamation suit in 1593 is typical. Richard Laminge and John Starkye argued in the parish church at Ewell, after morning prayer on St Stephen's Day. The churchwarden, apparently acting on behalf of Starkye, offered the vicar (Mr Sanders) 15d for the tithe of felled wood. The vicar refused to accept the money saying that he wanted the wood owed to him. At this point Richard Laminge intervened saying '… you have made the poore man (meaninge the said Mr Sanders) spend a thirtye or thirty two shillings about brablinge.'[21]

Laminge's reported use of the word 'brabling' is instructive. It is indicative both of quarrelling and of petty wrangling that had probably already reached the courtroom.[22] Another feature to note is the use of a go-between (the churchwarden) and presumably a man of some status in the parish. Starkye may have been concerned to avoid a direct confrontation with the vicar. The sense of events as portrayed in the deposition indicates that initially he remained in the background, but was inevitably drawn into the dispute when Richard Laminge intervened. Other witnesses referred to the cleric as 'troublesome' and warned against offering 'crosse counsell'.[23] The inference is that this confrontation took place against the background of a history of dispute.

In a number of cases the person intent on discussing tithe moved into the chancel of the church in order to confront the cleric. This was a particularly symbolic act since upkeep of the fabric of the nave of the church was the responsibility of the parishioners, but upkeep of the chancel was the responsibility of the clergy (or lay receivers of tithe). By negotiating tithe payment in this area – the chancel – tithe payers were able to insinuate a subtle reminder of the cleric's own material responsibilities towards the Church. This move into the chancel also represented resistance in the symbolic transgression it constituted. The tithe payer would almost certainly have had some sense of crossing a physical boundary (the rood screen), as well as a moral one. Moreover, the chancel was the area within which services might be read and where the Mass was celebrated.[24] Even after the Reformation the chancel may still have been regarded as one of the more sacred parts of the church with seating for members of the upper stratum of the parish. It is worth noting that, in the latter part of the sixteenth century, these confrontations over tithe often also addressed rights within the church, particularly with regard to seating.

When payment was intended, money was placed on the altar or communion table. This again was a peculiarly symbolic and a highly charged action, since if a parishioner persisted in withholding tithe, the cleric could resort to denying him or her the Mass. Furthermore, a deliberate placing of the money on the altar moved the onus away from the tithe payer. The cleric had to decide whether to pick up the money and complete the transaction, or to leave it and perhaps provoke a lengthy dispute. If the quarrel subsequently resulted in a court case, the tithe payer could reasonably claim that he or she had been willing to make payment. Placing money on the altar added a symbolic resonance to the transmission that had taken place.

---

[21]   See for example CCAL, PRC 39/15, fol. 119.

[22]   *Oxford English Dictionary*, Brabbling: a) cavilling, 'hair-splitting' (obs.), b) wrangling, noisy quarrelling; Brabble: a frivolous or paltry action at law (obs.).

[23]   CCAL, PRC 39/15, fol. 155.

[24]   Eamon Duffy, *The Stripping of the Altars: Traditional Religion in England 1400–1580* (London, New Haven,1992), pp. 110–13.

This was an action for which there was historic precedent. In the medieval period, symbolic objects, and later documents, were often presented on altars during conveyancing ceremonies.[25] Putting the money owed for tithe on the altar perhaps had a dual nature: it was the actual payment; but it also embodied a symbolic object or offering, signifying the reciprocal relationship between giver and receiver.

This evidence discussed above suggests that there were traditional arenas, times and places for public confrontation over tithe. In particular, the significance of the church as a venue for many of these exchanges suggests that it was regarded, especially by the middling stratum in society, as an appropriate arena for negotiation and the exploration of tension. Another location for the expression of resistance to tithe was in the harvest fields during the activities associated with 'tithing-out', the occasion when the tithe owner's share of the crop was set aside. This was an activity for which appropriate notice of intent was expected and which was closely overseen by the tithe-collector, their agents, family or servants to ensure that the tithed corn was assigned fairly and (a word often used by contemporaries) 'indifferently'. In Kent, the tithed crop was customarily indicated by a green bough, or less often by a clod. A statute in 1548 ratified these practices by affirming regulations for proper tithing practice and penalties for carrying away grain before it had been properly tithed.[26]

Despite the scrutiny theoretically afforded to the tithe collection process, many opportunities to defraud the tithe collector were available at this time. Belated or vague notice of the intention to tithe-out, for example, meant that the tithe collector missed the opportunity to oversee the process. Richard Culmer, a Kentish cleric provided a description of such practices in his seventeenth-century tract.[27] Culmer detailed many fraudulent practices utilized by tithe payers before, during and after tithing-out. These included ruses such as loading the tithe corn in a part of the field with a lesser quality crop, concealing poor quality corn in the middle of tithe sheaves, manoeuvring tithe collectors into the fear of trespass were they to collect their tithe, or reclaiming tithe which had not been promptly collected. If tithing-out had been overseen and agreed to have been fairly accomplished, the tithed sheaves might be replaced by poor quality ones during the night. These activities were characterized by Culmer as 'deeds of darkness' and as 'Black Art'.[28]

Manoeuvres such as these reveal both compliance and non-compliance. Though the right to collect tithe was not openly challenged, tithe payers found many ways in which to oppose and undermine the system. This was not overt resistance in the sense of direct challenge, but given the theoretical emphasis and insistence on

---

[25] Michael T. Clanchy, *From Memory to Written Record: England 1066–1307* (2nd edition, Oxford–Cambridge, Mass., 1993), pp. 254–60.

[26] *Statutes of the Realm*, 2 & 3 Edw VI, c. 13.

[27] Richard Culmer, *Lawles Tythe-Robbers Discovered Who Make Tythe-Revenue a Mockmayntenance* (London, 1655).

[28] Ibid., p. 5.

fairness at tithing-out, compliance at the level of actual behaviour was minimal.[29] While outward appearance suggested conformity, this helped to provide cover for many strategies of evasion. Deposition evidence from the sixteenth century frequently explores the conflict ensuing from activities of this kind, strategies which might be termed 'sharp practice' on the part of the tithe payer.[30] Culmer's tract was written in 1655, but these were long known, practised and even traditional ruses. Culmer himself declared them to be an '... [H]ereditary disease in many families being propagated from the unrighteous Father to the Son.'[31] This confirms the notion of consensual activity and again helps to locate behaviour within a continuum. The persistence of these activities as a process of constant testing and pushing of the boundaries of the system argues for traditions of dispute.

The continuity of the forms of resistance described above can be attributed to the verbal and behavioural transmission of strategies. The payment of tithe was very much concerned with practice and customary modes of behaviour, rather than having a basis in a written discourse. Custom was established in practice as part of the workday routine and its determination was usually reliant on memory and hearsay, informed by notions of tradition and time. The passing of time was an essential consideration when defining customary practice and in tithe suits witnesses frequently referred to the long duration of practice and to the views of their elders. The old had a valued role to play within the community as the trustees and custodians of the memory of past practice and their recollections subsequently became part of rehearsed community knowledge.[32] Information of this kind was most usually presented in the discussions concerning parish boundaries and the annual perambulations to delineate areas subject to the payment of tithe. Again, it was often conveyed as part of traditional ritual performance, usually in connection with perambulations, but also in the rituals surrounding death. Robert Barrowe of Willesborough, for example, described how he had been '... at the departing owt of this world of one Richard Spratt who in his death bedd declared that he had payde tythe hempe and that he knewe divers others which had like wise paid ...'[33] This recollection confirms that the old carried a knowledge with them that was important to pass on to succeeding generations.

---

[29]   James C. Scott, *Weapons of the Weak: Everyday Forms of Peasant Resistance* (Yale, 1985), p. 26.

[30]   For examples see Simpson, 'Custom and Conflict', pp. 99–116.

[31]   Culmer, *Lawles Tythe-Robbers*, Preface.

[32]   For detailed discussion see Keith Thomas, 'Age and Authority in Early Modern England', *Proceedings of the British Academy*, 62 (1976): 205–48.

[33]   CCAL, PRC 39/4, fol. 20v.

The longevity of much dispute is also apparent. An interesting case in this respect was Enyver *contra* Forde (1565–67).[34] This dispute concerned land known as 'twenty acres' or 'Great Pysing' in the parish of East Langdon, to which the nearby parishes of Whitfield and Guston also laid claim. Witnesses referred to perambulations of 12 years earlier and to a lease for the manor of Great Pysing held by David Forstall from the Abbey of Langdon before its dissolution. Most significantly, witnesses appear to have been asked whether they had any knowledge of the land having been in the ownership of a Philip of Pysing. The question indicates that, in framing the libel, the plaintiff had sought to trace the ownership of the land, and presumably rights relating to it, back to the thirteenth century. In the reign of Henry II, the manor of Pysing, together with lands called Pinham, had been held by Sir Philip de Pysing.[35] This was seemingly an attempt to draw evidence from over 300 years previously. Such disputes should, therefore, be understood within the context of long traditions, rights and conflict over those rights.[36]

The geographical concentrations identified above also suggest the importance of enduring patterns of dispute. For the Romney Marsh it has been possible to examine the act books of the ecclesiastical courts back as far as 1372.[37] The longer time period studied for this area has permitted the examination of family names for continuity of dispute through different generations of the same family. Many family names from the Romney Marsh parishes occur repeatedly as defendants in tithe suits. Sometimes there are up to 80 years between the instigations of the suits. Members of the Alane/Allen family of New Romney, for example, were cited in suits in 1472 and 1581; of the Brodenap/Brodnape family of Burmarsh in 1467 and 1551; of the Brokhill family of New Romney in 1464 and 1504; of the Sede family of New Romney in 1476 and 1544; and of the Whatman family of Old Romney in 1420 and 1471. If the consideration is extended to look at family names, not just in the same parish, but living on the Marsh, then there are many more instances. Members of the Strogell family living in Warehorne, New Romney and Snargate were involved in disputes instigated in 1466, 1477, 1480, 1562, 1563, 1591 and 1597; and members of the Symon/Symond family of Ruckinge and New Romney were defendants in suits in 1467, 1469, 1473, 1551 and 1552.[38] The implication of these findings is that some disputes may have been extremely long standing and that conflict over tithe payment may have been continued by successive generations

---

[34] CCAL, X.10.12 fols 189–96, 205v–8r; X.10.15, fols 14–5r, 16–18r, 64, 109–111r.

[35] Edward Hasted, *The History and Topographical Survey of the County of Kent* (12 vols,, Canterbury, 1797–1801), vol. 9, pp. 549–8.

[36] For discussion see Rosamund J. Faith, 'The "Great Rumour" of 1377 and Peasant Ideology', in Rodney H. Hilton and Trevor H. Aston (eds), *The English Rising of 1381* (Cambridge, 1984), pp. 43–73.

[37] This work was supported by a grant from the Romney Marsh Research Trust.

[38] For more examples see Paula Simpson, 'Tithe Litigation on Romney Marsh, 1371–1600', *Romney Marsh Irregular*, 22 (2003): 10–14.

of the same family. It reveals yet again strong traditions of dispute, as well as the possibility that certain rights or areas of land remained especially contentious.

Conclusion

Three distinct phases of tithe litigation in the sixteenth century have been identified: a period of relatively high incidence from the opening of the century until 1522; low levels of dispute between 1523 and 1547 (arguably a reflection of the years of religious disorientation and upheaval); and, thereafter, a steady rise in the number of suits entered to levels well in excess of the early years of the century. In the period 1548–1600, 79 per cent of the total number of disputes for the century as a whole was instigated. Furthermore, the indications are that tithe suits constituted an ever-increasing proportion of total court business.

While it is apparent that there was a positive relationship between the increasing incidence of tithe suits and inflation during the century, this was not a relationship of cause and effect. It is likely, however, that the climate of steadily rising prices created conditions conducive to an increased volume of dispute over tithe. Significantly, the most marked effect was on the pursuit of 'vicarial' (small) tithes by clerical plaintiffs. Indeed, the diocese of Canterbury exhibited a peculiarly distinct pattern of litigation in this respect. High numbers of clerically instigated suits were undertaken, particularly in the latter part of the century. Although the dissolution of the monasteries and the transfer of monastic tithe to the laity did have an effect on litigation in terms of an increase in the number of disputes instigated by lay plaintiffs, this should not be overstated. Certainly after 1580, the level of lay litigation was decreasing and there is little evidence from the deposition material offering an articulated opposition towards payment to lay collectors. Nonetheless, the rhetoric of Culmer's tract is also revealing about lay opposition to clerical tithes by placing it in the context of a sustained history. Evidence of the transmission of both knowledge and traditions of resistance between generations may have important implications for continuities of pious practice.

The geographical concentration of a high incidence of disputes – on the Romney Marsh, in north-east Kent and in the Weald – is marked. It is likely that the significance of these regional concentrations lies not in the soil, but in the conditions of agricultural change and land use. In postulating that marshland and woodland are the areas of real significance in terms of tithe litigation, interest lies in the fact that these were in many ways marginal economies. Consequently, it might again be argued that the pressure of rising prices was of considerable influence on dispute.

Payment of tithe was an inherent part of everyday social and economic relationships. Evidence from the deposition material reveals that the negotiation of these relationships often employed ritualized and symbolic behaviour, particularly in relation to actual payment and to methods of tithe collection. It signifies that ritual and symbol provided a means of exploring tension, expressing opposition and testing boundaries. Dispute over customary rates, payment and collection may well have originated with individual acts of defiance, but the evidence suggests that these confrontations were very much a matter of shared community concern and even intervention. Strategies of resistance employed had a long history of use and were part of common community knowledge that was passed between generations. The persistence of such strategies argues for traditions of dispute and disagreement reaching back prior to the sixteenth century as well as extending beyond it.[39]

Opposition to the payment of tithe was relatively disorganized, uncoordinated and neither firmly articulated nor overt. Resistance was usually characterized by acts of defiance that resulted in petty gains. This resistance was in the nature of the activities identified by J.C. Scott as 'a long-drawn-out, silent, and undeclared war of evasion, fraud, concealment, dissimulation, non-compliance, and quiet defiance answered by countermeasures, threats, and prosecutions.'[40] The range of tactics employed meant that tithe payers found all kinds of means to oppose and cheat the system. Outward conformity masked activities that were '... working the system to their minimum disadvantage'.[41]

The nature and extent of conflict outside the courtroom and the demonstrable longevity of many disputes is particularly interesting when viewed together with the evidence for the sustained and rising incidence of suits heard in court throughout the sixteenth century. Self-interest and preservation, especially in periods of inflation and economic hardship, will have influenced dispute. Yet opposition towards lay tithe collectors and censure of the moral behaviour of the parochial clergy indicate that contention also had its roots in convictions about the reciprocal nature of relationships between the individual, the community and the Church. These were relationships governed by mutual expectations, norms and responsibilities. When conflict occurred, these relationships were perceived to have broken down or to have been transgressed in some way. Court cases had origins in the local balance of power and were often informed by interpersonal rivalries and antagonisms. Suits were brought by those who perceived themselves to have lost out, either materially or morally, in encounters that had perhaps taken place over a long period of time.

While drawing attention to the everyday and persistent nature of dispute, the statistical analysis of tithe litigation reveals that there were concentrations of activity. It was in response to particular local circumstances and crises that concentrations of tithe litigation can be identified. As noted, the court case was

---

[39] For discussion of traditions of resistance see Christopher Hill, 'From Lollards to Levellers', in *Collected Essays of Christopher Hill*, II: *Religion and Politics in Seventeenth-Century England*, vol. 3 (Brighton, 1986), pp. 89–116.

[40] James C. Scott, 'Resistance without Protest and without Organization: Peasant Opposition to the Islamic Zakat and the Christian Tithe', *Comparative Studies in Society and History*, 29 (1987): 441.

[41] See Scott, *Weapons of the Weak*, p. 301 which paraphrases from Eric Hobsbawm, 'Peasants and Politics', *Journal of Peasant Studies*, 1/1 (1973): 13.

often the culmination of a series of petty confrontations and the courtroom provided a forum for re-examination as litigants sought workable ways of co-existence within local communities. While drawing attention to the local and regional influences on dispute over tithe, however, it is also apparent that dissension within local communities was also informed by issues of national significance, for example, in attendant controversies over the position of church furniture. We can note, for example in disputes that took place in the chancel, changes of reference from the 'altar' to the 'communion table' of reformed religion.[42] The continuity of these forms of resistance, and the implications for pious practice, within a period of religious adjustment and profound dislocation, is quite remarkable.

Finally, the complexity of the tithe payment system and the financial burden it constituted are clear, but the exacting nature of financial obligation toward the Church in addition to tithe was also very significant.[43] The prevalence and persistence over time of small-scale resistance to tithe has been discussed, but there are indications of a certain flexibility within the system and some forbearance of what might be termed 'slippage'. It seems likely that individuals may have delayed, staggered or re-negotiated payments on a regular basis.[44] This notion of slippage confirms the complexity of a system in which a level of lenience was in-built, a continuum in which a degree of contention was tolerated until crisis. Study of dispute over tithe at these times of crisis also highlights the nature of collective memory, the way in which 'forgotten' events found reiteration. These observations raise the question of whether it is really possible to point to the final resolution of conflict through use of the courtroom. The continuum of dispute reveals quite convincingly that matters, even between generations, were very rarely laid to rest and that moments of crisis often allowed grievance to resurface and be subjected to renewed exploration. It is clear, that there were very many strategies, of which use of the courtroom was only one, employed in seeking the resolution of conflict. Courtroom resolution when it did occur might be more sensitively understood, then, as the achievement of an only temporary compromise.

---

[42]   See Badcocke *contra* Gunnyll (1550): CCAL, X.10.4 fol. 105*v* and Partrich *contra* Bray (1597): CCAL, PRC 39/19 fol. 120*r*.

[43]   Peter Heath, *The English Parish Clergy on the Eve of the Reformation* (London, 1969), pp. 147–63.

[44]   The poorer parishioners may even have been excused from payments: ibid, p. 149.

Chapter 6

A Quantitative Approach to Late Medieval Transformations of Piety in the Low Countries
Historiography and New Ideas

Annemarie Speetjens

Late medieval devotion in the Low Countries is a subject that has attracted a great number of researchers during the past century. Many of these studies happened to reveal a significant transformation of medieval piety towards the age of Renaissance and Reformation. One of the first and most influential – and according to many also most attractive – studies which touches on this field is *Herfsttij der Middeleeuwen* by the Dutch historian Johan Huizinga, published in 1919.[1]

Huizinga's *Autumn of the Middle Ages*

Huizinga based his book on research into chronicles, poems, sermons and visual art, and thus his Dutch colleagues, who worked mainly on archival data, accused him of being an old-fashioned historian. He had adopted an intuitive historical method writing psychological history, instead of the then fashionable diplomatic scholarship, serving the history of institutions and state politics.[2] Meanwhile,

---

[1]   Johan Huizinga, *Herfsttij der Middeleeuwen. Studie over Levens– en gedachtenvormen der veertiende en Vijftiende Eeuw in Frankrijk en de Nederlanden* (Haarlem, 1919); Idem, *Verzamelde werken* III (Haarlem, 1949), pp. 180–278; published in English in 1924 as *The Waning of the Middle Ages: A Study of the Forms of Life, Thought and Art in France and the Netherlands in the XIVth and XVth Centuries*, trans. F. Hopman. See also note 4. [The editors are grateful to Dr. Jeroen Gunning, for assistance with proofreading this chapter].

[2]   F.W.N. Hugenholtz, 'Le Déclin du Moyen Age (1919–1969)', *Acta historiae neerlandica*, 5 (1971): 40–51; F.W.N. Hugenholtz, "The Fame of a Masterwork", in: W.R.H. Koops, E.H. Kossman, Gees van der Plaat (eds), *Johan Huizinga 1872–1972: Papers Delivered to the Johan Huizinga Conference, Groningen 11–15 December 1972* (Den Haag, 1973), pp. 91–3.

Huizinga was loudly praised by Dutch literary critics and his book was bought by a wide readership. *Herfsttij* was even awarded a literary prize.[3] Only in the 1960s, did the critical tide appear to have turned in Huizinga's favour. During the subsequent decades he was acclaimed a forerunner of the *en vogue* history of *mentalités* which was practised for example by the French *Annales* historians, and as a pioneering method in the fields of cultural anthropology and ethnography of the past.

His views on late-medieval culture in decline have caused a lively debate throughout the last century, and although his insights of an overall decline of late medieval culture no longer receive widespread support, Huizinga's book still forms a rich source of inspiration for many Dutch and foreign medievalists. The ongoing appraisal of this book is shown by the rather recent publications of a new English translation and an illustrated edition in Dutch.[4]

Although he did not found a Dutch school of *histoire des mentalités*, he appears to have discovered many topics in cultural history that since then have been studied by many medievalists, for example the field of late medieval devotion. His description of late medieval religious life in terms of an overload, or coexistence, of conflicting religious sentiments maintains its validity.[5] With regard to sources and methods, some medievalists of later generations took quite a different turn in exploring 'the (religious) waning of the Middle Ages' in the Low Countries. They preferred a quantitative approach.

Toussaert's Unchristian Flanders

The first of these scholars was Jacques Toussaert, a historian of French–Flemish descent. In 1959 he defended his thesis at the University of Lille on Flemish popular devotion in the period 1302–1526, which appeared in a commercial edition in 1963.[6] Whereas Huizinga had used literary and narrative sources, Toussaert employed administrative documents to do his research of Flemish late medieval

---

[3]   D.A. Thieme prize 1920, presented by the Dutch booksellers' association. W.E. Krul, *Historicus tegen de tijd. Opstellen over Leven en Werk van J. Huizinga* (Groningen, 1990), p. 214.

[4]   In 1997, a revised illuminated Dutch edition of *Herfsttij* appeared, edited by Anton van der Lem. A full translation of the book in English appeared under the adjusted title *The Autumn of the Middle Ages*, trans. Rodney J. Payton and Ulrich Mammitzsch (Chicago, 1996) to substitute the (abbreviated) English translation of *Herfsttij*, published in 1924 (see note 1 above). The *Autumn* in the new title renders the Dutch original better than the biased *Waning*. The new translation however lacks the original subtitle. For the history of the editions and translations of *Herfsttij*, see Edward Peters and Walter P. Simons, 'The New Huizinga and the Old Middle Ages', *Speculum*, 74 (1999): 587–620.

[5]   Huizinga, *The Autumn of the Middle Ages*, p. 205.

[6]   Jacques Toussaert, *Le Sentiment Religieux en Flandre à la fin du Moyen-Age* (Paris, 1963).

devotional life. In order to map out the religious practices in medieval western Flanders, he subjected his sources to the statistical methods of religious sociology conducted by Gabriel Le Bras.[7]

Toussaert used these quantitative methods for the analysis of serial material, like the churchwardens' accounts of Saint James church in Bruges. He made graphs of the church's annual revenues from offerings, its expenditures for hosts and for ablution wine.[8] Toussaert thus intended to calculate the number of persons that assisted at mass on Sundays and that participated in the Easter Communion. These three statistics showed important fluctuations in the frequency of the parishioners' churchgoing during the fifteenth and sixteenth centuries, which proved, according to Toussaert, the 'caractère spasmodique' of the religious sentiments of medieval Flanders. Furthermore, he discovered a lot of cases of violence, homicide and sexual abuse. Toussaert concluded that late medieval Flanders was not at all as Christian as it was thought to be: the Flemish lived in an impious, violent and licentious society, in which superstition and the remains of paganism played a large role.[9]

The reception of this book was divided in accordance with the Belgian–French border. Whereas French historians in general praised Toussaert's book, the Belgian historians disapproved of it.[10] The Flemish reviewers were familiar with the sources Toussaert had used, and were thus aware of the errors of reading and interpretation he made due to his – apparently – poor knowledge of the Dutch language,[11] in addition to a careless citing of the works of colleagues,[12] and simple

---

[7]　Gabriel Le Bras can be considered the inventor of the history of religious practice, studied by means of quantitative methods. Le Bras and his circle did not form part of the *Annales* group, but they inspired them and vice versa. See Peter Burke, *The French Historical Revolution. The Annales School, 1929–89* (Cambridge, 1990), pp. 74–5.

[8]　Ablution wine is the wine which was provided for the faithful after receiving the host. It should not be confused with consecrated wine, which in general was not taken by the laity.

[9]　Toussaert, *Le Sentiment Religieux*, pp. 136–7, 373–9, 414–28, 371, 596.

[10]　Ludo Milis, 'De devotionele praktijk in de Laat-middeleeuwse Nederlanden', in J.D. Janssen (ed.), *Hoofsheid en devotie in de middeleeuwse maatschappij. De Nederlanden van de 12ᵉ tot de 15ᵉ eeuw. Handelingen van het Wetenschappelijk Colloquium te Brussel 21–24 Oktober 1981* (Brussels, 1982), pp. 133–45, esp. pp. 137–8.

[11]　For example, a fight resulting in a homicide between the two gardeners (Middledutch: 'hofmannen') working for the Franciscan Friars in Bruges is cited as a proof of the violence among the convent's leaders or guardians (Middledutch: 'hooftmannen'). A cart loaded with stems of spruce trees (Middledutch: 'kerksparren') in the context of a caravan during warfare is interpreted by Toussaert as a load of church ornaments as spoils of war. See Toussaert, *Le Sentiment Religieux*, pp. 419, 790; A. Viaene, 'Lichten op rood. Aantekeningen bij een werk van Jacques Toussaert', *Biekorf*, 64 (1963): 145–296, pp. 145–50, 183–9, 294–6, esp. 145–6.

[12]　M. Stephanus Axters, 'l'Abbé Jacques Toussaert et l'Histoire du *Sentiment Religieux en Flandre à la Fin du Moyen-Age*', *Supplément de la Vie Spirituelle*, 16 (1963): 574–84, esp. pp. 579–80.

errors in counting.[13] With regard to the quantitative analysis of his sources, Toussaert was said to have made some odd assumptions: he supposed that at every mass all parishioners, rich or poor, offered the smallest coin that circulated at that time (while the semi-obligatory penny for seating did not yet exist), and that everyone took an exactly equal sip of wine, the size of which was based on a 'good guess'. Secondly, because the purchase of hosts and wine in the medieval accounts was sometimes notated in quantities and sometimes in unspecified sums of money, and hosts were available in large, small and unspecified sizes, Toussaert had to use some poorly founded calculations on quantities and sizes before making his graphs. In the end it appeared that the outcome of Toussaert's three sets of statistics did not correspond with each other: the highs and lows in the three measuring instruments for the frequency of churchgoing did not occur in the same periods.[14] Therefore, the legitimacy of his use of statistical analysis for religious history was questioned.[15] Moreover, Toussaert was accused of repeating his favourite cases again and again, thus giving the impression that a particular situation was representative for all of medieval Flanders. He omitted the reservations which he made in his preliminary conclusions, presenting his initial hypotheses as proven facts.[16] In addition, Toussaert was supposed to have failed to show a critical attitude towards his sources, some of which (e.g. confession mirrors and synodal prescriptions) had a regulating (thus one-sided) and not a descriptive purpose.[17] In short, it seemed Toussaert was only interested in indications of immorality and impiety,[18] and appeared to have drawn his conclusions before he had data at his disposal to prove his case.[19] Other reviewers did not so much doubt the methodology of Toussaert's book, but criticized his criteria for the overall evaluation of medieval Christians. Toussaert's reference point, supposedly, was nineteenth- and twentieth-century religiosity. Given the constant struggle for survival for many people and scarce education in religious matters, it should not

---

[13]   Viaene, 'Lichten op rood', 183–4.

[14]   S.J. Dierickx, 'Beoordeling van *Le sentiment Religieux à la Fin du Moyen-Age* van Jacques Toussaert', *Handelingen van de Koninklijke Zuidnederlandse Maatschappij voor Taal- en Letterkunde en Geschiedenis*, 19 (1965): 319–37, p. 327.

[15]   S.J. Mols, 'Emploi et Valeur des Statistiques en Histoire Religieuse', *Nouvelle Revue Théologique*, 86 (1964): 408; Anne-Marie Meyers-Reinquin, 'Proeve tot statistische benadering van de godsdienstpraktijk in de Late middeleeuwen en de moderne tijden (tot 1630) aan de hand van de Kerkfabrieksrekeningen', in *Handelingen der Koninklijke Zuidnederlandse Maatschappij voor Taal- en Letterkunde en Geschiedenis*, 23 (1969): 205–73, p. 206. Numbers derived from these kinds of sources should be examined in relation to the financial, economic and demographic situation.

[16]   J. Andriessen, 'De vroomheid in het middeleeuwse Vlaanderen', *Ons Geestelijk Erf*, 36 (1962): 423–31, p. 428.

[17]   Dierckx, 'Beoordeling van *Le Sentiment Religieux*', p. 337.

[18]   Stephanus Axters, 'L'abbé Jacques Toussaert et l'Histoire du *Sentiment Religieux*', pp. 580–4; L. Gaillard, Review in *Revue d'Histoire Ecclésiastique*, 59 (1964): 307–8.

[19]   Adriaan Bredero, *De ontkerstening der middeleeuwen* (Kampen, 2001), pp. 386–7.

surprise us that medieval people could not satisfy these requirements.[20]

Because of these objections, and a perceived disdain for the Flemish people, as experienced by the reviewers, Toussaert's book as a whole could not count on any goodwill in the Low Countries. The series of short reviews by Antoon Viaene reveal especially, and in a very edgy style, the extent to which Belgian historians felt offended by Toussaert's book and responded by ridiculing his mistakes.[21] After the appearance of these articles, the sale of Toussaert's book in Bruges came to a halt.[22] However, in their alacrity to pull down this book, the Belgian critics failed to notice its positive methodological achievements, Toussaert being the first to adopt historical statistics in the study of (medieval) religion in the Low Countries.

On the other hand, in France Toussaert's book was received with enthusiasm for the very reason of his unusual and pioneering methodology. Therefore, in the non-Dutch speaking countries, where only the laudatory French reviews were read, Toussaert's book was and is often cited without any reservation.[23] His conclusions are readily cited in important French and English studies on late medieval religious life; in particular, his doubtful findings about the poor observance of Sunday mass and the irregular Easter communion are eagerly repeated.[24]

In the Dutch speaking Low Countries, though, after the extremely critical reviews, *Le sentiment religieux* was practically neglected.[25] Most books on the religious life of the Middle Ages in the Low Countries perfunctorily list Toussaert's book in the bibliography, in general without taking its content very seriously.[26] In this way, unfortunately, the negative points concerning

---

[20] Dierickx, 'Beoordeling van *Le Sentiment Religieux*': 335–7; M. Pacaut, Review in *Revue du Nord*, 46 (1964): 107–110; A. Latreille; Review in *Le Monde*, 5 October 1963; L. Gaillard, Review, p. 307. More recently Arnold Angenendt, *Geschichte der Religiosität im Mittelalter* (Darmstadt, 2000), p. 73.

[21] Antoon Viaene, 'Lichten op rood'.

[22] S.J. Dierickx, 'Beoordeling van *Le Sentiment Religieux*', p. 330.

[23] John van Engen, 'The Christian Middle Ages as an Historiographical Problem', *The American Historical Review*, 91 (1986): 519–52, p. 526.

[24] R.N. Swanson and Francis Rapp cite Toussart's results with regard to church-going and Easter communion: Swanson, *Religion and Devotion in Europe, c.1215 – c.1515* (Cambridge, 1995), p. 99, and Rapp, *L'Eglise et la Vie Religieuse en Occident à la Fin du Moyen Age* (Paris, 1971), p. 316. Jacques Le Goff calls the work of Toussaert 'un livre tres dru', and refers to his conclusions considering the primitive nature and irregularity of the religious sentiments of late medieval people: Le Goff, *La Civilisation de l'Occident Médiéval* (Paris, 1984), p. 447, and Le Goff, *Medieval Civilisation 400–1500* (Oxford, 1988).

[25] Milis, 'De devotionele praktijk', p. 138.

[26] Exceptions are J. van Herwaarden and R. de Keyser, 'Het Gelovige Volk in de Late Middeleeuwen', *Algemene Geschiedenis der Nederlanden*, 4 (Haarlem, 1980), pp. 405–20, 489–90; and J. van Herwaarden, 'Religion and Society: The Cult of the Eucharist and the Devotion to Christ's Passion', in van Herwaarden, *Between Saint James and Erasmus: Studies in Late-Medieval Religious Life: Devotion and Pilgrimage in the Netherlands*

misinterpretations and mistakes prevailed over the positive ones of exploring new methodologies. This resulted in a prolonged and deep aversion among medievalists from the Low Countries for quantitative methods for religious history.[27]

After Toussaert's Syndrome

In 1969, Anne-Marie Meyers-Reinquin tried to wrest Flemish historiography free from the post-Toussaert syndrome: she subjected the accounts of the parish (Saint Martin) and collegiate churches (Our Lady, in the borough) of the city of Courtrai and of the countryside pilgrimage centre Lede to quantitative research.[28] More than one third of her article is used for a critical evaluation of Toussaert's book, in which she shows the shortcomings of his methods. Meyers explains how these types of serial source material could be used in a more responsible manner, while applying this to the accounts from medieval and early modern Courtrai and Lede. Without trying to deduce numbers of communicants, like Toussaert did, she analysed the offerings on certain holidays, and the revenues from the boxes at the altars and statues of particular saints.

The outcome of her research did not meet with her initial expectations. Meyers established that there were considerable fluctuations in the level of revenues in the churchwardens' accounts, but she did not find any correspondence with economic, financial, demographic or religious events of the period 1400–1630.[29] Whether the abrupt and therefore highly interesting disappearance from the accounts of the mention of income from devotion to the saints at altars and statues in the Courtrai parish church after 1540 had its correlative in the collegiate church or not, could not be checked because of incompleteness of the source material. In any case, the countryside parish of Lede seems not to have suffered from this decline of devotion and shows continuous fluctuating revenues during the whole period. Meyers suggests that the devotion to saints in the Courtrai parish church dropped because of the religious troubles, and signals that it did not recover until after the Catholic Counter Reformation. This analysis of churchwardens' accounts thus seemed to raise more questions than it gave answers.

Unfortunately, Meyers did not succeed in ridding Flanders of the post-Toussaert syndrome. She did, however, publish an inventory of church accounts from the fourteenth to the seventeenth century from Flanders.[30] Nobody followed her example or responded to her call to study church accounts in order to get a better understanding of the source material. While from the 1970s onwards, in

(Leiden, 2003), pp. 174–207.
27 Milis, 'De Devotionele praktijk', p. 142.
28 Meyers-Reinquin, 'Proeve tot statistische benadering', pp. 205–73.
29 Ibid., p. 216.
30 Anne-Marie Meyers-Reinquin, 'Repertorium van de kerkfabrieksrekeningen in Oost- en West-Vlaanderen. Einde 14de eeuw tot 1630', *De Leiegouw*, 12 (1970): 29–48.

France the historians of the *Annales* school adopted statistics in the study of religious mentality (primarily based on the analysis of testamentary wills),[31] in the Low Countries only a few medievalists used quantitative methods in their research into religion.

Quantitative Research in the Low Countries: Church Accounts and Miracles

One of those rare quantitatively oriented medievalists is the art historian Wim Vroom who, in 1981, published a study on the financing of medieval cathedral construction, particularly the Dom church of Utrecht.[32] Two years later, this book was followed by a study of the building campaign of the church of Our Lady in Antwerp.[33] As Vroom wrote from a background of architectural history, his main scope was to reconstruct the origin of the funding of the construction of the Utrecht cathedral. The most important sources for this part of his study are the almost complete series of accounts of the church fabric from 1395 to 1580, which had already been edited, but of which no extensive study had thus far been made.[34] An important share of the revenues for the building campaign of the Utrecht Dom church was formed by 'quests' (itinerant alms collections in the diocese), instituted in the name of Saint Martin and other saints, whose relics were employed for the purpose. Thus, a part of this book touches the field of religious mentalities, as the fluctuations in this important share of the income of the cathedral can be considered as an indication of religious zeal. Vroom's study shows that at the end of the fourteenth century almost half of the income of the fabric originated from the itinerant diocesan collections made by pardoners, while by around 1500 this number had grown to almost 80 per cent. During the 1520s, the share of the 'quest' in the income of the cathedral fabric dropped to 40 per cent, from 1554 even to under 20 per cent. In absolute numbers, the picture becomes even more dramatic: an almost continuous increase took place until the peak year 1518–19, when suddenly these resources collapsed, and came to a final end after 1563–64. The building activity of the cathedral therefore was stopped.[35]

Similar conclusions are drawn by Gerrit Verhoeven in his study of the late medieval devotion to a crucifix and three miraculous statues of Our Lady in the city of Delft.[36] From the fourteenth century onwards, the two parish churches in

---

[31]   See note 40.

[32]   W.H. Vroom, *De financiering van de kathedraalbouw in de middeleeuwen, in het bijzonder van de dom van Utrecht* (Maarssen, 1981).

[33]   W.H. Vroom, *De Onze-Lieve-Vrouwekerk te Antwerpen. De financiering van de Bouw tot de Beeldenstorm* (Antwerpen, 1983).

[34]   L. Van Tongerloo, 'De financiering van de Dom', *Maandblad Oud-Utrecht*, 54 (1981): 167–9.

[35]   Vroom, *De financiering van de kathedraalbouw*, pp. 300, 508–12, 360.

[36]   Gerrit Verhoeven, *Devotie en negotie. Delft als bedevaartplaats in de Late*

Delft had become regional pilgrimage centres that attracted the faithful from the County of Holland. Almost 340 miracle stories had been recorded by the churchwardens. These miracle books were used as evidence to obtain indulgences from the pope, and served as an inspiration for sermons to stimulate the spread of the cult. The financial interest of the pilgrimages for the churches is evident from the churchwardens' accounts.

The popularity of the Delft pilgrimages changed dramatically during the first quarter of the sixteenth century. The last miracle recorded in the miracle books had taken place in 1519.[37] Likewise, the gifts from the pilgrims, as registered in the churchwardens' accounts, rapidly declined after 1519–21.

Quantitative Research in the Low Countries: Last Wills

In the late 1980s, Hans Mol published an article on the pious bequests in medieval Frisian last wills.[38] This appears to be the first – and so far only – publication of a quantitative analysis of the religious aspects of last wills in the Netherlands. Traditionally, wills used to be considered of scholarly interest only by historians of law. However, as early as 1959 they were discovered as a source for social history by W.K. Jordan in his quantitative study of London late medieval social care, and as a source for research on the concept of gift exchange by Joel T. Rosenthal in 1972 in *The purchase of paradise*, in which he studied medieval English noble wills.[39]

Not much later, testamentary research was taken up by the French historians of the *Annales* school, who applied statistical methods to the history of mentalities: Michel Vovelle (1973) and Pierre Chaunu (1978) on early modern Provence and Paris, and Jacques Chiffoleau in 1980 on the medieval Avignon area.[40] The

---

middeleeuwen (Amsterdam, 1992).

[37]   OLV der 7 Smarten. The other miracles had already stopped: Maria Jesse, 1439; Heilige Kruis, 1511; Maria ter Nood Gods, 1516. Verhoeven, *Devotie en negotie*, p. 182.

[38]   J.A. Mol, 'Friezen en het hiernamaals. Zielheilsbeschikkingen ten gunste van kerken, kloosters en armen in testamenten uit Friesland tot 1580', in N. Lettinck and J.J. van Moolenbroek (eds), *In de schaduw van de eeuwigheid. Tien studies aangeboden aan prof. dr A.H. Bredero* (Utrecht, 1986), pp. 28–64; revised in J.A. Mol (ed.), *Zorgen voor Zekerheid. Studies over Friese Testamenten in de Vijftiende en Zestiende Eeuw* (Leeuwarden, 1994), pp. 175–214.

[39]   W.K. Jordan, *Philanthropy in England 1460–1660. A Study of the Changing Pattern of English Social Aspirations* (London, 1959); Joel T. Rosenthal, *The Purchase of Paradise. Gift Giving and the Aristocracy, 1307–1485* (London & Toronto, 1972).

[40]   Michel Vovelle, *Piété Baroque et Déchristianisation en Provence au XVIIIe Siècle. Les Attitudes Devant la Mort d'Après les Clauses des Testaments* (Paris, 1973); Pierre Chaunu, *La Mort à Paris 16e 17e 18e Siècles* (Paris, 1978); Jacques Chiffoleau, *La Comptabilité de l'Au-delà: les Hommes, la Mort et la Religion dans la Région d'Avignon à la Fin du Moyen Age (vers 1320–vers 1480)* (Rome, 1980).

American scholar Samuel Cohn combined the fields of socio-economic history and history of mentalities in his 1988 book on medieval and early modern Siena.[41]

The study of Dutch medieval last wills by Hans Mol takes as its point of departure the question of whether religious sentiments and behaviour during the fifteenth and sixteenth centuries were influenced by humanism and Reformation. He analysed some 212 testamentary documents from late medieval Frisia. His main conclusions are that some significant changes took place in the phrasing of the clauses and in the type of bequests made in the wills around 1520–30. The number of chantry foundations and of obit masses dropped, as did the donations to parish churches and convents, while the charitable bequests grew in number as well as in size. Furthermore, the poor also gained in ranking as they were no longer mentioned as a residual figure, but appeared at the beginning of the list of bequeathed persons and institutions. Another type of change was the disappearance of references to the saints and to Mary from the *commendatio animae*.[42]

Quantitative Research in The Low Countries: Confraternities

Another area that has attracted quantitative medievalists from the Low Countries is that of religious confraternities. During the 1970s, several studies on religious confraternities were published, which aimed mainly at gathering genealogical data of members of one particular brotherhood. Many of these publications also had a minor quantitative component concerning the religious mentality of its members, as expressed in applications for membership and in participation in common activities. The only publication in the Low Countries in which not only the confraternities of one city as a whole were studied, but also quantitative methods were used, is the dissertation by Paul Trio. Trio analysed the archival material concerning the brotherhoods that existed during the Middle Ages in the Flemish city of Ghent.[43] Between the twelfth and sixteenth centuries no less than forty religious brotherhoods appear to have existed in Ghent; mostly founded during the fifteenth century. Trio distinguishes two periods in the development of the Ghent brotherhoods: a first period until around 1400, in which the membership of a confraternity implicated a strong personal commitment, such as attendance at masses and ceremonies, and participation in funeral services of deceased *confratres*. During the second period, starting at the beginning of the fifteenth century, the bond with the brotherhood diminished for most brothers and sisters, except for the members of the board. The social and religious obligations of the common brothers and sisters slowly disappeared: common members paid a fee to

---

[41] Samuel Cohn, *Death and Property in Siena, 1205–1800: Strategies for the Afterlife* (Baltimore and London, 1988).

[42] Mol, 'Friezen en het hiernamaals', pp. 36–8, 55–8.

[43] Paul Trio, *Volksreligie als spiegel van een stedelijke samenleving. De broederschappen te Gent in de late middeleeuwen* (Leuven, 1993).

profit from the spiritual benefits, but were excluded from the other confraternal activities. According to Trio this membership *à deux vitesses* developed because of the growing number of members, which inhibited the equal participation of all. Trio signals a first average bloom period for the Ghent confraternities during the second half of the fifteenth century which lasted until the years 1480–85, when it was followed by a nadir. After 1492–93 there was a revival, which went on until the first quarter of the sixteenth century. In most confraternities this second bloom is followed by decay in *c.* 1525.[44]

Dutch Devotions in Decline: Two Explanations

From the studies by Vroom, Verhoeven, Mol and Trio a picture arises of a late medieval declining popularity of some of the popular devotions, concentrated in the 1520s. The explanations for this sudden change in devotional life are sought in either the field of socio-economic and political developments or in changes in belief and mentality. Without excluding the influence of the sixteenth-century religious debate, Paul Trio points at the synchronism between the periods of decline in the number of new members of the Ghent confraternities and the various socio-economic and political crises during the fourteenth, fifteenth and sixteenth centuries.[45] Trio argues that during periods of crisis, the financial obligations attached to membership of a religious brotherhood became too heavy a burden for a large part of the town's inhabitants. He demonstrates how at each crisis the number of new members dropped dramatically, and increased afterwards at the recovery of the market. This happened after the crises of 1447–53 and 1482–92. Also in 1520, economic decline is echoed by a diminishing number of new Ghent confraternities. After the crisis that had started during the 1520s, however, the economic situation in Ghent did not recover quickly: it was only in 1560 that purchasing power reached the same level as before. After this long period of neglect of the confraternal spirit, the old level of applications for the brotherhoods never returned. Trio suggests that the confraternities themselves had suffered from this long crisis: the governors had had to cut down the expenses to survive during the financial downturn, which had an intensifying negative impact on the image of the brotherhoods.[46] This would explain the fact that the Ghent confraternities never recovered from the 1520 crisis.

A few remarks have to be made about these two explanations of the 1520 devotional decline in the Low Countries. With regard to the general economic developments in the Low Countries, some authors state that the 1520 crisis did not last long: already from the second half of the 1530s onwards an economic recovery

---

[44]   Ibid., pp. 190–92.
[45]   Ibid., pp. 189–97.
[46]   Ibid., p. 194.

took place in most parts of the Low Countries.[47] However, the old spirit of offerings did not return as might have been expected. It is argued, therefore, that economic developments alone cannot account for the devotional change.

The second explanation of the 1520 devotional decline, which looks to the early signs of the Reformation and the penetration of humanist ideas, is supported by Vroom, Verhoeven, and Mol. They and other historians who interpreted the 1520 devotional change in terms of signs of a 'pre-reformation' usually deny the possibility of a socio-economic explanation.[48] As an explanation for the sudden drop in income for the Utrecht Cathedral from quest and indulgences Wim Vroom quotes directly from his sixteenth century sources. In a document from 1522, the canons of the Utrecht Cathedral chapter blame the economic problems, political distress and also the spread of the teachings of Luther. Of these three factors, Vroom argues that the penetration of Reformation ideas was by far the most important. He sees a confirmation of his ideas in the fact that in the same year, 1522, the canons summoned the pardoners to distribute a pamphlet with miracle stories against Luther's doctrine.[49]

With regard to the cult of the miraculous Delft statues, Verhoeven also argues that the decay was favoured by the penetration of reformist sentiments and denies a connection with economic developments. Also in Delft, the cult of saintly objects became more and more subjected to overt criticism. As proof of the vehement clashing of these religious sentiments, Verhoeven refers to the appearance in Delft of several preachers with 'heretical' sympathies from 1515 onwards, and a non-incidental disturbance of a procession in 1528 by a future leader of the Anabaptists. When one decade later a fire destroyed a large part of the town and damaged the Delft churches, generous donations to the churches revived during a short period, but the cult of the shrines had stopped definitively.[50]

The various changes in the Frisian last wills are explained by Mol with two complementary developments. The increasing attention to charities after 1510–20 is seen as a symptom of the growing fear among the rich about the spread of pauperism and vagabondage caused by demographic and economic developments.[51] Institutionalized and rationalized charity is often considered to be

---

[47]   The main studies of economic trends in the Low Countries, though, are less positive than is often suggested by the opponents of an economic explanation of the early sixteenth-century devotional decline: see J. Noordegraaf, *Hollands welvaren? Levensstandaard in Holland 1450–1650* (Bergen, 1985). An interesting detail is that half of his statistics relating to the purchasing power of masons in the county of Holland on which the quantitative data of the book is based, derive from religious or charitable institutions.

[48]   C.I. Kruisheer, *De Onze Lieve Vrouwe-Broederschap, c. 1397–1580* (Annheim, 1976), pp. 43–4; Verhoeven, *Devotie en negotie*, p. 181.

[49]   Vroom, *De financiering van de kathedraalbouw*, pp. 320, 316.

[50]   Verhoeven, *Devotie en negotie*, pp. 182, 183, 190.

[51]   Mol, 'Friezen en het hiernamaals', pp. 54–5.

a humanist innovation.[52] Regarding the diminishing of the quantities and importance of donations to convents and churches, of the number of chantries and of obit masses, and the disappearance from the wills of the *commendatio animae* phrase, and of the mentioning of the saints and Mary, occurring around 1530, Mol too points at the relation between these changes and the spread of reforming ideas.[53] He argues that around 1530, influenced by new religious ideas among the reform-minded and orthodox Catholic Frisians alike,[54] the attitude towards the hereafter as expressed in the last wills had changed.[55]

In short, according to these supporters of the 'early-Reformation-explanation' for the devotional change of 1520, late medieval people had lost their faith in the Church as the provider of eternal salvation, which resulted in a retreat of many faithful from the popular traditional devotions.

The supporters of this interpretation mention the influence of writings by humanists, such as Erasmus of Rotterdam and, of course, Martin Luther, as carriers of a change in attitude towards religion and devotion. It is true that in 1518, the earliest texts of Luther already circulated in the Low Countries among a small group of humanists, theologians and Augustinian monks, who are said to have spread these ideas among lay people through sermons.[56] Moreover, during the 1520s, some writings by Luther (for example his *Sermon vom Ablass und Gnade*) were translated into Dutch and printed in Antwerp or Leiden.[57] On the other hand, criticism of certain outwardly devotional practices had existed in the Low Countries long before 1520. To quote but one example: Erasmus of Rotterdam published his *Enchiridion militis christiani* in 1504,[58] in which he mocked people's faith in indulgences.[59] It seems strange that this pre-existing urge for reform was not heard until it was joined by Luther in the years around 1520, when all of a

---

[52]   The main reference made is to the pamphlet by Ludovico Vives, *De Subventione Pauperum*, first published in 1526. The importance of this pamphlet is given a different shade in the current research of Ad Tervoort, Vrije Universiteit, Amsterdam.

[53]   Strangely, Mol does not refer to humanist ideas in this respect, whose influence he had announced he would study in the introduction of his article.

[54]   For a discussion of the difficulty of distinguishing between these groups, see Eamon Duffy, *The Stripping of the Altars. Traditional Religion in England c. 1400–c. 1580* (London, New Haven, 1992), pp. 504–15.

[55]   Mol, 'Friezen', pp. 56–7.

[56]   See also C.Ch.G. Visser, *Luther's geschriften in de Nederlanden tot 1546* (Amsterdam, 1969).

[57]   Johan Decavele, 'Vroege Reformatorische bedrijvigheid in de grote Nederlandse steden. Claes van de Elst te Brussel, Antwerpen, Amsterdam en Leiden (1524–1528)', *Nederlands archief voor kerkgeschiedenis*, 70 (1990): 24–5.

[58]   Léon Halkin, *De biografie van Erasmus* (Baarn, 1987), pp. 78–86; available in English translation as *Erasmus: A Critical Biography*, trans. J. Tonkin (Oxford, 1993).

[59]   Jan van Herwaarden, 'Medieval Indulgences and Devotional Life', in van Herwaarden, *Between Saint James and Erasmus. Studies in Late-Medieval Religious Life: Devotion and Pilgrimage in the Netherlands* (Leiden, 2003), p. 121.

sudden it caused such an important change. A major change in mentality, resulting in a different approach to devotions, does not take place within a few years, as explanations which seek a direct correlation with Lutheran ideas would suggest.[60]

The 1520-Thesis

The publication of these studies within a short period of time and their similar outcome concerning the late medieval religious mentality in the Low Countries was signalled by Koen Goudriaan who, in 1994, published an essay in which he brought together the results from this – then – recent research.[61] He established that, independently from each other, the series of quantitative data in these above-mentioned studies showed a sudden decline in enthusiasm for the traditional devotions around the years 1520–30. Goudriaan, wittingly, suggested that these historians had discovered 'the end of the Middle Ages',[62] and launched what, since then, has been known as the so called '1520-thesis'. In his essay, Goudriaan dismisses the one-sided accounts of both the economic and the religious explanation. Goudriaan cites additional evidence of a changing mentality regarding religious matters: in the city of Gouda in the County of Holland the willingness among the members of the guilds to participate in the annual processions of the Holy Sacrament and Saint John diminished, as indicated by the falling numbers of persons to whom the local government offered free drinks on these occasions in the city's accounts after 1513. At the same time, the number of novices in the Rotterdam convent of Carmelites dropped dramatically after 1520. Other indications for changing mentalities, according to Goudriaan, lay in the lowering of status and appreciation for the Franciscan friars. Furthermore, the towns and the sovereign tried to limit the tax freedom of the convents and other religious houses within their respective territories. Although fluctuations in the popularity of devotions and instances of anticlericalism had already occurred before 1520, a simultaneous fall in one and rise in the other had never occurred. Therefore in his 1994 essay, Koen Goudriaan opted for a third explanation for the 1520 devotional change. He argued that the phenomenon of a fall in participation in traditional religious activities, in 1520, was neither caused by socio-economic problems nor should it be seen as an early result of Luther's writings. It was, rather, an indication of a large cultural reversal, which he called a 'religious burn out'. An increasing number of citizens became 'fed up' with the overkill of devotional obligations.

---

[60]   Trio, *Volksreligie als spiegel*, p. 196; See also the discussion in Paul Trio, 'Friese Testeerpraktijken', Review of J.A. Mol (ed.), *Zorgen voor zekerheid. Studies over Friese testamenten in de vijftiende en zestiende eeuw* (Leeuwarden, 1994), *Signum*, 8 (1996): 47–58, p. 55.

[61]   Koen Goudriaan, 'Het einde van de Middeleeuwen ontdekt?', *Madoc*, 8 (1994): 66–75.

[62]   The title of his essay translates as, 'The Discovery of the End of the Middle Ages?'.

Luther's teachings of justification through faith offered an alternative to compulsory good works in late medieval society, which was based on religious merit. In the end, as Goudriaan's argument shows, religious experience itself had changed.[63]

A few remarks should be made about the explanation models for the 1520 devotional crisis. First of all, it seems that evidence that does not fit in the picture is left out. Although sometimes it is necessary to focus in order to get a clearer look, the blurred edges also form a part of the view. For example, the number of new members of the confraternity of Our Lady in 's-Hertogenbosch (Brabant) already declined slowly from 1510.[64] The fall in membership of the brotherhood of St Mary in Bergen op Zoom (Brabant) had started in 1489,[65] and the popularity of one of Ghent's confraternities detailed in Paul Trio's book fell from as early as 1485 onwards. These can be considered as changes in 'devotional attitude' *far* before 1520. The confraternity of Our Lady in Heusden (Brabant), however, did not loose popularity until the decade 1540–50.[66] The income from offerings in the Buurkerk, the eldest parochial church in the city of Utrecht, after 100 years of heavy fluctuation, stabilized only from 1542 at a more moderate level,[67] while the offerings in the parochial church of Kortrijk did not change throughout the fifteenth and sixteenth centuries.[68] With these additional data in mind, the changes that did take place during the years around 1520 appear to have happened less suddenly.

A second remark on the 1520-thesis is that it conflates many different types of pious utterances. To use a Dutch expression, it is like comparing apples with pears. All these different kinds of devotions have their own peculiarities, which could easily be overlooked in a broad overview. Using these parameters, we risk ignoring their own value. Comparing the trends in the numbers of new members of a confraternity with those of the income from the offerings in a parochial church seems risky. Even the comparison between the applications for two confraternities is not always without problems, if one knows that the confraternity of Our Lady in 's-Hertogenbosch had 15,000 members in its heyday (not only living in the town and its surroundings, but all over the Low Countries, the German cities and even in England). The motivations that are hidden behind the participation in one particular

---

[63]   Goudriaan, 'Het einde van de Middeleeuwen', pp. 68–70, 73–4.

[64]   G.C.M. van Dijck, *De Bossche Optimaten, Geschiedenis Van de Illustere Lieve Vrouwebroederschap te 's-Hertogenbosch, 1318-1973* (Tilburg, 1973), p. 209.

[65]   K. Slootmans, 'De Hoge Lieve Vrouwe van Bergen op Zoom', *Jaarboek Oudheidkundige Kring 'De Ghulden Roos'*, 24 (1964): 46–7.

[66]   R.C.M. Hoppenbrouwers, 'De broederschap van Onze-Lieve-Vrouw te Heusden', in D.E.H. de Boer and J.W. Marsilje (eds), *De Nederlanden in de late middeleeuwen* (Utrecht, 1987), pp. 199–235.

[67]   Vroom, *De financiering van de kathedraalbouw*, pp. 344–52, 542–6.

[68]   Meyers-Reinquin, 'Proeve tot statistische benadering', pp. 216–17.

devotion or another often diverge too much for a sensible and responsible comparison or even equalization.[69]

Another point of concern is the question: what exactly is the object of our study, by counting the participation in these various pious practices? To what extent is it really 'devotional enthusiasm', or is it mixed with other aspects connected with a certain devotion? It is very likely that it was not only 'religious zeal' that made people choose *that* particular form of devotional utterance. Apart from the economic factors, pious choices can, for example, be influenced by considerations of charity, prestige, and family bonds. All of these motivations influence each other in a certain (continuously changing) manner. As it is not possible to separate these factors, in the end it is not clear which aspect of the devotional action is currently under study. For example, when people join religious confraternities, do they do so out of pure devotion to the patron saint, or is it because all of their families or colleagues always do so, or do they want to secure themselves a good burial and prayers for their souls, or are they mainly attracted by the annual banquet and the prospect of being part of a community?

Transformations Within Devotion

The most important remark to be made on the implementation of a quantitative approach to devotion, however, is that in general it tends to ignore the changes that took place within the religious practices themselves. The religious practices and the significance they bear for the believers are treated as concepts that remain stable during an often very long period of time. Also, reformist sentiments are read into medieval behaviour. An example is the highly debated issue of the testamentary preambles.[70] The absence of invocations to Mary and the saints, and the emphasis on Christ, is often regarded as a sign that the testator tended towards Protestantism, renouncing the cult of the saints. But this interpretation ignores the fact that during the late medieval period the role of the veneration of the saints was changing, and that Christocentric piety gained importance.[71] Another example: for the brotherhood of Our Lady in Liege, there is the rather unique situation of four consecutive versions of the Confraternity Rule, dating from 1457 until 1529. The functions of this brotherhood changed considerably.[72] Comparison of the rules of 1457 and 1529 show that the participation of the members in funeral ceremonies became less important: in 1457 the brotherhood functioned around the

---

[69]   Van Dijck, *De Bossche Optimaten*, p. 211.

[70]   For example, Cohn, *Death and Property in Sienna*, pp. 58–60; Duffy, *Stripping of the Altars*, pp. 504–15.

[71]   Christine Peters, *Patterns of Piety. Women, Gender and Religion in Late Medieval and Reformation England* (Cambridge, 2003), p. 4.

[72]   David Henry Dieterich, *Brotherhood and Community on the Eve of the Reformation: Confraternities and Parish life in Liege, 1450–1540* (Michigan, 1982), pp. 56–68.

remembrance of the deceased members, while in 1529 it was merely directed at the living. Further, the rule of 1529 prescribes an increased number of masses, and the confraternity's accounts show more expenses for sumptuous liturgy after 1530. In 1457, the confraternity was an organization for members only, while in 1529, its activities aimed at the parish as a whole.

Transformation within the devotions themselves is a neglected aspect of the study of religious developments. In the remainder of this paragraph, devotions related to the commemoration of the dead are taken as an example. The care for one's own soul and the souls of ancestors, relatives and friends is at the core of late medieval devotional culture. Unlike many other quantifiable devotions, the medieval foundations of chantries and memorial services in the Low Countries have previously not been studied from a quantitative point of view.[73] The incidence of foundation of new chantries and of simple memorial services shows an enormous boom between 1500 and 1510.[74] All types of memorial foundations had been gaining popularity during the last decades of the fifteenth century, and slowly started to decline after 1510, and fell rapidly from 1520 onwards. This is nothing to be surprised by, as the year 1520 has already been identified as a breaking point in the popularity curves of many traditional devotions. However, after detailed analysis of these data, some changes that took place on the *inside* of these curves can be discovered.

A neglected field in the study of commemorative devotion are memorial services in charitable institutions. Bequests to hospitals and almshouses usually consist of an annual liturgical (or para-liturgical) commemoration and the distribution of alms to the poor and sick, and often a combination of both.[75] The changes in religious attitude of 1520 and the subsequently approaching Reformation are said to have caused a shift from devotional practices towards charity. As a result of pre-reform sentiments, the surplus of religious good works is supposed to have been used for social care.[76] The memorial books of St Catherine's hospital in Leiden (Holland) show a shift in the type and contents of bequests that took place during the fifteenth and sixteenth centuries. In the anniversaries of the benefactors who died during the first half of the fifteenth century, alms to the poor and sick were included only in one-third of the cases. Of the benefactors who made their bequests between 1480 and 1530, more than two-

---

[73]   This is the subject of my Ph.D thesis: 'A Quantitative Study of the Transformations of Two Forms of Late Medieval Memorial Piety: The Foundations of Chantries and Charitable Piety in the Northern Low Countries, 1400–1580' (in progress, Vrije Universiteit, Amsterdam).

[74]   The incidence over time of memorial foundations in the individual towns is much less clear, depending on local circumstances, such as the growth of the town's population, a devastating fire, an outbreak of the plague or other disease, local warfare or political intrigue.

[75]   For example, visits at the benefactor's grave, with prayers, psalms, candles etc.

[76]   Mol, 'Friezen en het hiernamaals ', pp. 206–07, 214.

thirds requested the distribution of food to the poor as a part of the commemoration of the anniversary of their death. This development shows that, well before we can speak of any 'proto-reformist' sentiments (at least in Leiden), the shift from liturgical memorial services to charity had started.

Analysis of the memorial book of another hospital, the Holy Spirit in Deventer (Oversticht/Overijssel) shows that another development is to be discovered. In 1450, the distribution of food to the poor from bequests of the benefactors were reformed: their funds were put together and the almsgiving was redistributed at regular intervals during the year, dissolving the alms from the commemoration date. The names of the old benefactors disappeared from the accounts once their alms were joined together. From that year on, the benefactors who made endowments for alms chose one or a few dates on which the distribution had to be made, which did not coincide with an obit. In the yearly accounts of the Deventer hospital, year after year we find the names of these new benefactors at the entries concerning the alms distributions they asked for. This development might indicate that benefactors not only wanted the poor to have a meal, for the benefit of their own souls, but also desired to have their names remembered, on paper and probably also spoken at the occasion of almsgiving. It looks as if another idea, which usually is ascribed to Protestantism,[77] might have at least some fifteenth century roots: the remembrance in 'here and now' gained importance over merely prayers for the hereafter.

The first women to found a chantry appear in the last quarter of the fourteenth century, while men had been founding chantries since 1250. The female share in the total amount of foundations is some 20 per cent. During the period of decline in the amount of new chantries after 1510, the percentile participation of women grew: from a little over 20 per cent it doubled to 40 per cent. From a feminist point of view, one could argue that the growing participation in this type of devotion is a sign of emancipation. But I suspect that it is more accurate to interpret the appearance of a high number of women at the moment devotion declined, as a sign of the *loss of status* for the chantry, which in turn might have had further implications for its popularity.

Every chantry was served by at least one priest, who was appointed for life. Usually, the first priest was chosen by the founder, but to ensure the continuance of duties after the chaplain's death or resignation, the chantry's founder had to make provisions. They thus created not only a chain of priests to sing mass, but also a chain of patrons, whose tasks consisted in nominating and supervising the priest. The founder had three main options: he or she could appoint a relative and his or her offspring, the holder of an ecclesiastical office, or a combination of both. During the period between 1250 and 1350, only 20 per cent of the new founders put the chain of advowson in the family. Between 1350 and 1450 this was 40 per cent. During the years of the boom of chantry-foundations, 1460–1510, 66 per cent

---

[77]   Peter Marshall, *Beliefs and the Dead in Reformation England* (Oxford, 2002).

of new chantries had a relative of the founder as patron.[78] This growing role of the family in chantry foundation might be considered an indication not so much of growing family consciousness but, in a certain way, of the tendency of a partial subtraction of devotions from clerical supervision. It was laymen and women who paid for the liturgical services, and the clergy who carried out their instructions.[79]

Conclusions

Although this is only the result of work in progress, I would like to make two final remarks. When studying late medieval devotional practices with a quantitative approach, it is necessary not only to look at religious and socio-economic circumstances, but to include, also, certain other aspects: changes in the importance of family ties, prestige, gender, charity, and commemoration.

Further, the 1520-thesis, on closer inspection, does not point at changes that took place in one year or one decade. It appears that the various changes in devotional attitude took place in the period between 1450 and 1550 with, however, a remarkable but not exclusive concentration around 1520.

---

[78] This is high, especially if we take into account that in some churches it was very difficult to have a family chantry established, especially in the collegiate churches with strong colleges of canons.

[79] See also Duffy, *The Stripping of the Altars*, p. 114.

PART III
Reading and Representation: Material Cultures of Piety

Chapter 7

'Some Tomb for a Remembraunce'
Representations of Piety in Post-Reformation Gentry Funeral Monuments

Claire Bartram

This chapter seeks to investigate the significance of the Elizabethan funeral monument as a material object that reflected changes in piety and pious representation. In a post-Reformation culture which had ambivalent attitudes towards images and church decoration and which – with the abandonment of purgatory and value of intercessory prayer – had negated the primary function of the monument, elaborate tombs to members of the élite and professional classes proliferated, blocking aisles and sight lines within the church and making sometimes exaggerated statements concerning the status and authority of the deceased.[1] Such monuments with their emphasis on status, wealth and family, their use of secular iconography and composition appear to have little to do with expressions of piety or to have lent themselves to the transaction of religious polemic.[2] This chapter seeks to re-complicate the interpretation of such monuments and argues that historians have been too quick to assume the dominance of secular practices and imagery in post-Reformation processes of remembrance. Instead, it argues that not only were there strong strands of continuity between pre- and post-Reformation monument style, but that a richer cultural contextualization of the funeral monument is required. Using examples from Kent, it will put forward a

---

[1]   On the monument as 'obstacle' see David Cressy, *Birth, Marriage and Death: Ritual Religion and the Life-Cycle in Tudor and Stuart England* (Oxford, 1997), p. 472.

[2]   See Nigel Llewellyn, '"Plinie is a weyghtye witnesse": The Classical Reference in Post-Reformation Funeral Monuments', in Lucy Gent (ed.), *Albion's Classicism: The Visual Arts in Britain 1550–1660* (London, 1997), p. 147 for the argument that such '… funeral monuments were public statements, essentially orthodox phenomena, not likely or suitable sites for the transaction of religious polemic'; Nigel Llewellyn, *Art of Death: Visual Culture in the English Death Ritual c.1500–c.1800* (London, 1991), p. 118.

reading of the Elizabethan monument within broader processes of remembrance and the formation of identity in gentry culture.

Gentry Monuments and Sacred Space

Extant monuments in Canterbury Cathedral and in parish churches across Kent suggest that the laity and specifically the gentry dominated post-Reformation sacred space. Striking aspects of this style of monument included the appearance of almost life-sized wooden or alabaster effigies often depicted kneeling in prayer before a lectern. The use of classical architectural trims as opposed to the decorative friezes that had echoed medieval church architecture and the increasing use of inscriptions also seemed to mark a distinctive change of style. The use of heraldry and armorial achievements and the depiction of mourning family members might also be considered as significant facets of this style.

The place of the gentry funeral monument within post-Reformation church space needs to be carefully evaluated. Prominent local families had always dominated church space both within the congregation and in the erection of tombs and brasses.[3] Norris reminds us of the medieval precedent for displays of wealth and status, recording the use of life-sized monumental brasses in the medieval period.[4] Burgess also highlights the role played by parishioners in defining the decoration of church interiors through bequests of moveable goods such as altar or hearse cloths, vessels and vestments as well as more substantial alterations to the fabric of the building itself including the commissioning of an elaborate roodloft, the gilding of, or gifts of, hangings for altars, or the painting of religious scenes on pillars.[5] There was much less scope to perpetuate processes of commemoration or to express piety materially within a post-Reformation church space that had a communion table instead of an altar, that had removed the roodloft and many holy images and had whitewashed the stonework.[6]

---

[3] See for example, Peter Fleming, 'Charity, Faith and the Gentry of Kent 1422–1529', in Anthony Pollard (ed.), *Property and Politics: Essays in Late Medieval English History* (Gloucester, 1984), pp. 36–57.

[4] Malcolm Norris, 'Late Medieval Monumental Brasses: An Urban Funerary Industry and its Representation of Death', in Steven Bassett (ed.), *Death in Towns: Urban Responses to the Dying and the Dead 100–1600* (London, 1995), p. 195.

[5] Clive Burgess, '"Longing to be prayed for": Death and Commemoration in an English Parish in the Middle Ages', in Bruce Gordon and Peter Marshall (eds), *The Place of the Dead: Death and Remembrance in Late Medieval and Early Modern Europe* (Cambridge 2000), p. 59.

[6] For a description of the interior of Canterbury Cathedral in the 1560s see Patrick Collinson, 'The Protestant Cathedral, 1541–1660', in Patrick Collinson, Nigel Ramsay and Margaret Sparks (eds), *A History of Canterbury Cathedral* (Oxford, 1995), pp. 162, 167.

What is striking about the effigy monument is that it remained an accepted form of church decoration in a period that was highly ambivalent about the depiction of the human form. This ambivalence is seen no more clearly than in the acts of iconoclasm that occurred from the 1530s onwards. What was admissible in Protestant church interiors and culture remained a vigorous forum for debate across Elizabeth's reign. Those iconoclasts who had previously defaced the images of saints in line with the strictures of the second commandment 'Thou shalt not make to thy selfe any graven Image nor the likenes of any thing that is in heaven above' continued to object to other media, imagery in stained glass, crosses in graveyards and elsewhere, maypoles and organs.[7] Yet, not all images were deemed idolatrous and Protestantism was not hostile to art per se. Only those images venerated as having spiritual powers were removed. The fact that images remained a valid means of instruction was evident in the extensive use of woodcut illustrations in such works as Foxe's *Acts and Monuments*.[8]

However, Collinson has argued that Protestants became increasingly iconophobic as Elizabeth's reign progressed. He highlights 1580 as a watershed in Protestant culture in which a second generation of Protestants reacted against the use of the mimetic media of drama, music and pictorial art.[9] The Protestant divine Edward Dering condemned such media, enumerating the '… great licenciousnes of printing bookes full of all sin and abhominations that have now filled the world' and drew parallels between the current publication of:

> Many baudy songs (I am loth to use such a loathsome word save that it is not fit enough for so vile endeavours) … our songs and sonets, our pallaces of pleasure, our unchast Fables & Tragedies and other such sorceries, mo then any man may reckon.

Dering also referred to the role of such works in the Catholic past as '… the subtle sleights of satan to occupy Christian witts in heathen fantasies … [and to] … kindle in mens harts the sparkes of superstition'. Such 'vanities', continued Dering should be 'burned up' and replaced by 'Holy readings.'[10] The absence of illustration of the type seen in Foxe in similar religious works of the 1590s reflected this desire to promote holy readings and represented the capacity of the written word to communicate the visual.[11] Indeed, given Dering's strict line against the use of images 'to be the better put in mind of God', he might have been pleased

---

[7]   Margaret Aston, 'Iconoclasm in England: Official and Clandestine', in Peter Marshall (ed.), *The Impact of the English Reformation 1500–1640* (London, 1997), p. 182.

[8]   Aston, 'Iconoclasm in England', pp. 177, 180; Patrick Collinson, 'From Iconoclasm to Iconophobia: The Cultural Impact of the Second English Reformation', in Marshall (ed.), *The Impact of the English Reformation 1500–1640*, p. 299.

[9]   Collinson, 'From Iconoclasm to Iconophobia', p. 297.

[10]   Edward Dering, *A Briefe and Necessarie Catachisme or Instruction*, in *Maister Dering's Works* (1590), unpaginated 'Address to the Reader'.

[11]   Collinson, 'From Iconoclasm to Iconophobia', p. 295.

with the sentiment expressed in the collation of his works for posthumous publication:

> But thowe that nowe, of him woldest have a perfecte sighte and vewe / Peruse his bokes, there ar his lokes purtracted faier and trewe. / These are to him his monumentes whilest he doth lie in grave.[12]

Dering was representative of a policy which sought to define more closely and separate the realms of the sacred from the secular. Trends towards this policy were apparent in the 1570s with the removal of the portraits of royal and courtier patrons from editions of the Bible and in the pressure to separate the scripturally sanctioned aspects of the funeral service from the secular desire for commemoration. Thomas Cartwright stipulated that a pause should be made in the increasingly popular funeral sermon to differentiate between the section of the sermon which offered praise to God and that which commemorated the life of the deceased.[13] This divide was also to be marked in any subsequent publication of the sermon, even though, as Archbishop Whitgift and others argued, the commemorative aspects of the sermon provided the perfect opportunity to:

> Entreat of the mortality of man and the shortness of his days, of the vanities of the world, of the uncertainty of riches, of the resurrection, of the judgement to come, of eternal life and of everlasting death, and of infinite other most necessary points than that wherein we have a present example [i.e. corpse] before our eyes.[14]

Concerns about iconoclasm also proliferated in secular art forms. From at least as early as the 1550s, debates about the propriety of portraiture, its form and function were evident. Aston records the attempts by Christopher Hales in 1551 to obtain portraits of leading Zurich reformers whom he had known in his time abroad. Hales argued that the placing of the portraits in his library and the depiction of the reformers with book in hand offset the possibility of the imputation of vainglory on the part of the sitters or of veneration of the deceased. 'Who ...', exclaimed Hales, '... is so senseless as to worship a painting or a picture deposited in a library?'[15] As Aston points out, the presence of books in the portraits and the designated space for the portraits in a room of books was also significant. These reformers were men who lived by the word of the bible; depicted in this way the image of the reformer

---

[12]   CKS, U350 C1/2.

[13]   Patrick Collinson, 'A Magazine of Religious Patterns: An Erasmian Topic Transposed in English Protestantism', in Derek Baker (ed.), *Renaissance and Renewal in Christian History*, *Studies in Church History*, 14 (1977): 223–49, pp. 246–7.

[14]   Eric Carlson, 'English Funeral Sermons as Sources: The Example of Female Piety in pre-1640 Sermons', *Albion* 32/4 (2000): 567–97, p. 571.

[15]   Margaret Aston, 'Gods, Saints and Reformers: Portraiture and Protestant England', in Lucy Gent (ed.), *Albion's Classicism*, pp. 187–8.

promoted and was subordinate to the text he carried, the image urged study not contemplation.[16] Aston also highlights the capacity of a portrait to aid recollection of speech. She identifies not only portraits and woodcuts of reformers such as John Calvin actively preaching, but also a trend in funeral monument design, consonant across the sixteenth century, that depicted a bust of the deceased preaching from a pulpit, book in hand.[17] It could be argued that there is a similar trend in post-Reformation effigy monuments which move from depicting the deceased in recumbent prayer to kneeling before a lectern actively inciting the reading of scripture.

Not enough research has been undertaken concerning the capacity of post-Reformation effigy monuments to reflect changing modes of pious expression. Indeed, although highlighting the role of the post-Reformation monument as a form of Protestant *memoria*, Llewellyn does not draw out the significance of the monument within this religious context stating that monuments had little to do with religious belief and were almost entirely secular in their iconography and composition.[18] Gittings has also argued that the simplification of the burial service led to greater emphasis on secular social rituals such as feasting. She suggests, further, that the advent of the prescriptive heraldic funeral in the late fifteenth century stressed the transfer of title and authority to the heir within the context of the State, with the implication that this secular emphasis gained further currency after the Reformation.[19]

The perception of the secularization of processes of commemoration is visually reinforced by knowledge of changes in church decoration such as the replacement of the crucifix with the royal arms. This has perhaps had the effect of making more apparent the role of the élite funeral monument as a symbol of status and order. Llewellyn's work has demonstrated the role of the monument in maintaining social differentiation and of establishing the memory and social reputation of the deceased.[20] Finch has drawn attention to the role of the monument in the construction of social hierarchies and identities, paying particular attention to the social geography of church space and the ways in which the monuments differentiated social strata within the élite. The meaner sort of gentry had ledger

---

[16]   Aston, 'Gods, Saints and Reformers', p. 188.

[17]   Ibid., p. 191.

[18]   Llewellyn , *The Art of Death*, p. 118.

[19]   Clare Gittings, 'The Urban Funeral in Late Medieval and Reformation England', S. in Bassett (ed.), *Death in Towns: Urban Responses to the Dying and the Dead 100–1600* (London, 1995), pp. 173, 175–7.

[20]   Llewellyn, *The Art of Death*, p. 104 and Llewellyn, 'Honour in Life, Death and Memory: Funeral Monuments in Early Modern England', *Transactions of the Royal Historical Society*, 6th series, 6 (1996): 180. See also Nigel Llewellyn, 'Claims to Status through Visual Codes: Heraldry on Post-Reformation Funeral Monuments', in Sidney Anglo (ed.), *Chivalry in the Renaissance* (Woodbridge, 1990).

slabs and the nobility raised tombs with full-sized effigies.[21] Parker Pearson has also drawn attention to the role of the monument in social strategies of aggrandizement and social advertisement arguing that material artefacts associated with commemoration were not objective reflections of static roles within society but represented instead idealized relationships between groups and individuals.[22]

Such studies rightly establish the dynamic role of monuments in the negotiation of social position, power and authority within the community. They encourage us to think about the local social and familial context of the monument, the ways in which the monuments reflected local marriage ties or the arrival and integration of a new family into the region, as well as the fabrication or misrepresentation of lineage and longevity.[23] As such, we should also consider the narratives that the monuments promote through the use of inscription, heraldry, classical motif and effigy as part of broader processes of forming identity. Indeed, as Parker Pearson has suggested more recently, funerary rituals are simply one arena of representations among many.[24]

Remembrance and the Formation of Identity

The second section of this chapter proposes to contextualize the effigy monument within Protestant and humanist-inspired processes of remembrance and the formation of identity. It will argue that the 'secular' facets of monument design had a concomitant spiritual meaning and will similarly highlight the ideologies of Christian humanism and Protestantism that informed the identity constructed by the gentry in life and for perpetuity in their tombs. It seeks to contextualize the effigy monument by examining it in relation to textual forms of remembrance such as the representations of the gentry in histories, in prefatory dedications to patrons of early printed books and commemorative tributes in sermons and elsewhere. Situated within these literary discourses of identity formation, the effigy monument also needs to be considered within the context of Puritan and Christian humanist processes of self-examination which placed emphasis on the capacity of the individual to externalize their inner spiritual and moral well-being and to act as an example to others through their lifestyle.

---

[21] John Finch, '"According to the Quality and Degree of the Person Deceased": Funeral Monuments and the Construction of Social Identities 1450–1700', *Scottish Archaeological Review*, 8 (1991): 105, 111.

[22] Michael Parker Pearson, 'Mortuary Practices, Society and Ideology: An Ethnoarchaeological Study', in Ian Hodder (ed.), *Symbolic and Structural Archaeology* (Cambridge, 1982), pp. 110–12; Finch, '"According to the Quality and Degree"', p. 108.

[23] Finch, '"According to the Quality and Degree"', pp. 110–11; Llewellyn 'Claims to Status', pp. 152–3.

[24] Michael Parker Pearson, *The Archaeology of Death and Burial* (Stroud, 1999), p. 33.

There is a strain of writing across the early decades of the Elizabethan period, perhaps most famously evinced in Foxe's *Acts and Monuments*, which sought to establish not only a Protestant past but also the place of the recent members of, in some instances, Kentish gentry families within that history.[25] This Protestant process of remembrance had a complex evolution. In some respects it provided a hagiography to rival that of the Catholic past, but it was also linked to classical rhetorical traditions of history writing and panegyric. The growing custom of providing an account of the life and achievements of the deceased at the funeral – a precedent established in the late medieval heraldic funeral but which became more common from the late 1530s – was also a significant aspect of this discourse of remembrance.[26]

In the first edition of his translation of *Heresbach's Four Books of Husbandry* (1577) Barnabe Googe paid tribute to his maternal grandmother Lady Margaret Hales, recalling:

> Her special love and delight in God, and in his service, her helpful hand and comfort of the poore and distressed ... her milde and sweete disposition, her great humilitie & carelesnesse of the vaine worlde and other such vertues. I would to Christ that all other Gentlewomen that professe Christ outwardly, were as well geven to followe him in deede as she was unfaynedly.[27]

This sentiment was echoed almost identically by another of her grandchildren, Dean Thomas Neville who erected a plaque to her memory in St Mildred's church, Canterbury, in 1599, some twenty years after her death. As members of a Protestant élite in Kent, both men were keen to establish their links with 'the wife of Sir Walter Mantyll of Northamtonshire', executed for his part in Wyatt's rebellion and whose widow had been active in keeping the name of respectable Protestantism alive in Canterbury in the 1550s.[28]

Lady Hales was not only written into a Protestant past, but her life could also stand as an example for the living. In this respect, the tributes by both grandsons

---

[25]   For further discussion of this see my doctoral thesis: 'The Reading and Writing Practices of the Kentish Gentry: The Emergence of a Protestant Identity in Elizabethan Kent.', unpublished Ph.D Thesis, Canterbury Centre for Medieval & Tudor Studies, University of Kent (2004).

[26]   Collinson, 'A Magazine of Religious Patterns', pp. 225, 243; Claire Gittings, *Death Burial and the Individual in Early Modern England* (London, 1984), pp.166–87; and Carlson, 'English Funeral Sermons as Sources, p. 569.

[27]   Barnabe Googe, *The Foure Bookes of Husbandry, Collected by M. Conradus Heresbachius Counceller ... Newely Englished and increased by Barnabe Googe* (1577), fols 167v–168r.

[28]   Barnabe Googe, *The Foure Bookes of Husbandry, Collected by M. Conradus Heresbachius Counceller ... Newely Englished and increased by Barnabe Googe* (London, 1577), fol. 167v; Peter Clark, *English Provincial Society from the Reformation to the Revolution: Religion, Politics and Society in Kent 1500–1640* (Hassocks, 1977), p.100.

are recognizably of the type that became published genres of spiritual writing in the seventeenth century: the printed funeral sermon and the spiritual biography. The value of the exemplary life was to become well established in such literature. The work *Ten Eminent Divines* (1662), for example, contained many instances of ministers who '… lived religion while many only make it the subject of their discourses.'[29] But John Foxe was also certain of the didactic values of such lives, acknowledging a form of history writing which drew together the moral imperative of classical histories with the spiritual imperative of a martyrology to create a history that would, '… conserve in remembrance the lives, acts and doings not only of bloody warriors but of mild and constant martyrs of Christ'. This form of history writing would serve, '… not so much to delight the ear as to garnish the life, to frame it with examples of great profit and to encourage men to all kinds of Christian godliness.'[30]

The classics were also a significant influence on the writing of spiritual biographies in the sixteenth and seventeenth centuries. As Collinson has demonstrated, for instance, the moral framework of Plutarch and more specifically the ethics of Aristotle underpinned many of the descriptions of the Protestant martyrs in Foxe's *Acts and Monuments*.[31] Classical values and rhetoric also infused Kentish history writing; another medium through which the Kentish gentry were commemorated. Kentish gentlemen such as Sir Roger Manwood and Sir Thomas Scott received special mention in William Lambarde's *Perambulation of Kent* or *Holinshed's Chronicles* as '… worthie remembrance for that which [they] hath doone in [their] own countrie of Kent.'[32] Manwood in particular was lauded by Lambarde, for his founding of a '… a faire Freeschoole … for the increase of godlynesse and good letters' on the site of an old Carmelite friary in the town of Sandwich; a fine example of knowledge overcoming the ignorance and superstition of a Catholic past.[33]

Writing in the mid 1570s, a Kentish gentleman, Thomas Wotton explained the importance of history, ranking it second only to study of 'the sacred word of Almightie God' as a 'profitable' subject of study. Wotton established the edifying principles of history describing how through the study of '… other folks experience are we taught largely …' to commend and follow the virtuous actions of the good and '… Christianly to bewaile … and wisely beware …' of the foolish actions of the lewd and ignorant. For, through the careful reading of histories, concluded Wotton '… are we taught and brought out of danger to settle ourselves,

---

[29] Quoted in Collinson, 'A Magazine of Religious Patterns', p. 234.

[30] John Foxe, *Acts and Monuments of these Latter and Perilous Dayes*, 8 vols (London, 1843), vol.1, p. xxv.

[31] Collinson, 'A Magazine of Religious Patterns', p. 235.

[32] Raphael Holinshed, *Holinshed's Chronicles*, 6 vols (London, 1807–08, repr. with an introduction by V. Snow, New York, 1965), vol. 4, p. 551.

[33] William Lambarde, *A Perambulation of Kent Conteining the Description, Historie and Customes of that Shire* (London, 1826), p. 119.

as it were, in a seat of suretie.'[34] Both Wotton and Foxe shared a perception of the value of history as a means through which to incite virtuous or godly behaviour. Aston, amongst others, has highlighted the capacity of portraits of worthy ancestors to inculcate virtuous behaviour in the living.[35] The tracing of signs of virtue through generations of Kent families was also a common narrative thread in Francis Thynne's contributions to *Holinshed's Chronicles*. In recording '... the singularity of wit and lerning ... [the] ... honour and government in and of the realme about the prince and elsewhere at home and abroad' of recent generations of the Wotton family, Thynne published in full the epitaph from Dean Nicholas Wotton's memorial which detailed '... his birth, his parents, his honors at home, his embassages abroad' as sufficient testimony to his 'worthinesse'.[36]

Sir Roger Manwood, Lady Hales and the Wottons were representative of what Foxe termed, 'The lively testimony of God's mighty works in the life of man.'[37] Their public acts of charity signified an inner spiritual purity as members of God's elect. The trends of spiritual biography and history writing outlined above are linked to the perception that the individual could externalize their inner piety and virtue and serve as a didactic example to the wider community.[38] The inward spiritual peace of the regenerate Protestant was displayed in the ways they conducted their life and was to be read in their, '... continency of life, sobriety in apparel, moderation in meats and drinks, temperancy in pastimes, labour in our several callings and equity in all our deeds and dealings'.[39] Man's inherent sinfulness dictated that this cleansed status was a state of being to aspire to throughout life. 'We must ...,' urged Lambarde:

> ... line and square our words and works together...But to be and become the very same in work and deed that we desire to be called by name, but to be transformed and fashioned into that which we do hear and learne. But to fructify through the moisture of that heavenly dew and influence that we receive; and never to depart from that which we see in the glass and book of this truth of God.[40]

The above quotation taken from William Lambarde's *Charges to the Quarter Sessions* underscores the links between Puritan self-examination and the social

---

[34]   Lambarde , *A Perambulation of Kent*, p. ix.

[35]   Aston, 'Gods, Saints and Reformers', p. 197; Llewellyn also argues that heraldic imagery was thought to instil virtue in 'Claims to Status', p. 148.

[36]   Holinshed, *Holinshed's Chronicles*, vol. 4, pp. 600–602.

[37]   Foxe, *Acts and Monuments*, vol. 1, p. xxv.

[38]   Anna Bryson, 'The Rhetoric of Status: Gesture, Demeanour and the Image of the Gentleman in Sixteenth and Seventeenth Century England', in Lucy Gent & Nigel Llewellyn (eds.), *Renaissance Bodies: The Human Figure in English Culture c.1540–1660* (London, 1990), pp. 145–6.

[39]   Lambarde, *William Lambarde and Local Government: His Ephemeris and Twenty Nine Charges to the Juries and Commissions*, ed. Conyers Read (New York, 1962), p. 78.

[40]   Lambarde, *Charges*, pp. 76, 82.

activism of Christian humanism. Using classical moralists such as Cicero and Seneca, humanists urged the inculcation of virtuous behaviour in society at large through the reform and the social activism of the individual. As Todd summarizes, the new Biblicism conditioned by revived classical moralism defined a new social type, the pious, self-controlled, industrious lay person, active in civic and ecclesiastical affairs, seeking always the common good. Influential within this ideology were the writings of Erasmus, whose manuals of self-improvement were characterized by a deep concern for sin and a stoic conviction that self-understanding and self-control were essential in order to overcome evil.[41]

In Erasmus's writings, the internal/external corollary is again apparent. As Bryson has highlighted, Erasmus's *De Civilitate* stressed the manifestation of good manners as the exterior signs of one's inner character. Civility was equated with an 'outward honestie' which mirrored the inner, virtuous qualities of the soul. The body became an interpretative site through which the 'habyte and apparyle of the inward mind' could be read.[42] The body was a text through which good and bad character could be read and which through speech and gesture, deportment and demeanour communicated the inner nobility of the élite. As such, membership of the social élite was distinguished by a superior control of both body and impulses.[43]

This section has sought to provide a cultural context in which to consider the significance of the effigy monument. By looking at trends in historical writing and the burgeoning genre of spiritual biography, it has suggested that the lives of the gentry could be exemplary and incite virtuous behaviour in others. By highlighting both Puritan and Christian humanist processes of self-reformation and the capacity of the body to express the internal spiritual and moral purity of the individual, it has also suggested that the demeanour and behaviour of the individual (as well as, or perhaps instead of the attire) was expressive of social and spiritual election. The funeral effigy certainly did represent the social self but in post-Reformation society there was scope for that social self to reflect a status and authority that had a moral and spiritual dimension.

Moral and Spiritual Significance

This final section proposes to examine the moral and spiritual significance of the effigy monument by considering one case study within the context of the élite forms of forming identity outlined above. Sir Roger Manwood, son of a well-established merchant family in Sandwich rose to social and political prominence in

---

[41] Margaret Todd, *Christian Humanism and the Puritan Social Order* (Cambridge, 1987), pp. 27–30.
[42] Bryson, 'The Rhetoric of Status', pp. 144–5.
[43] Bryson, 'The Rhetoric of Status', pp. 145, 137, 152.

the county and beyond through his pursuit of a legal career. He represented Sandwich as MP for 12 years, stood as recorder for that town and later was appointed as a Justice of the Peace (JP). His extensive knowledge of the privileges of the Cinque Ports and his place on county commissions made him a prominent defender of Kentish interests. His successful legal career, which saw him rise from sergeant at law to judge and finally to Lord Chief Baron of the Exchequer, his contacts at court and his own wealth and property made him a natural target for patronage in the county and elsewhere.[44]

Sir Roger Manwood's monument has been chosen not only for its striking design, but also for the potential that exists to contextualize the monument within discourses of remembrance and reputation (see Plate 7.1). Other representations of Manwood composed by his Kentish contemporaries included the account of his life by Francis Thynne in the second edition of *Holinshed's Chronicles* (1587) and tributes paid by William Lambarde in *A Perambulation of Kent* (1576) and by Reginald Scot in the dedication of his *Discoverie of Witchcraft* (1585). In addition, Manwood himself contributed to this textual process of remembrance, incorporating an extensive (and favourable) account of his role in the restoration of Rochester Bridge among the Bridge Wardens' papers. He also provided detailed accounts of active processes of remembrance including sermons and rituals of gift- and alms-giving and feasting linked to his charitable institutions at Sandwich and Canterbury in his last will and testament.

With its displays of heraldry and armour and the imposing bust of the deceased in his scarlet robes of state, the monument is a ready statement of secular power, wealth and status. Beneath the bust of Manwood kneel his first wife and children on one side and his second wife on the other. Manwood presides over them all, representing the power of the State in his capacity as Lord Chief Baron of the Exchequer and patriarchal authority over the household. Flanking the bust of Manwood on either side are two tablets complete with Latin inscriptions, a central tablet below records his legal career and charitable foundations. Beneath, on the table-top lies a naturalistic sculpture of a skeleton.

Visually, the monument contrasts the wealth and professional power of Manwood in life with the stark image of death; and the Latin inscriptions encourage this interpretation, challenging the viewer to reject the very materiality of the monument itself:

Cum tumulum cernis cur non mortalia. / Spenis tali namque domo remanebit / Quilibet homo mors sceptra, et ligones aequat.

When you see this tomb, why do you not scorn mortal things? For in such a home any man becomes a worm. Death rules and he is made equal to the worms.

---

[44] For a recent summary of Manwood's career see Sybil Jack's entry in the new *ODNB* (online edition, May 2005).

Plate 7.1 Roger Manwood's Monument, St Stephen's Parish Church, Canterbury

The Latin inscriptions coincide almost exactly with Whitgift's description of the instructive capacity of the funeral sermon. In death, Manwood represents the fate of all men:

> O vir sum speculum, mortis imago, tuum / Nunc flens prospicito; stans ora, saepe memento / Magnificam vitam mors inopina rapit.

> Oh Man, I am the mirror image of your death. Now weeping gaze, now standing pray. Often remember that unexpected death snatches away a splendid life. [45]

The inscription dramatizes Manwoods's resurrection, Judgement and hoped for entry into eternal life:

---

[45] I am grateful to Marten Rogers for making available the translation of this inscription from his pamphlet *Sir Roger Manwood: St Stephens, Hackington 1525–1592* (privately published, 1999).

Ante fui judex, iam judicis ante tribunal / Respondens paveo judicor ipse modo / Transit lux, ubi lex ubi laus, mea fama silescunt; imo vix nomen, vox semiviva sonat / Non sum qui fueram viduata caro sepelitur; / Ac privis acta male mens renovanda luit / Nam post, carne mea, dotatus luce superna / Cernere, spero deum te salutare meum.

Before I was a Judge, now I am before the tribunal of the Judge. As I answer, I fear. I myself am judged now. Light passes. Where there is law, where there is praise, where there is fame, they are silent. Indeed the half dead voice scarcely pronounces my name. I am not the man I was. My widowed flesh is buried. The mind due to be renewed atones for earlier deeds badly done endowed after my flesh with heavenly light. I hope, O God to see Thee who art my health.[46]

Manwood's life was also instructive. The inscriptions urge courage, industry, equity and the pursuit of virtue in an amalgam of Christian humanist values. His achievements in public office and his founding of the school at Sandwich and almshouses at Canterbury were evidence of civic duty born of his status as a virtuous gentleman and as one, as he described himself in his will, '... of the nomber of His electe'.[47] Manwood's sense of the exemplary qualities of his own life are apparent in his choice of attire on the monument and the theme of Judgement that pervades the inscriptions. In his position as a judge, Manwood sought to ensure that 'Justitia est ratio approbata ... viz malis poenam, bonis praemium uncvique suum tribvere justitia est anima civitatis et reipublicae.' ('What is done should be done justly ... That is, punishment for evil doers, reward for good men, to give to each man what is his.'). Manwood's temporal judgements were part of a broader system of justice:

Ante fui judex, iam judicis ante tribunal / Respondens paveo judicor ipse modo ... In judicio non est personarum respectus / Memorare novissima et iterum non peccabis / Ante obitum nimo reatus.

Before, I was a judge, now I am before the tribunal of the Judge ... At the Judgement, there is no respect of persons. Remember the last things and you will not sin again.

In his self-fashioning as an equitable Judge and protector of the less fortunate, Manwood may well have had a biblical ideal in mind:

For I delivered the poore that cryed, and the fatherless, and him that had none to helpe him. The blessing of him that was ready to perish came upon mee and I caused the widowes heart to rejoyce. I put on justice and it covered me, my judgement was as a

46   Ibid.
47   Francis Thynne in *Holinshed's Chronicles*, vol. 4, p. 551; CCAL CC/S7, fol. 1r.

robe and a crowne. I was the eyes to the blind and I was the feete to the lame. I was a father unto the poore and when I knew not the cause I sought it out diligently.[48]

Manwood's perception of himself as a Job-like figure was reinforced in other media. In the prefatory dedication of *The Discoverie of Witchcraft* (1584), Reginald Scot described his patron Manwood as, '[A] father to orphans, an advocate to widows, a guide to the blind, a stay to the lame, a comfort and countenance to the honest, a scourge and terror to the wicked'; an account which bears close resemblance to Job 29 12–16 quoted above.[49] This identity was also perpetuated through the funeral and later annual memorial sermons and in the rituals of commemorative feasting and gift giving that he had established which included the weekly gifts made to his alms folk:

> Everye Fridaye twelve pence in monney and every sondaye & wednesdaye one pennye wheat loafe att the parishe church upon some shelf or boorde in the ile where my tome is.[50]

Manwood's monument occupies a significant place within a system of the formation of identity and commemoration that covered a diverse range of media. To examine the effigy monument within this context is to situate it not only within a culture of display in which social, moral and spiritual status was read through appearance and behaviour but within a culture of remembrance which was informed by classical rhetorical forms and biblical resonances.[51] It also questions the extent to which any Elizabethan funeral monument can be perceived as only commemorating the secular attributes of status, power and allegiance as Llewellyn argues, in a culture in which the literary and figurative arts measured the lives of the great and the good against biblical and classical precedents; and when those of a Puritan bent in particular sought to emulate that which '... we see in the glass and book of this truth of God'.[52]

---

[48]   *The Bible* (second edition, 1582), Job 29 12–16.

[49]   Reginald Scot, *The Discoverie of Witchcraft* (London, 1584), unpaginated prefatory material.

[50]   CCAL CC/S7, fol.6r–v.

[51]   For further discussion of this form of writing see Collinson, 'Truth, Lies and Fiction in Sixteenth Century Protestant Historiography', in Donald Kelly and David Harris Sacks (eds), *The Historical Imagination in Early Modern Britain* (Cambridge, 1997), pp. 65–7.

[52]   Nigel Llewellyn, 'Accident or Design? John Gildon's Funeral Monuments and Italianate Taste in Elizabethan England', in Edward Charney and Peter Mack (eds), *England and the Continental Renaissance: Essays in Honour of J.B. Trapp* (Woodbridge, 1990), p. 151; Lambarde, *Charges*, p. 82. For examples from the period see *Mirror for Magistrates* (1563), and also the commemorative poem attributed to Christopher Marlowe in which Manwood is described as 'Noctivagi terror, ganeonis triste flagellum. / Et Jovis Alcides, rigido vulturque latroni, / Urna subtegitur' ('Here lies the dour scourge of the profligate, /

To argue for a didactic interpretation of the lay effigy monument is perhaps to agree with Aston's comment, that in some respects, images of the gentry in portraits of worthies and ancestors became for the reformed world what saints had been for the pre-reformed.[53] Perhaps one of the most remarkable aspects of the design of Manwood's monument is precisely that capacity to reinvent pre-Reformation media in a reformed world. In design the monument closely resembled the pre-Reformation monument to the humanist and schoolmaster John Colet. It also invoked the medieval *memento mori* trope so powerfully employed in the design of the double decker monument to Archbishop Chichele in Canterbury Cathedral (*c.* 1426) in which the life-like effigy of the Archbishop is accompanied by another of equal size beneath representing a naked, decaying cadaver.[54] As such, Manwood's tomb signals the complexity of post-Reformation effigy monuments both in design and reception. The monument itself is testament to Manwood's ability to manipulate the visual vocabulary of the monument to express his wealth and status as a new gentleman and his authority in the public weal only to undercut this materialism by providing a didactic reading of his life. In so doing Manwood uses the suggestive, almost archaic image of the skeleton, redolent of a pre-Reformation culture of images and remembrance through intercession, but controls the interpretation of the *memento mori* theme through the Latin inscriptions, thus demonstrating his grip on the current politics of images.

Finch argues that funeral monuments should be seen to be active, operating in many simultaneous contexts and discourses and this chapter has similarly argued for a more detailed contextualization of the post-Reformation funeral monument.[55] In seeking to recomplicate the interpretation of the Elizabethan effigy monument in particular, it has sought to more strongly contextualize the monument within Protestant and humanist-inspired processes of remembrance and identity formation. By stressing the didactic capacity of the effigy monument and in highlighting the complex place of the image and the figurative arts in a post-Reformation culture, the chapter has also sought to demonstrate the extent to which such monuments provide evidence of pieties in transition.

Instrument of the hardened criminal's fate, / Fearsome to vagrants, Hercules from Jove sent.'): Christopher Marlowe, *The Poems*, ed. Millar Maclure (London, 1968), p. 111.

[53]   Aston, 'Gods, Saints and Reformers', pp. 181, 197.

[54]   See Christopher Wilson, 'The Medieval Monuments', in Collinson et al. (eds), *A History of Canterbury Cathedral* (Oxford, 1995), pp. 476–81; Llewellyn, *Art of Death*, p. 132.

[55]   Finch, '"According to the Quality and Degree"', p. 113.

Chapter 8

'The Dayes Moralised'

Reconstructing Devotional Reading, *c.* 1450–1560

Elisabeth Salter

Introduction

The purpose of this chapter is to examine devotional reading practices at the level of popular culture across a period of immense ideological and material transition, *c.* 1450–1560. This is a period that, in spanning our traditional categories of late medieval to early modern, is usefully called the 'early English renaissance'. The ideological transition is 'the Reformation'; the material transition is that from manuscript to print; the books being read are Primers and Prayer Books (both in manuscript and in print); and the popular culture is, in this instance, Kentish.

Large numbers of relatively cheap devotional books survive.[1] Evidence from Kent (as elsewhere) indicates that such books became available to the non-élite reader through a number of different channels. They might be owned personally, shared through networks of lending, loaned by clergy to laity, and also bought by groups of laypeople for public use in churches as 'common profit' books.[2] The detailed attention to practice, here, constitutes an ethnographic approach to reading: individual books are treated as the subjects whilst also looking beyond the books, to ask detailed questions of *how* readers used their books in the culturally creative processes of reading.[3] As an investigation of reading in a particular historical context, this investigation is connected to the growing field in studies of The History of Reading, which is often associated with The History of the Book.[4] However, in pursuing the subject as a detailed reconstruction of practice with

---

[1]   Tessa Watt, *Cheap Print and Popular Piety, 1550–1640* (Cambridge, 1991); Ian Green, *Print and Protestantism in Early Modern England* (Oxford, 2000).

[2]   See Paul Lee, *Nunneries, Learning and Spirituality in Late Medieval English Society: The Dominican Priory of Dartford* (Woodbridge, 2001); Elisabeth Salter, *Cultural Creativity in the Early English Renaissance: Popular Culture in Town and Country* (London, 2006).

[3]   Jonathan Boyarin (ed.), *The Ethnography of Reading* (London, 1993).

[4]   See for example, Guiglielmo Cavallo and Roger Chartier (eds), *A History of Reading in the West* (Cambridge, 1997). Lotte Hellinga and J.B. Trapp (eds), *The Cambridge History of the Book in Britain 1400–1557*, 5 vols (Cambridge, 1999).

evidence not usually considered in detail, this chapter moves beyond current approaches to reading or reception. It raises questions about whether it is plausible to think in terms of any overarching transition in devotional reading practices, *c.* 1450–1560. Questioning this transition addresses several historiographies, including: the impact of the invention of printing; the idea of rising literacy; and the issues associated with the chronology and popular experience of the English Reformation.[5]

An Introductory Issue of Method

There are a number of issues of method that are associated with the reconstruction of practice at the level of popular culture. This is a necessarily interdisciplinary endeavour, which also necessarily involves dealing in fragmentary evidences. One issue is that there is an apparent disparity between a local focus on Kent and the material objects examined here. There is plentiful evidence that legitimizes the proposition that books such as Primers were owned, used, borrowed and could even be read in North Kent in the early English renaissance and significant numbers of books were bequeathed in wills.[6] Following national trends, educational opportunities in Kent included university, school, informal teaching, and apprenticeship.[7] G.M. Draper's chapter in this volume adds significantly to the

---

[5] For the seminal initial hypothesis, see Elizabeth Eisenstein, *Printing Press as an Agent of Change: Communications and Cultural Transformations in Early Modern Europe* (Cambridge, 1980); on Reformation (from a Catholic perspective), see, Eamon Duffy, *The Stripping of the Altars: Traditional Religion in England, c. 1400–c. 1580* (London, New Haven, 1992); also Francois Gilmont, 'Protestant Reformations and Reading', in Cavallo and Chartier (eds) *History of Reading*. For a critique of the historiography of rising literacy, see G.M. Draper, 'Educational Provision and Piety in Kent, *c.* 1400 – 1640', this volume.

[6] See Elisabeth Salter, 'Cultural Appropriation and Transmission in Town and Country in Late Medieval England', unpublished Ph.D Thesis, Canterbury Centre for Medieval & Tudor Studies, University of Kent (2003); Margaret Deanesly, 'Vernacular Books in the Fourteenth and Fifteenth Centuries', *Modern Language Review*, 15 (1920): 349–58; Joel Rosenthal, 'Aristocratic Cultural Patronage and Book Bequests, 1350–1500', *Bulletin of John Rylands University Library of Manchester*, 64 (1982): 522–48, pp. 535–48; Jo Ann Hoeppner Moran, *The Growth of English Schooling, 1340–1548: Learning, Literacy, and Laicization in Pre-Reformation York Diocese* (Princeton, 1985), pp. 150–56, 175, 196–7, for a comparison with the York diocese; Carol Meale, ' "… alle the bokes that I have of latyn, englisch, and frensch": Laywomen and their Books in Late Medieval England', in Carol Meale (ed.), *Women & Literature in Britain, 1150–1500* (Cambridge, 1993), pp. 130–33, on will evidence for book ownership; Mary C. Erler, 'Devotional Literature', in *The Cambridge History of the Book, 1400–1557*, p. 497.

[7] Nicholas Orme, *English Schools in the Middle Ages* (London, 1973), p. 194; Margaret Spufford, *Small Books and Pleasant Histories: Popular Fiction and its Readership in Seventeenth-Century England* (Cambridge, 1981), esp. ch. 2, and pp. 28–9 on the use of

current understanding of educational provision in local society between the twelfth and the sixteenth centuries; and Paul Lee's thorough scrutiny of the testamentary provision of education in the Rochester diocese, *c.* 1400–1560, indicates the importance of benefaction from clerics, religious institutions and wealthy laity.[8] The books examined in this chapter, however, cannot have a Kentish provenance proved. But, although the detailed evidence for reading practices is based on non-Kentish material, it is clearly contextually appropriate to consider such reading practices as occurring in Kent.

The other introductory issue of method is also concerned with the nature of the evidence for popular reading, but more particularly with its relatively discontinuous and sporadic nature. Recently, various cultural historians have stressed the importance of examining what are often 'fragmentary' evidences of popular culture. There is often only 'fragmentary' evidence for the way the majority of the population lived and thought; yet the word 'fragmentary' is sometimes used, negatively, to suggest 'implausible'.[9] However, it is important to stress that the detailed consideration of individual fragments of evidence actually provides special access to popular culture. As Roger Chartier suggests, 'the ways in which an individual or a group appropriates an intellectual theme or a cultural form are more important than the statistical distribution of that theme or form'.[10] And, as Robert Darnton suggests, it is only through the detailed consideration of such evidence that the language of the historical subject is enabled to 'speak for itself'.[11]

Primers; J.W. Adamson, 'The Extent of Literacy in England in the Fifteenth and Sixteenth Centuries', *The Library*, 4th Series, 10 (1930): 162–93, pp. 174–9, for a discussion of the role of clergy in 'informal' education; also see Paul Lee, 'Monastic and Secular Religion and Devotional Reading in Late Medieval Dartford and West Kent' unpublished Ph.D Thesis, University of Kent (1998), ch. 7, p. 220, for caution about terminology, where 'schoole' may refer to either a grammar school or university education.

[8] See Lee, 'Monastic and Secular Religion', ch. 7, esp. p. 227; Moran, *The Growth of English Schooling*, pp. 164–70, for comparable evidence from York diocese.

[9] I would like to thank Felicity Riddy for a recent discussion regarding the issue of fragmentary evidences.

[10] Roger Chartier, *Cultural History: Between Practices and Representations*, trans. L.G. Cochrane, Oxford, 1988), pp. 5, 35; see also Carlo Ginzburg, *The Cheese and The Worms: The Cosmos of a Sixteenth Century Miller*, trans. J. and A. Tredeschi (London, 1981), p. xxii.

[11] Robert Darnton, *The Kiss of Lamourette: Reflections in Cultural History* (London, 1990), pp. 195, 213.

The History of Reading

Interest in the study of reading in late medieval and early modern society is currently growing.[12] However, there has long been an interest in reading literacy, as distinct from writing literacy,[13] and in a reading public.[14] Jo Ann Moran, for example, gives detailed consideration to how reading was taught to provide basic knowledge of both Latin and English. She suggests that Primers played a significant role in the process of learning to read.[15] Moran also notes the difficulty of identifying what people actually read before the advent of printing, although others, such as Carol Meale, have found evidence for expansion in certain forms of reading, particularly Romance reading, in fifteenth-century England.[16] Devotional reading has received attention, particularly in the context of the role of religious houses in the promotion of lay literate devotion, particularly in the period approaching the Reformation.[17] Carol Meale, Felicity Riddy and Julia Boffey have also specifically traced manuscript evidence that such books were owned and shared by laywomen of gentle and mercantile status, together with women in religious orders.[18] And, Paul Lee has made detailed investigation of evidence for

---

[12]   See Kevin Sharpe and Stephen Zwicker (eds), *Reading, Society and Politics in Early Modern England* (Cambridge, 2003).

[13]   Adamson, 'The Extent of Literacy in England', pp. 163–5.

[14]   H.S. Bennett, 'Printers, Authors, and Readers, 1475–1557', *The Library*, 5th Series, 4 (1949): 155–65, pp. 161–3; Jocelyn Wogan-Browne, Nicholas Watson, Andrew Taylor and Ruth Evans (eds), *The Idea of the Vernacular: An Anthology of Middle English Literary Theory, 1280–1520*, Exeter Middle English Texts and Studies (Exeter, 1999), esp. part 3. See also Joyce Coleman, *Public Reading and the Reading Public in Late Medieval England and France* (Cambridge, 1996).

[15]   Moran, *The Growth of English Schooling*, pp. 44–6; also, Orme, *English Schools in the Middle Ages*, pp. 62–3; Lee, 'Monastic and Secular Religion', p. 221; Spufford, *Small Books and Pleasant Histories*, pp. 28–9, Adamson, 'The Extent of Literacy in England', pp. 166, 170, 150, 155.

[16]   Moran, *The Growth of English Schooling*, p. 186; Carol Meale, ' "gode men/ Wiues maydnes and alle men": Romance and its Audiences', in Carol Meale (ed.), *Readings in Medieval English Romance* (Cambridge, 1994), p. 217.

[17]   Michael Sergeant, 'The Transmission by the English Carthusians of Some Late Medieval Spiritual Writings', *Journal of Ecclesiastical History*, 27 (1976): 225–40; Vincent Gillespie, 'Vernacular Books of Religion', in Jeremy Griffiths and Derek Pearsall (eds), *Book Production and Publishing in Britain, 1375–1475* (Cambridge, 1989); Vincent Gillespie, 'Cura Pastoralis in Deserts', and Anne Hutchinson, 'Devotional Reading in the Monastery and in the Household', Michael Sergeant (ed.), *De Cella in Seculum: Religious Secular Life and Devotion in Late Medieval England* (Cambridge, 1989); Lee, 'Monastic and Secular Religion'; Lee, *Nunneries, Learning, and Spirituality*.

[18]   Carol Meale, '"… alle the bokes that I have of latyn, englisch, and frensch"'; Felicity Riddy, ' "Women talking about the things of God": A Late Medieval Sub-Culture', in Carol Meale, (ed.), *Women & Literature in Britain*, pp. 106–111; and Julia Boffey,

reading amongst the nuns of Dartford Priory in Kent, and their associates.[19] There has also been some useful recent work on laypersons' attitudes to devotional reading. Vincent Gillespie has closely analysed mystical poetry to assess the nature of a medieval lay reader's ecstatic mystical experiences.[20] And, Paul Saenger made a convincing, if overarching, case for the significance of the private ownership of devotional books in the development of silent reading, as well as the broader political implications associated with lay independence from the clergy.[21]

Theory and Practice in Reading

It has recently been proposed that amassing evidence for the ownership of books is a valuable precursor to the analysis of reading practices, but evidence for book ownership is not evidence for reading, or reading practice.[22] And, in carving out a space for the interpretation of reading practice, there is a necessary negotiation between the various contemporary theories about reading and the various measures that dictated what was included and removed from devotional books, especially *c.* 1520–60.[23] It should be assumed that these theories and statutes had some affect on readers, but also that they do not in themselves tell the whole story of reading practice. There is a danger of confusing *theories* of reading with *practices* of reading. Theories of reading are taken to mean either theories prevailing in a particular historical context or theories produced subsequent to that context. The authors of *The Idea of The Vernacular*, for example, distinguish clearly between theory and practice by claiming their interest to be in contemporary theories – of writing, reading and the construction of audience.[24] Other evidence for scholarly

---

'Women Authors and Women's Literacy in Fourteenth- and Fifteenth-Century England', in Meale, *Women & Literature in Britain, 1150–1500*, pp. 165–6, 169–75.

[19] Lee, *Nunneries, Learning and Spirituality*, chs 4 and 5.

[20] Vincent Gillespie, 'Mystic's Foot: Rolle and Affectivity', in M. Glascoe (ed.), *The Medieval Mystical Tradition in England* (Exeter, 1982), pp. 212–20.

[21] Paul Saenger, 'Books of Hours and the Reading Habits of the later Middle Ages', in Roger Chartier (ed.), *The Culture of Print: Power and the Uses of Print in Early Modern Europe* (Cambridge, 1989), pp. 143–4, 145.

[22] Cavallo and Chartier (eds), *A History of Reading in the West*, p. 4.

[23] On statutes, see Margaret Aston, *England's Iconoclasts* I: *Laws Against Images* (Oxford, 1988); Green, *Print and Protestantism*. For a recent summary of reading theories see Michael Clanchy, 'Images of Ladies with Prayer Books: What do they Signify?', in Robert Swanson (ed.), *The Church and the Book*, *SCH*, 38 (Ecclesiastical History Society, London, 2004).

[24] Wogan-Browne, et al. (eds), *Idea of the Vernacular*, pp. xiv, 220. Other approaches claim to be about reading practice but tend to be based in theory. See, for example, Andrew Taylor, 'Into his Secret Chamber', in James Raven, Helen Small, and Naomi Tadmor, (eds) *The Practice and Representation of Reading in England* (Cambridge, 1996).

models of reading provides very useful insight into scholarly practice.[25] But, the popular reading and popular practice analysed in this chapter is intended to be distinct from this élite sphere of highly educated reading. Theoretically based assessments of reading and reception constructed in the last decade have also recently been applied to medieval and renaissance reading practices.[26] But, for this study of reading in a particular cultural situation of pre-modern Kent, overmuch recourse to theoretical views of reception tends to detract from the immediate concerns with the reading practices and experiences of ordinary renaissance individuals. What therefore drives this investigation of devotional reading practice in the popular culture of the early English renaissance is the detailed evidence provided by the books themselves, rather than theoretical abstraction.

The theoretical stimulus for this chapter is Johannes Fabian's consideration of the role of 'oralisation' in the literate practices of newly literate groups.[27] Fabian is not actually talking about reading practices, but he *is* talking about ethnographic attitudes to literate practice; and emphasizing the need to take seriously the literate practices of 'traditional/oral societies'.[28] This is part of the response to the 'reflexive turn' in anthropology.[29] Thus, Fabian notes that there is a requirement for modern ethnographers to take into consideration the uses of literacy by societies previously considered 'traditional' or 'oral' (where these terms have previously tended to imply 'primitive'). Fabian uses the term 'people-writers' to describe the attitudes to text of individuals previously considered to be members of oral societies. His analysis relates to the relatively recent work acknowledging that people-writers manipulate literacy for their own means.[30]

---

[25]   Lisa Jardine and Anthony Grafton, *From Humanism to Humanities: Education and the Liberal Arts in Fifteenth- and Sixteenth-Century Europe* (London, 1986). See, especially, ch. 1 on 'Ideals and Practice', where in pp. 9–13 Jardine and Grafton address 'what actually went on' in the classroom of Guarino Guarini of Verona. See also p. 161 for the intention of this volume to get to grips with 'humanist *practice*' rather than its theoretical and idealistic promises.

[26]   Cavallo and Chartier (eds), *A History of Reading in the West*, p. 1, which begins by citing Michel de Certeau's generalized claims concerning the role of readers as 'travellers'.

[27]   Johannes Fabian, 'Keep Listening: Ethnography and Reading', in Jonathan Boyarin (ed.) *The Ethnography of Reading*, pp. 80–97.

[28]   Brian Street, *Literacy in Theory and Practice*, Cambridge Studies in Oral and Literate Culture (Cambridge, 1984), pp. 94–125.

[29]   James Clifford and George Marcus (eds) *Writing Culture: The Poetics and Politics of Ethnography* (Berkeley, 1986).

[30]   Niko Besnier, *Literacy, Emotion, Authority: Reading and Writing on a Polynesian Atoll*, Studies in the Social and Cultural Foundations of Language, 17 (Cambridge, New York, Melbourne, 1995); also Andrew Butcher, 'The Functions of Script in the Speech Community of a Late Medieval Town, c.1300–1550', and Alexandra Walsham, 'Preaching Without Speaking: Script, Print, and Religious Dissent', in Alexandra Walsham and Julia Crick (eds) *The Uses of Script and Print, 1300–1700* (Cambridge, 2004), pp. 150–70, and 211–34.

The originality of this chapter lies in the examination of 'oralized' responses made by readers of the early English renaissance during their devotional reading. Oralization is not here used to represent reading aloud. This chapter is not concerned with now widely criticized assumptions that orality was vital for a supposedly pre-literate pre-modern society.[31] Instead, oralization is understood as an imaginative process. This enables an analysis of the subtleties of process in popular reading practices. The concept of oralization is also closely related to 'visualization'. Michael Clanchy has recently explored 'visualization' in relation to the interpretation of images, suggesting that images were more open to interpretation by readers because they left meaning '… unsaid and perhaps unsayable'.[32] This chapter suggests that both visualization and oralization were part of pre- and post-Reformation devotional reading practice.[33]

The concept of oralization is very appropriate to a consideration of reading in the Early English Renaissance because it was used in medieval and renaissance theories of reading mnemonics. Here it was proposed that the reader ought to listen to the pronunciation of each word on the page.[34] But to maintain the focus on practice, there is useful recent work on the extent to which oral and literate cultures interact in early modern society. This work indicates that a consideration of oralization is also legitimate in relation to the cultural production of perception and experience in the daily lives of ordinary individuals in this period.[35] The concept of oralization therefore takes up some of those contextually and culturally appropriate issues of how text and reading is perceived, and refers to a process involved in the practice of reading. Alongside the evidence for the self-consciousness of popular devotional texts about relationships between writing, reading, speaking and hearing, I return to the role of marginal annotations with a renewed attention to their implications for the oralization process in the practice of reading. This is described here as the 'rhetorics of annotation'.[36]

The process of oralization in reading is particularly relevant to the limited literacy of what (adapting Fabian's phrase of 'people writers'), are described here as 'people-readers'. It is important to make it clear that I do not suggest there is something simpler about orality and oralization than about literacy and being

---

[31]   For seminal work proving the rise and extent of literacy in post-conquest England, see Michael Clanchy, *From Memory to Written Record: England 1066–1377* (2nd edition, Oxford, 1993).

[32]   Clanchy, 'Images of Ladies', p. 115.

[33]   See Emily Richards, 'Writing and Silence: Transitions between the Contemplative and the Active Life', this volume.

[34]   Clanchy, 'Images of Ladies', p. 114.

[35]   Adam Fox, *Oral and Literate Culture in England, 1500–1700* (Oxford, 2000); Watt, *Cheap Print*.

[36]   See Stephen Zwicker in Jennifer Anderson and Elizabeth Sauer (eds), *Books and Readers in Early Modern England (Material Studies)* (Pensylvania, 2001), on 'poetics of annotation'.

literate.[37] Fabian suggests that new literates or new readers have a more free kind of literacy, less constrained by conventional rules of grammar and syntax. Here, I investigate the nature of an oralized response made by readers during their devotional reading. But just to reiterate: talking about oralization might seem dangerously close to the rather out-dated talk of popular literatures, where poems rhymed for reading aloud and in order to help with memory in a pre-literate pre-modern society. The purpose of this chapter is definitely not to repeat that argument, but it does return to this interest in the interactions between orality and literacy, in order to qualify the issue in terms of the reading practices of ordinary individuals in English local society, including North Kent.

Introducing the Examples of Evidence for Reading Practices

Huge numbers of devotional books survive. My intention in the following discussion of examples is not to survey these, but to engage in detailed analysis of reading practices. The examples that are cited should, of course, be seen in the context of the plethora of manuscript and printed books which exist for the period *c.* 1450–1560. The great extent of the production and survival of printed books in the remaining years of the sixteenth century, and the increase in variety, also explains the cut-off date taken here. It would be in Helen White's words 'a large undertaking', or in other words another chapter, to consider 1560–1600.[38]

Helen White's work remains a seminal text for the consideration of devotional literature, and how it changed in the period immediately before and after the English Reformation. She proposed of such 'private' devotional literature that it:

> ... may well be expected to afford a more direct and more dependable way to the understanding of the religious consciousness of much of sixteenth century England than any other single avenue of approach now available to us.[39]

White proposes the Primer as possessing a 'tradition of flexibility and adaptability', which had antecedents in the ways that medieval religious literature was compiled. And, her detailed discussion of what might now be called textual transmission in the different editions of Primers, published by various different printers, indicates some of the complexities of tracing the changing contents of these books across the reformation period. Of particular significance are, first: issues of translation, particularly between English and Latin text, but also French

---

[37]   I choose to side-step a detailed consideration of Walter Ong's approach. For recent brief summaries of Ong's contribution to scholarship see Coleman, *Public Reading*, pp. 4, 14, 17; also Fox, *Oral and Literate Culture*, pp. 36–7.

[38]   Helen White, *Tudor Books of Private Devotion* (Madison, WI, 1979), p. 84.

[39]   Ibid., pp. 1–2.

and English vernaculars; and second: the interactions between books produced abroad, particularly in France, and in England.[40]

My emphasis in this ethnography of reading is not so much on tracing textual forms, but on two aspects of the detailed evidence for reading practices: the first type of evidence arises from the 'official literature' initially contained in the book; and the second type of evidence arises from moments of reception. So, I begin with some detailed considerations of a selection of specific texts found within a group of religious books, loosely called Primers. I then proceed with an examination of the marks and traces left on these by their readers, in order to assess the rhetoric of annotation. There are several issues that these examples seek to demonstrate. First, that devotional books of this kind were intended for the popular market of people-readers – those not very experienced in reading; second, that there is an emphasis on orality in the literature (that is to say, the Primers drew on a popular oral discourse); third, that readers responded to this oral literature in an oralized manner. So, I propose that both the production and the reception of this devotional literature, as evidenced by the texts and the reader-responses of annotation, give us access to *how* readers thought and read in the early English Renaissance.

Primers as Literature for People-Readers

That printed Primers were devotional books for beginners is particularly clear in versions published by Robert Redman, *c.* 1530–40, which contain instructions about aspects of the service. The example given below treats the reader as if they were a beginner in the use of a private service book. These instructional texts, and others like this, provide basic tuition on the nature and origins of a particular piece of litany or rite.

The Evynsong of Our Lady
What is mente by this worde
Evensonge
Lyke as the service that we be dayly accust–
omed to saye in the morning is called Ma. tyns eveyn so is the
service used to be sayd or sungen towarde evening called Evynsong
And this is the true signification and meenyng
of the same worde whiche we call Evynsong of our lady
because it is specially done in y' laude and praysyng
of her[41]

---

[40]   Ibid., ch. 4.

[41]   See, CCAL H/L W–2–X–2–7 (Robert Redman Primer, 1537), fol. L. ii, r. This version is discussed, as STC 15997, in Charles C. Butterworth, *The English Primers (1529–1545): Their Publication and Connection with the English Bible and the Reformation in England* (Philadelphia, 1953), ch. 8.

Popular Oral Discourse

Alongside the intentional role of these books as teaching texts for beginners, there is persuasive evidence to suggest that early printed Primers were intent on popularizing religious concepts and issues concerning litany.[42] The term popularizing, in this instance, refers particularly to the production of versified text concerning various aspects of daily and yearly religious practice. I call these versified liturgical texts 'doggerel verse', but although using this term for these versifications may seem elitist, it is not intended in that way: this is not *bad* literature or poetry; but it certainly is distinctively obvious in its attempts to make rhyme. Where doggerel rhyme is used, it often seems to be for non-scriptural prayers. Helen White suggested that the absence of non-scriptural prayers or the presence of strong warnings against such prayers, are a characteristic of some of the early reformed Primers. For example, some editions of the *Godly Primer* printed by Biddle and Marshall in English in 1535, engaged in invectives against such:

> ... peryllous prayers, sclanderous both to god and to all his holy saintes ... promising moche grace and many yeres, days, and lentes of pardon, whiche they could never in ded performe to the great decepte of people and the utter destruction of theyr soules.[43]

However, even this Primer kept some of the favourites of non-scriptural private devotion, such as the repetitive – not to say ecstatic – invocatory verses known as 'O Bone Jesu'.

In the Primers of the pre- and post-Reformation period, there appears to be a conscious effort to incorporate texts which engage the popular imagination, using 'contemporary personal needs or occasions' as an access route into the popular mentality.[44] One such apparently popular form of doggerel verse is a set of poems relating to that traditional aspect of the Books of Hours, the yearly calendar.[45] Another apparently popular form of doggerel verse is the selection of texts called 'The Dayes Moralised'. Both of these examples clearly feed into an important aspect of lay devotional reading, which is the structuring of a daily, monthly and yearly devotional cycle. A further aspect of this popular oral discourse of devotional literature is the interest in themes of seeing, hearing, speaking and

---

[42] See White, *Tudor Books*, p. 33, on the 'evolution' of the Primer out of the Psalter through the addition of non-scriptural prayers and more directly pedagogical material.

[43] Ibid., p. 92.

[44] Ibid., pp. 62–3.

[45] The occurrence of the calendar poems is frequent; it probably had antecedents in manuscript devotional books. It certainly occurs in printed primers dating between 1502 and 1555. See White, *Tudor Books*, p. 59, for her description of the same set of verses in the 1527 Regnault Primer as follows: 'The more solemn admonitions of the calendar were relieved by conventional but pleasant little quatrains bringing out the parallels between passing months and the passing seasons of human life.'

listening. In a number of printed devotional collections (which date between *c.* 1502 and 1560), there is a series of prayers that focus on different aspects of the body and mind, by taking subjects such as the hands, thoughts, mouth and speech, heart and so on. These prayers illustrate the strong emphasis on what might best be described as the sensual or corporeal nature of devotional reading. There follow four examples: the first two are doggerel verse, the following two are ecstatic verse.

Popular Oral Discourse: Example 1 (Doggerel Verse)

Both an English Primer printed for Francois Regnault in 1538 at Rouen and an English Primer printed by Robert Valentin at Rouen in *c.* 1554, have the monthly calendar rhyme in almost exactly the same version.[46] Each month represents an age of man, and for each there is a quatrain on the characteristics of that month in human terms, followed by a quatrain on the saint days marked in that particular month.

March

March behovith the vi yeres following
Arraying the erthe with pleasant verdure
That season youth careth for nothing
And without thought doth his sporte and pleasure

David of wa-les lo-veth. Well. Lekes
That wyl make gre-gory. Lene. Chekes
Yf. Ed-ward.do.eat some with them
Mary send him to bed-lem

[...]

Maye

As in the monthe of Maye all thing is might
So at xxx yere man is chiefly king
Pleasant & lusty to every mannes sight
In beaute & strength to women pleasing

James toke crosse masters John to kill
Nycolas sayd do hym no yll
But with that came fayre Helayne
And Franceys to departe them twayne

---

[46] CCAL H/L–4–8 and H/L–3–6 respectively. This collection of verse is certainly printed from 1533, and probably earlier.

Popular Oral Discourse: Example 2 (Doggerel Verse)

In the doggerel rendition of 'The Dayes Moralised', each day of the week is given a particular characteristic which relates to biblical and liturgical issues and which also provides a model for how the reader should behave on that particular day. Friday's biblical reference, for example, is to Good Friday and the reader is encouraged to think that this is a day for fasting and praying. Charles Butterworth proposed of this collection that it '… seems to have been introduced for the first time in a Latin Primer published early in 1531 by the same Christopher of Endhoven who formerly printed certain lost editions of the Tyndale New Testament'; and that it was first printed in England in 1537, in a Primer produced by Robert Redman which was itself substantially copied from a Primer printed in Rouen in 1536.[47] Helen White seems to suggest that the idea of a reader engaging in private daily devotional morality has something of a Protestant ring to it.[48] It is therefore interesting to mention that these verses are found in Primers dating across the whole spectrum of Henrician, Edwardian, Marian and Elizabethan religiosity.[49] The issue of daily devotional practice across the Reformation is discussed below.

Fryday
Named I am devout Fryday
The whiche careth no delyte
But to mourn / fast / deale and praye
I do set all my hole appetite
To think on the Jewes despite
How they did Christ on the tre rent
And thinking how I may be quitte
At the dreadful iudgement

Saterday
Saterday I am comyng last
Trussyn on the tyme spent well
Havyng ever mynde stedfaste

---

[47]   See Butterworth, *English Primers*, p. 141.
[48]   See White, *Tudor Books*, p. 101, for the suggestion that the collection of prayers 'for every day of the week' in a 'reforming primer' printed by John Gowhe, is a devotional element which becomes increasingly popular with the establishment of the Protestant Primer. 'Medytacions' for each day of the week are also found in BL C 106.a.21, *A Spirituall Counsayle, Very Necessarye for Every Persone to Have* (printed in 1540).
[49]   'The Dayes Moralised' was certainly printed in primers dating between 1531 and 1555. See Thielman Kerver's 1531 version (e.g. BL C 35.a. 14); as well as the Redman Primer printed in 1537, mentioned by Butterworth in *English Primers*, p.141, and the English Primer printed for Francois Regnault in 1538 at Rouen (e.g. CCAL H/L 4–8) and an English primer printed by Robert Valentin at Rouen in *c*. 1554 (e.g. CCAL H/L 3–6). It is likely that manuscript antecedents of these verses will be found in due course, perhaps in French.

On the Lorde that harrowed hell
That he my sinnes will expel
At the instaunce of his mother
Whose goodnesse dooth ferre excel
Whome I serve above all other

Popular Oral Discourse: Example 3 (Ecstatic Verse)[50]

The emphasis on aspects of the individual reader's own body and senses was not a new invention of the printed devotional literatures. Corporeal, sensual or ecstatic devotional literatures formed an important part of the medieval affective tradition. Such literature was circulating in the fifteenth century, with antecedents stretching back to thirteenth century lyrics.[51] In an early fifteenth-century manuscript collection of devotional literature is a poem that uses many well-known conventions of affectively pious writing such as the writing on the heart theme. Issues of speech and text are mentioned frequently. This example also gives some insight into the connections between oralization and another process, which is usefully explored as visualization by Emily Richards in this volume.[52] The theme of visualization recurs repeatedly in this poem, but this is done through metaphors of writing and orality and not through metaphors of reading.

Jesu that haste me dere bought
Write now goostely in my thought
Then I may with devocion
Think upon thy passion
For yf my herte be hard as stoon
Yet may thow goostely **write** theron
With nayles and with speer kene
And so schul the **letters wele be sene**
Write in my herte thy **speeches swete**

Popular Oral Discourse: Example 4 (Ecstatic Verse)[53]

In a series of sensual prayers is an ecstatic verse with the very interesting title of 'A fruitfull medytacyon not to be sayde with the mouthe lightly but to be cryed with

---

[50] BL MS Add. 39574, fols 1–4 (my emphasis). This manuscript was edited by M. Day, as *The Wheatley Manuscript*, *Early English Text Society*, Original Series 155 (London, 1921).

[51] See, BL MS Harley 2253; Thomas H. Bestul, *Texts of the Passion: Latin Devotional Literature and Medieval Society* (Philadelphia, 1996).

[52] See Richards, this volume.

[53] BL C. 106.a.24 (*A Spirituall Counsayle*), fol. E viii, v.

herte and minde often and exyghtely'.[54] The title of this meditation explicitly emphasizes the issues of corporeality to which the other examples of ecstatic verse allude. There is also something startlingly ecstatic about this silent prayer, which is to be *cried out* in the heart. Its invocatory form is also intensely oral.

A fruitfull medytacyon …
O mooste excellent goodness withdraw not thy mercy o moste myghte maker dispyse not thy work, o most prudent redeemer suffer not to perysshe the pryce of thy redempcion o most gentyll ghostly and heavenly host and gest, puryfye, save, dresse, and kepe thy howse and dwellyng place, the whiche thou dedicatest & sanctifydest, to the in the sacrament of baptism O most blyssed jesu, O most charitable jesu O most swete jesu O most bounteous jesu O most excellent jesu O most glorious jesu O moste innocet jesu O most merciful jesu O most dere jesu have mercy on me when shall I love the when shall I be sorry and contrite for my synnes when shall I forsake my synnes when shall I tourne unto the by grace when shal I remember thy benefytes thy mekenes thy poverte and payneful & most bytter passion thy pacience thy obedience thy love and thy charyte …

Summary of Evidence for a Popular Oral Discourse

The examples of evidence for a popular oral discourse belong within a range of many possible kinds of devotional literatures available in manuscript and printed Primers and Prayer Books in the period *c.* 1450–1560. These particular examples were chosen to show two different but linked ways in which the spoken word is emphasized in this literature. The doggerel verse of the first two examples indicates the actual orality, which would be involved with the acts of reading such doggerel rhyme. The three examples of ecstatic verse indicate a focus on *concepts* relating to modes of vocalization, such as speaking, listening and crying out. But these modes of vocalization are made special by being presented in ways that modify normal usage, such as crying out silently. I suggest, therefore, that the ecstatic prayers encourage the reader to think conceptually about issues of oralization in reading whereas the doggerel rhymes, through their emphasis on popular speech, direct the reader to a heightened awareness of the relationships between reading and poetic diction.

The Oralized Responses of Readers

The following consideration of the rhetoric of annotation has been particularly stimulated by Fabian's proposition that newly literate groups use language freely, in a way that mimics spoken forms. The following examples of annotation each

---

[54]   Ibid.

indicate how the reader responds in an oralized manner. Such oralized responses are stimulated by the emphasis on issues of orality in the 'official literature' initially written or printed into a book. Some examples also correspond with Fabian's proposition that people-writers (people-readers) express a more free sense of grammar and syntax.

The Oralized Responses of Readers: Example 1 (Rhyming Couplets)

One of the most common types of annotation is the rhyming couplet. While these are ubiquitous, when viewed in the context of this chapter, the production of a rhyming couplet becomes an interesting aspect of the reader's process of oralization.

> This is my wyle and my deed.
> It be spared his harte that this doth reed [55]

The Oralized Responses of Readers: Example 2 (Proverbialization)

Some annotated couplets suggest an engagement of the reader with the text that goes beyond sensitivity to poetic forms. The following example provides evidence that the reader has used the official text of a prayer to form the basis of a proverb.[56]

The annotation:
Where the tree fallath ther he lyeth
Everey tree is knowen by his fruit

The official text:
Let us Praye
Graunt (we beseche the lorde god)
That thy servaunt may enioye con
tinuall helthe of body & soule, & throughe
The gracious intercession of the v'gin thy
Mother, yt we may be delivered from this
Present hevynes, & to have **the fruition of**
Eternall gladness By Christ our Lorde. So
Be it. Blesse we the lorde. Thake we god.[57]

---

[55] CCAL H/L–3–6, fol. B iv, r.

[56] On the prevalence of 'Proverbial Wisdom' in local society see, Fox, *Oral and Literate Culture*, ch. 2; and Spufford, *Small Books and Pleasant Histories*, ch. 1 on the ubiquity of proverbs in English and Scottish society in the sixteenth and seventeenth centuries; especially pp. 15–16 on creative mis-rememberings.

[57] CCAL H/L–W–2–X–2–7, fol. F. iiiv.

The Oralized Responses of Readers: Example 3 (Poeticization of a Memo)

Annotations that are apparently irrelevant to the matter of the book are probably the most common. This example is written into a fifteenth-century Psalter. Most of the annotation is in a sixteenth-century hand, although the italicized 'which is willing' has been added subsequently, probably by a seventeenth-century reader. This poeticized memo tends to confirm the tendency of readers to think in terms of rhyme – or at least to write their thoughts in terms of rhyme. The addition of the later line into this rhyme also provides evidence for the possibility of a continued interaction between reader, or readers, and annotations.

> My mother owethe
> Unto me seven and
> Twenty shillings
> *Which is willing*
> Which is willing
> That I should get it
> Done to remember [58]

Conclusion: Everyday Popular Reading Practices Across the Reformation

Having provided some evidence to legitimate the examination of devotional reading at the level of popular culture in local English society this chapter goes on to propose a rather chicken-and-egg model for the interaction between reading process and popular literature. It is no coincidence that the compilers and printers of the devotional books used doggerel verse: they knew the popular market of people whose lives were conducted through a world of interactions between orality and literacy – proverbs, sayings, and songs. The use of doggerel and proverbs by printers and by readers in their annotations indicates that connections between oral and literate spheres are culturally embedded. But it also indicates something about reading process. In other words, this emphasis on oralization provides access to the ways that ordinary people practised reading in this period, and how they conceptualized reading. I have sought to demonstrate how a detailed ethnographic approach to popular literature opens to interpretation these practices and processes. This approach treats as significant in their own right both the individual books *and* the individually produced marks and traces of their readers, which are in them.

It seemed necessary to justify the fact that the evidence for reading in popular culture is difficult, crumbling, sporadic, and what might be termed 'fragmentary'. Rather than making an apology for engaging with such a subject and such material, I propose that in several ways these very little local examples also impinge on some much bigger issues. In particular, these examples ask questions about the

---

[58] BL MS Add. 35284, end flyleaf.

popular experience of the massive ideological shifts associated with the English Reformation. The emphasis on various aspects of orality and oralization in both manuscript and printed books of popular devotional literature persisted during the sixteenth century and spanned across the reformation period; such literature also had a long history stretching back into the medieval (affective) tradition. This persistence of forms of literature such as the doggerel rhymes and the ecstatic verses lies within a context of numerous changes in the nature of devotional literature and religious ideology more broadly. A primary cause of many changes was the legal requirements imposed on the publication of religious literature in the climate of changing religious ideologies across the reformation period.

Helen White described the (printed) Primer as '... charting the development of various stages of the English Reformation'.[59] In her comprehensive examination of the changing attitudes towards religious devotion, and specifically to images, Margaret Aston described Primers as being 'specifically insidious'. In the period prior to the Reformation, the early 1530s, this is because 'it was easy to slip packets of advanced thought inside the cover of such conventionally ordered texts of popular religious reading'.[60] In 1538, there were rigorous attempts to stop the entry of English Primers produced outside of England because 'sundry contentions and sinister opinions have by wronge teaching and naughtye printed bokes, encreased and growen within this realm'.[61] And, in periods of aggressive reform such as the late 1540s, there were determined efforts to remove all religious literature except for that specifically sanctioned by the Crown. The statute of 1549 is as follows:

> That all Books called Antiphoners, Missals, Grailes, Processionals, Manuals, Legends, Pies, Portuasses, Primers in Latin or English, ... other than such as or shall be set forth by the King's majesty, shall by authority of this present Act clearly and utterly be abolished, extinguished, and forbidden for ever to be used or kept.[62]

Such strong attempts to regulate this popularly available devotional literature certainly indicate that it was perceived by the authorities to be a powerful force in forming the beliefs of the populous. But, the evidence of the popular devotional literature examined here shows that a focus on practice, rather than on the theoretical position expounded by statutes, indicates that people prayed and read in a very similar way before and after the Reformation. So, a study of reading practices across this immense ideological transition provides an interesting insight into everyday experiences of religious re-formation. To refer back to the examples of 'The Dayes Moralised' and 'The Calendar of Months', my proposition is that from day to day, month to month and year to year between about 1502 and 1560,

---

[59] Ibid., p. 9.
[60] Aston, *England's Iconoclasts*, p. 416.
[61] Butterworth, *English Primers*, p. 167.
[62] Cited in White, *Tudor Books*, p. 57.

practices of popular reading remained remarkably consistent. The tendentious suggestion therefore is that at the popular level, the re-formation of religious ideology was conducted through this literature but that this is not a literature invented by Protestantism. It arises from deep structures of a popular discourse of English (and French) Catholic devotion stretching back at least as far as the thirteenth century. This asks questions about the attribution of meaning to the ritualized practices associated with popular piety across the reformation period. As the work of Caroline Humphrey and James Laidlaw would suggest, '… variety, discordance, and even absence of interpretation' are all integral to the devotional rituals associated with popular reading practice (in Kent) in the early English renaissance.[63]

---

[63] Caroline Humphrey and James Laidlaw, *The Archetypal Actions of Ritual: A Theory of Ritual Illustrated by the Jain Rite of Worship* (Oxford, 1994), p. 264.

Chapter 9

Writing and Silence
Transitions Between the Contemplative and the Active Life

Emily Richards

In 1976, Michael Sargent wrote:

> From its foundations the Carthusian Order cultivated letters as the most fitting form of labour for those who dwelt apart in the desert; for although they lived and worked in strict solitude, they still spoke to the Christian world through the books which they wrote, copied and transmitted.[1]

In this chapter, I would like to take up this statement and examine its implications. One is that the transmission of writing by the Carthusians involved a strict separation of the place of production (a place of 'strict solitude') from the place of reception ('the Christian world'). Carthusian houses were indeed significant in the copying and dissemination of books into the wider community. But their apparent distance from the communities they served in this way raises questions about the relationships between the contemplative life, reading and writing. The purpose of this chapter is to explore some of these questions by considering the very important role of language in the reception and the transmission of spiritual meaning. What happened when spiritual writings were 'transmitted' from their site of production in a contemplative order to sites of reception amongst the lay religious? Who were the recipients of such transmission and how might they have read? These types of questions must be asked in order to understand how the lay people of local communities in Kent, Yorkshire and elsewhere used the devotional literature which was most readily available to them. In this chapter, I will use a fifteenth-century Carthusian manuscript, British Library Additional 37049 (hereinafter Additional 37049), which depicts a number of themes and motifs characteristic of late medieval (monastic) spirituality, to look at these questions further.

---

[1]   Michael Sargent, 'The Transmission by the English Carthusians of some Late Medieval Spiritual Writings', *Journal of Ecclesiastical History,* 27/3 (1976): 225–40, p. 225.

Defining Terms

It is important to note that it is difficult to distinguish satisfactorily between 'mysticism' and 'contemplation'. S.S. Hussey suggests that 'they themselves [that is, writers of mystical texts in Middle English] called it contemplation'.[2] This is borne out by contemporary texts; medieval people did not describe themselves as mystics. Literally, contemplation of God was the goal of the contemplative life. In this chapter, for the sake of clarity, I shall use the term 'contemplation' to refer to the conscious practice of meditation and prayer directed to this goal, and 'mysticism' to refer to the experience of God which may result from such practice and which was communicated to others as such. I will use the term 'mystic' in our modern sense to refer to those who stood out as individuals and were usually perceived by their contemporaries to have some special status, setting them apart from their social and religious context, in terms of their personal relationship with God.[3]

The differences between medieval and modern meanings of terms such as 'mysticism' and 'contemplation' is an example of the possible loss of understanding if a specific use of language is ignored. Such confusion may also lead to a forgetting of how language both shapes and is shaped by spiritual experience. In this chapter, I argue that any historical or geographical transition is marked by specific semantic changes which in turn create new linguistic milieus, these in turn creating new possibilities for experience by reflecting different realities and modes of describing these realities. What one person means by 'affective piety', for example, is not necessarily what is meant by another. This needs to be borne in mind when we look at different kinds of pieties and devotional practices. A book's transition between one place and another, and its reception throughout the trajectory of that transition, need to be analysed bearing in mind specific theological, historical and semantic contexts. Especially, the potential differences in language use between those writing and those reading need to be borne in mind. All of these issues of linguistic – and hence subjective – meaning, have important implications for the transmission of the devotional literature and concepts of piety discussed in this chapter, especially when discussing the transmission of such literature from a contemplative to a non-contemplative environment.[4] Who were the recipients of such transmission, and how might they have read?

---

[2]   S.S. Hussey, 'The Audience for the Middle English Mystics', in Michael G. Sargent (ed), *De Cella in Seculum: Religious and Secular Life and Devotion in Late Medieval England* (Cambridge, 1989), pp. 109–22, 109.

[3]   See Clifton Wolters's introduction to *The Cloud of Unknowing, The Cloud of Unknowing and other works*, translated with an introduction by Clifton Wolters (London, 1967 and 1978), for a general background to these terms.

[4]   See below for a discussion of the 'mixed' life, i.e. the life combining both active and contemplative elements.

Contemplation, Mysticism and Writing

In terms of the contemplative life, if the goal of contemplation was (at least temporarily) reached, the mystic was confronted with the difficulty of how to communicate this without losing the attained state of near-perfection. Writing may be, among other things, a way of verbalizing a potential conflict between the active and the contemplative life, and this verbalization can itself be controversial: although the contemplative life of silent prayer (as also the mystic experience) may be perceived to be of higher spiritual value than the active, it is first of value to others when it is spoken about or written down. Mystics, who may or may not have belonged to a contemplative order, frequently suffered both internal and external conflicts regarding their own communication of their experiences – Margery Kempe is the most obvious example. Richard Rolle, a Carthusian, who is presented in Additional 37049 as a holy and exemplary figure, was in his own time criticized by his order for his self-revelatory works and his claim to authorship – Carthusians then as now were expected to remain anonymous.[5]

Mystics emphasize the subjective nature of their experiences – Ralph Hanna III describes how Rolle, in naming himself and his experiences, created his own vocabulary.[6] Hence, mystics also invite conflict, as the expression of mystical experience in one's own language questions the whole concept of authority. While mystics are usually anxious to be seen to be operating within orthodox thought, the fact that they base their writings on experience rather than on teaching means they are, by implication, allowing their readers to question the role authority plays in directing their beliefs.[7] On the other hand, the mystic or contemplative generally views themselves as only a channel for God's message, which by implication therefore requires communication in either a textual or oral form. This paradox is one which raises the question of what authorship, and authority, might be, a point illustrated by Nicholas Watson with reference to the experiences of Julian of Norwich. Julian's role as visionary is inherently paradoxical: she must not succumb to pride and to the closely related danger of unorthodox thought, and yet she is also the chosen recipient for the divine visions. Further, by insisting that the visions are for everyone, she paradoxically emphasizes her own special role as mediator, as it is only through her book that others can apprehend the revelations for themselves. Julian's book thus becomes an authoritative text, but its authority might be described as deriving from the paradox which so troubles her: her status

---

[5]   See for example *The Wound of Love: A Carthusian Miscellany*, eds anonymous (London, 1994).

[6]   Ralph Hanna III, '"Meddling with Makings" and Will's Work', in A.J. Minnis (ed), *Late Medieval Religious Texts and their Transmission. Chapters in Honour of A.I. Doyle.* (Cambridge, 1994), pp. 85–94.

[7]   See Nicholas Watson, *Richard Rolle and the Invention of Authority* (Cambridge, 1991), pp. 1–2.

at the interface of a subjective relationship to God which must also be recognized as having universal application.[8]

Mystics, while not necessarily identical with contemplatives, operated in a context of the contemplative life, the goal of which was to leave language behind and to experience God directly. Hence this paradox – the necessity of communicating that which is incommunicable, as well as the conflict between the opposing requirements of *solitudo* and *utilitas* – was something inherent in the conflict between an active and a contemplative life. Such anxiety as Watson describes, therefore, may not only be related to the spiritual dangers of authority (such as pride or the risk of heresy) but also to awareness on the part of the mystic of how, as Watson describes in another context, '... experience is formalized and deflected by language'.[9]

One way of responding to this awareness was the attempt of many contemplatives to attain a state in which linguistic paradigms were overcome or altered. This can still be seen in Carthusian writings today, where words such as 'poverty', 'chastity' and so on are used with a number of meanings; they are free-floating signifiers, intended to encourage a state of mind in which their meanings are subject to endless re-inscription according to the level of understanding attained by the disciple.[10] This is not a new practice; the fifteenth-century Carthusian mystic Richard Methley, for example, also took the term 'solitudo' and redefined it to imply a solitude of the spirit, not necessarily of the body.[11]

Similarly, monastic reform in the later Middle Ages with its emphasis on *affectio, identificatio, imitatio, meditatio* rather than on forms of political or missionary activity, led to the development, via a specialized vocabulary, of ideals that many outsiders saw as passive and weak.[12] The monastic emphasis on what is now termed affective piety was seen as feminine because its principal aim was to develop one's longing for Christ (*desiderio*) by becoming aware of the lack in oneself. The concept of *desiderio* was especially developed by St Catherine of Siena and the kind of vocabulary developed by mystics such as Teresa of Avila has been described as deriving essentially from such a principle of femininity. Such affective theology required that one 'speak like a woman';[13] and this ideal, first developed in ascetic monasticism, required a rewriting of theological and other terms such as *virilitas, otium* and *discretio* '... to counter the simplistic gender–

---

[8]   Ibid., p. 4.

[9]   Ibid., p. 2.

[10]   See *The Wound of Love*, and also Robin Bruce Lockhart (ed.), *"O bonitas!" Hushed to silence: a Carthusian Monk*, (Salzburg, 2000).

[11]   James Hogg, 'Richard Methley – To Hew Heremyte a Pystyl of Solytary Lyfe Nowadayes', *Analecta Cartusiana*, 31 (1977): 91–119, p. 102.

[12]   See, especially for a discussion of affective piety and the origins of this term, Dennis D. Martin, *Fifteenth Century Carthusian Reform. The World of Nicholas Kempf* (Leiden–New York–Cologne, 1992), pp. 8ff.

[13]   Quoted in Martin, *Fifteenth Century Carthusian Reform*, p. 13.

specific categories of the "world"'.[14] For this reason, Carthusians in particular were often accused of inappropriate 'weakness' and lack of activity in ecclesiastical politics.[15] Carthusian belief and its linguistic expression implied that the life of the *via negativa* involved redefining language and vocabulary, contrasting with what Dennis Martin calls 'the investigating, outward-looking, linear, speculating logocentric theology of the schools'.[16] It is important, therefore, to recognize that different theological contexts required different vocabularies, and hence different reading.

Language may thus play a central role not only in describing spiritual experience at the place of production, but also to guide reading practice or to create a new reading vocabulary. Language therefore strongly contributes to creating the (spiritual) milieu in which reception occurs. However, this in turn hides another paradox: the reader may find themselves within a textual world with fixed values and meanings, which appears to direct their spiritual behaviour towards normative goals; yet this textual/semantic world has itself been developed in a setting where spirituality and its semantic expression are in a process of intense change. This continual rethinking of language, and the implication that spirituality itself is not 'fixed', may become hidden as the text passes from its writers to its readers. But the readers in turn may respond to the text in unexpected ways. This can lead to an increased dialogic interaction between writers and readers and hence, perhaps, to further changes in language and thought. It can also lead to a hardening of certain opinions and a greater defence of the 'official' language of spirituality with the concurrent fear and punishment of 'heretics' who use language differently – the punishment of those who advocated the translation of Scripture into the vernacular is the most obvious case.

Such dialogic interaction may seem unlikely to have occurred between the Carthusians and the lay community around them if we accept the prevailing belief that, as Sargent suggests, they kept themselves remote from their readers. But in fact, the Carthusian order was not in reality closed, even if its ideals emphasized the necessity of distance. It was an order in which the world was intensely interested, and which reciprocated this interest both through its dissemination of vernacular books and through vernacular instruction of the laity or semi-laity. It

---

[14] Ibid., p. 217.

[15] For an example of such criticism and how it might have been refuted by a monastic theologian, see the description of correspondence between Johann of Eych, bishop of Eichstaett 1445–64, and Bernard of Waging, prior of the Austin canons at Tegernsee from 1452, in ibid., pp. 203–24. Martin uses their debate to examine more closely what he calls the 'rise of misogyny' (p. 221) associated with a more active, bureaucratic and scholastically oriented Church in the later Middle Ages.

[16] Ibid., p. 13. One question might be how far this differs from our academic need to define meanings of words in a discursive, possibly polemic context. I would surmise that our own tradition as academics is principally derived from 'logocentric theology', and this means that we may have difficulties in approaching texts which are not written to be read in this way.

also received numerous men from outside the charterhouse for shorter or longer periods of time, who did not necessarily themselves live contemplative lives. Through this combination of willed interaction with some aspects of the outer world and simultaneous rejection of others, I suggest, the Carthusians developed their own spirituality and their own semantic coding of this spirituality.

Far from simply 'transmitting' writing from an untouchable place of solitude, the Carthusians made creative use of the contemplative/active dilemma. The ideal of solitude, rather than the reality, would seem to have led to a 'contemplative community' made up not only of those official contemplatives, but also of those who partook in other ways in Carthusian life, creating linguistic paradigms of affective and contemplative piety which in turn entered into the lay/vernacular world in a dialogic form.

The Carthusians and their Books

Additional 37049 appears to have been produced in Yorkshire, but its context is that of continuous exchange of books and ideas between charterhouses, especially between London and the North of England. There are no surviving catalogues of Carthusian libraries, but contemporary lists of books sent from one house to another do exist. These book lists can be found in the excellent edition by Ian Doyle, who, together with Vincent Gillespie, provides a thorough examination of the evidence of how Carthusians contributed to the dissemination of literature in England in the Middle Ages.[17] Although, of course, we cannot know whether the extant lists are representative, and most of those surviving are of loans from London to other charterhouses, they are particularly interesting in that they show a high proportion of Middle English mystical works being passed between charterhouses, including works by Richard Rolle and translations of St Bridget's *Revelations*. Other evidence of the transfer of books can be found in the *chartae* published after each annual meeting of the Grande Chartreuse, which frequently mention such loans and gifts.[18] Gillespie attributes Additional 37049 possibly to Axholme or Hull; it is of interest to note that probably in the late fifteenth century, the English translation of Guillaume de Deguileville's *Pelèrinage de l'Ame* was sent from London to Hull, and there is an English version of this work in Additional 37049.[19]

Additional 37049 is generally held to be a fifteenth-century miscellany of religious writings produced most probably in a Northern charterhouse; this attribution is due to its language (Northern English) and to its mention of Mount Grace. It was obtained by the British Library from the Rosenthal family in Munich

---

[17] Vincent Gillespie with Ian Doyle (eds), *Catalogue of Syon Abbey with the Libraries of the Carthusians*, Corpus of British Medieval Library Catalogues, 9 (London, 2001).
[18] Gillespie and Doyle (eds), *Catalogue of Syon Abbey*, p. 609.
[19] Disputation between the soul and the body, fols 82r–84r.

in 1905, but its history is otherwise completely unknown. The manuscript has been ascribed to Mount Grace's scriptorium, but there is no satisfactory evidence for this.[20] It was produced probably during the first half of the fifteenth century, in the context of highly politicized debate around the nature of religious imagery and the use of the vernacular in religious texts.[21] It is a unique, richly detailed manuscript with pages full of words and pictures, and includes several religious dialogues, numerous prayers and poems and excerpts from religious texts.[22] The attribution of the manuscript to the Carthusian order is based on excerpts in it from Henry Suso's works and on a poem which narrates the story of how the charterhouse was founded, and also on the numerous pictures of probably Carthusian monks. The poem emphasizes the importance of solitude and retreat into a metaphorical desert, isolated from ordinary communities.[23]

The manuscript is known for its pictures. Given its assumed Carthusian provenance, the manuscript has a particular significance when looking at how pictures and text interact; the use of imagery is of particular interest in investigating the relationship between the contemplative life and reading/writing. Charterhouse statutes of the time in England restricted the use of imagery for monks, while allowing it for lay people.[24] At the same time, however, there is much evidence of imagery being a part of the daily lives of the monks after a new decree in the fourteenth century allowed them to place such images in their churches and monasteries.[25] The images preserved are mainly those of the suffering Christ known as *imagini pietatis*. Additional 37049 contains numerous

---

[20]   Glyn Coppack and Mick Aston, *Christ's Poor Men. The Carthusians in England* (Stroud, 2002), caption to Figure 1 of the coloured plates (unnumbered pages). For possible attribution and dating see also: R.H. Bowers, 'Middle English Verses on the Founding of the Carthusian Order', *Speculum*, 42/4 (October 1967): 710–13; T.W. Ross, 'Five Emblem Verses in BL Additional 37049', *Speculum*, 32 (1957): 276–9; and the entry in the electronic Middle English Dictionary (http://ets.umdl.umich.edu/m/med/).

[21]   For the historical background and discussion of the controversies on the use of the vernacular in religious writing from the fourteenth century on, see especially Jocelyn Wogan-Browne et al. (eds), *The Idea of the Vernacular. An Anthology of Middle English Literary Theory, 1280–1520* (Exeter, 1999), pp. 339–45.

[22]   For a detailed list of the contents see the British Library Catalogue; the use of dialogue is particularly notable in well-known poems such as the 'Querela divina' (fol. 20v), in formal disputes such as that between the Body and Worms (fol. 33r) and in shorter dialogic pictures where the subjects are given scrolls bearing words to 'converse' with each other.

[23]   BL MS Add. 37049, fol. 22v.

[24]   E. Margaret Thompson, *The Carthusian Order in England* (London, 1930), pp. 106, 266; Rev. Robert A. Horsfield, 'The Pomander of Prayer: Aspects of Late Medieval Carthusian Spirituality and its Lay Audience', in Sargent (ed.), *De Cella in Seculum*, pp. 205–14.

[25]   Thompson, *The Carthusian Order in England*, p. vi.

such pictures.[26] At Mount Grace a so-called 'pardon panel' is also preserved on a wall of what would have been cell ten of the monastery, a picture of Christ showing his wounds similar to pictures in the manuscript. There is a famous version of the *imago pietatis* at the charterhouse church of Santa Croce in Gerusalemme, Rome, and a copy of this image was sent from the London charterhouse to Hull in the late fifteenth or early sixteenth century along with a number of books.[27] The list also includes, out of twenty-five items, four works by Richard Rolle, and it is the same list which includes the edition of *Pèlerinage de l'Ame*.

Eugene Honée argues that the use of pictures for what he terms 'private devotion' did not really become widespread until the advent of 'visual theology' with Aquinas and Bonaventura, where the principle of *imitatio*, the imitation of Christ and emotional identification with His suffering, became a leading principle in devotional practice.[28] The height of such practice was reached in the fifteenth century, with the rise of the *devotio moderna*, translations from Latin for pastoral use, and the creation of libraries and anthologies (e.g. *rapiaria*) based on the individual needs of those who would use them. At this time, Honée claims, a separate 'culture of prayer' began to evolve in Italy and quickly spread to the rest of Europe, a culture that was less 'normative'.[29]

The private use of books and reading is often perceived as leading to a less 'normative' kind of piety (although, as I shall argue later, this perception does not take into account the possibility of interiorized norms of affective behaviour). The Carthusians were particularly famed for their book production and dissemination. Gillespie argues that this was in part a response to the requirement of their early statutes that they do not neglect pastoral care of souls (the 'curam animarum'), although the statute at this time mentions only 'animarum nostrarum', that is those souls directly within the care of the charterhouse – the lay brethren, the *conversi* and the *clerici-redditi* (those who were allowed to take part in the life of the charterhouse as brothers, but whose vows allowed them to leave if there was a good reason to do so) and so on.[30] These statutes were developed from the *Consuetudines* of Guigo, the first Prior, in which he made the famous statement

---

[26] BL MS Add. 37049, fols 20r, 23r, 24r, 26r, 45r. For more on the *imago pietatis* see Henk van Os et al. (eds), *The Art of Devotion in the Late Middle Ages in Europe 1300–1500*, trans. from the Dutch by Michael Hoyle (London, 1994), pp. 110–12.

[27] Gillespie and Doyle (eds), *Catalogue of Syon Abbey*, p. 620.

[28] Eugene Honée, 'Image and Imagination in the Medieval Culture of Prayer: A Historical Perspective', in van Os et al. (eds), *The Art of Devotion*, pp. 157–74.

[29] Honée, 'Image and Imagination', p. 130.

[30] Vincent Gillespie, 'Cura Pastoralis in Deserto', in Sargent (ed.), *De Cella in Seculum*, pp. 163–89 (p. 162). The statute referred to is the *Statuta Antiqua* of 1259.

that, as the Carthusians could not preach with their mouths, they should preach with their hands, that is, through the creation of books.[31]

This evokes Pope Gregory's suggestion that the illiterate should be provided with pictures so that they may 'read by seeing'.[32] The spiritual requirements of those who are unable to follow the highest form of religious life must be met in different ways. Certainly there are implicit references to Gregory by later writers such as, for example, Jean Gerson. His phrase concerning the availablity of vernacular books for the laity is 'ut doceretur per se legendo eos' (that they would learn through the reading of them). Gerson also considered the roles of speaking and reading in the salvation of the soul, and suggested that although the speaking of the preacher played an important role, for some the availability of writing was important because 'vox intrans per unam aurem exit per alteram' (a voice entering through one ear exits through the other).[33]

The transmission of spiritual care and instruction, therefore, is perceived as taking place on a number of different levels (writing in Latin; writing in the vernacular; oral preaching; pictures), and to these levels different values may be attached. Among Carthusians (and between Carthusians and other religious orders) books and learning were disseminated, particularly in the fourteenth and fifteenth centuries, via copying, translation, import and physical transfer.[34] Any instruction of the laity, and care of the lay brethren within the charterhouse, took place probably in the vernacular, possibly with the use of books of pastoral care or prayer books; Gillespie maintains that the illiteracy of the lay brethren (in Latin) was encouraged.[35] By the end of the fifteenth century, there is also much evidence for the transmission of books in both directions between the (usually wealthy and/or learned laity) and the charterhouses.[36] It should also not be forgotten that a number of book donors were men who had been 'active' religious, for example priests, before they entered the contemplative life in the Carthusian order, or who

---

[31] 'Libros quippe tanquam sempiternum animarum nostrarum cibum cautissime custodiri et studiosissime volumus fieri, ut quia ore non possumus, dei verbum manibus predicemus' : quoted in Gillespie, 'Cura Pastoralis', p. 172.

[32] See Wogan-Browne et al (eds), *Idea of the Vernacular*, p. 216.

[33] Gillespie, 'Cura Pastoralis', p. 176.

[34] Thompson, *The Carthusian Order in England*, pp. 313–34.

[35] Gillespie, 'Cura Pastoralis', p. 166.

[36] On this see the introduction in Gillespie and Doyle (eds), *Catalogue of Syon Abbey*. Notably, Henry V, establishing the charterhouse at Sheen and the Bridgettine house at Syon, made especial provision for libraries at both houses (*Catalogue of Syon Abbey*, pp. xxx–xxvii). See also Thompson, *The Carthusian Order in England*, pp. 313–34, Sargent, 'The Transmission of some Late Medieval Spiritual Writings', and Gillespie, 'Cura Pastoralis', p. 173, for evidence of Carthusian libraries and the kinds of bequests made to them. See Horsfield, 'The Pomander of Prayer', p. 209, for evidence of textual transmission from the Carthusians to the laity.

lived for a period of time within the charterhouse before returning to the active life (the most famous example being, perhaps, Thomas More[37]).

The provision of books and/or instruction for those outside the charterhouse, however, especially for the less learned, was a politically ambiguous point. While Gerson held book-reading to be advantageous for the suppression of heresy, Arundel's *Constitutions* of 1409, and the corresponding ecclesiastical legislation in the York diocese, were a deliberate response to threats of Lollardy and indicate an anxiety that the wrong kind of book may encourage heresy in the newly literate.[38] Hence, the emphasis on imitation and emotive identification with Christ in 'private' devotion which Honée sees as evidence of a greater affective piety, and which may also have been a result of the dissemination of monastic practice among the laity, was also of political importance. Arundel approved (and possibly commissioned) the Carthusian Prior Nicholas Love's *Mirror of the Life of Jesus Christ*, a highly influential book written at Mount Grace and intended to encourage meditative practice among the laity, in part as a way of influencing pious reading: it was to encourage a more emotive response to reading and thus discourage heretical thought and discussion.[39]

Provision of pastoral care and/or spiritual instruction through texts, therefore, may be linked to quite specific, politically motivated aims and objectives on the part of those providing it, in their attempts to influence and form reception and create new 'norms' of piety. However, those who eventually read the texts may not read them as they are intended to be read, and there is usually no certainty as to who, in fact, will read pious and devotional material. One certainty, however, is that such texts were fairly accessible to a relatively wide range of people in the local communities of Kent and elsewhere through personal ownership and inheritance of books, as well as private borrowing, and the function of the parish church as a library.[40] In terms of production, the writing of contemplative texts, or the writing of texts within a contemplative setting, may embody the very doubts, conflicts and ambiguities which officially the dissemination of such texts may be supposed to dispel.

---

[37] Peter Ackroyd, *The Life of Thomas More* (London, 1999), pp. 93–101. See also Gillespie, 'Cura Pastoaralis', p. 164.

[38] On Gerson, see Gillespie, 'Cura Pastoralis', p. 176; on literacy and heresy see, Wogan-Browne et al. (eds), *Idea of the Vernacular*, p. 216.

[39] Wogan-Browne et al. (eds), *Idea of the Vernacular*, p. 252.

[40] See Elisabeth Salter in this volume and the works to which she refers, pp. 148–9.

The Active and the Contemplative Life: Some Considerations

The potential conflict between the active and the contemplative Christian life, and the difficulties of bridging the gap between the two, has been a common subject of discussion by Christian writers from Augustine and Gregory to the present day, but was of especial – acute – interest in medieval societies. Watson writes that '[c]oenobites and solitaries were ... assumed to be essentially superior to others in their way of life'.[41] The life of solitude represented the highest form of living, but by the fourteenth century more models of the mixed or 'medled' life had become available, as evidenced by the writings of Walter Hilton, Richard Rolle and others. In these models, the concept of preaching played an especially important part; the need to minister to the spiritual needs of others (*utilitas*) had to be balanced with the need to gain a greater intimacy with God through solitude (*solitudo*).[42]

It is generally agreed that the Carthusians met this potential conflict by reference to the rules set out by Guigo I, as described above.[43] The Carthusians perceived themselves, and were perceived, as serving the lay community and other religious communities via textual activity, providing those outside the individual charterhouse with devotional reading matter. The lists of the 'inter-library loans' carried out between Carthusian houses mentioned above, and the evidence of endowments of libraries through legacies or gifts, lend credence to the idea that the medieval Carthusians were perceived by contemporaries as playing an important role in the collection and preservation of literature.[44] Such textual activity represented the *utilitas* required of the spiritual life in a form which did not threaten the monks' belief that being apart from the world was necessary for their spiritual welfare. However, as I have argued above, the implication may be that the Carthusians themselves were already in a position which was of greater spiritual value, as the solitary life was held to be more valuable than the active. Book-making and book-writing might represent, then, a compromise by which the outer community was served but did not impinge upon the monastic life, a form of compromise between the active and the passive life. But what is then the spiritual status of words in a context where oral communication is (to a point) forbidden, while the written word is not?

According to the medieval ideal of contemplation, the use of words was a lower rung on the ladder of salvation, inferior to contemplative visualization, where

---

[41]   Watson, *Richard Rolle*, p. 22.

[42]   Ibid., pp. 11–15. Watson also points out that, as the status assigned to the mixed life became greater, so did its definitions become more inclusive (p. 16).

[43]   Ibid., p. 15.

[44]   On the role of the Carthusians in introducing new devotional literature into England through copying and borrowing books, see Paul Lee, *Nunneries, Learning and Spirituality in Late Medieval English Society: The Dominican Priory of Dartford* (York, 2001), pp. 183–5, 215–16.

ultimately there are no words.[45] A ladder, the 'Scala Celi' is pictured on fol. 49v of Additional 37049; the rungs of the ladder are, from the bottom up, 'Humiliacione', 'Conuersacione', 'Meditacione', 'Contricione', 'Confession', 'Satisfaccion', 'Orison', 'Deuocion' and finally 'Contemplacion'; other ladders of spiritual advancement are found on fols 37r and 65v. However, reading, while not an end in itself, did have an important role to play to guide the soul to perfection. Richard Methley named the 'redyng of holy englisshe bokes' as one of the five things demanded by God for a holy life, the other four things being contemplation, good prayer, meditation and devotion.[46] Like Nicholas Love earlier in his life, Methley was known for what Hope Emily Allen terms 'sensory devotion'[47] and was compared by contemporary sources to Richard Rolle and John Norton, two other Carthusians. Such devotional behaviour was frequently criticized by contemporaries who found the verbalization of such emotive experience controversial.[48] Yet the books describing many variations of such experience were eagerly read. Paul Lee suggests that books may have gone some way towards helping people solve the conflict between activity and contemplation. He suggests that the problem for the laity was the integration of the insights of the 'monastic contemplative life' provided by the available vernacular and translated books, into the active life in the world. Some widely available books, however, such as those by Walter Hilton, actually gave advice on living the mixed life.[49] But how are the insights of contemplation transformed into a form which can be helpfully read, and what does that process of transformation involve? To answer these questions, it is necessary to consider the process by which contemplatives themselves might turn an experience which is potentially non-verbal, and certainly felt to be beyond the bounds of ordinary experience, into a verbal communication. This may require a different kind of language from that which is used in non-contemplative discursive contexts.

---

[45] For the role of visualization in medieval belief, see especially Rosario Assunto, *Die Theorie des Schönen im Mittelalter* (2nd edition, Cologne, 1996). For the concept of mystic experience as 'not knowing', and the difference between 'vocal' (i.e. verbal), and 'mental' prayer (that practised by the contemplative, in which words are ultimately unnecessary), see *Cloud of Unknowing*, pp. 21–6, and Horsfield, 'The Pomander of Prayer', pp. 210–11.

[46] Hogg, 'Richard Methley', p. 118.

[47] Ibid., p. 92.

[48] The comparisons can be seen in annotations made in the late fifteenth or early sixteenth century on Mount Grace's manuscript of the *Booke of Margery Kempe*, where all three monks are also compared to Margery. 'Sensory devotion' continues to be criticized by some modern writers, too; see Hogg, 'Richard Methley', pp. 92–3.

[49] Lee, *Nunneries, Learning and Spirituality*, p. 141.

Different Languages for Different Behaviours? How Mystics Write

Ralph Hanna III has described a difference between 'discursive' and 'non-referential' language in approaching medieval religious experience. 'Non-referential' language was the linguistic behaviour favoured by hermits and mystics, who, if they did not prefer silence, tended to describe their experience in what Hanna calls '… a meditative sequence of approximations like [Richard] Rolle's "dulcor"/ "calor"/ "candor" [sweetness/ heat/ light]'.[50] In writing of his own experience, Rolle defied, or subverted, the Carthusian ideal that as a contemplative one leaves one's own language and self behind. Although Hanna is writing about Langland when he describes the importance of the act of creating a personal language to describe personal experience, his words might equally be applied to Rolle. Rolle was not only a Carthusian; as evidenced by the book lists above, his works played an important role for the Carthusians, despite his atypical and controversial (for a Carthusian) rejection of anonymity.

Rolle is pictured in Additional 37049 as 'Richard hampole' (*sic*).[51] The picture forms part of a sequence (the 'Desert of Religion') which continues for 20 pages.[52] In this sequence the pattern described below can be observed.

The introductory poem, on the recto side, describes how a man, seeking the holy life, enters the wilderness – the 'desert of religion'.[53] The verso side of this folio is divided vertically into two aspects: on the left, a poem describes how the man in the wilderness encounters the Tree of Virtues, and what each leaf on this tree means. On the right, a picture shows 'paule þe first hermet', who kneels on the ground looking up to the Holy Ghost in the shape of a bird, and above the Holy Ghost to an angel who bears the shield of Christ's wounds. This picture is framed by a short poem: 'Fourty yer in Wyldernes I dwelled in a caue: Whare god of his gret godenes graunted me for to haue. And ilk day to me gun dres/Wth[with] a raven halfe a lafe [loaf]. þar my clathes ware mare & les. Of leues þat me gun save'. On the facing recto folio, the page is taken up by a tree bearing a number of inscribed leaves, here the 'Tree of Virtues'. This sequence is repeated throughout: as the reader holds the book open, they see on the far left a long poem, then on its right a picture of a human being – in nearly all cases a religious or a saint – on the ground, looking up to a supernatural being (an angel, saint or one of the Trinity) who is looking down to him and linked to him via various symbolic objects; a shield, a bleeding Heart, a ladder, trees, church spires, scrolls of text or the Holy Spirit. On the facing page is then the picture, taking up a whole page, of that which the long poem describes.

The smaller pictures on the verso folio, however, do not appear to be related directly to the poems, which refer to the trees on the facing side. What then might

---

[50] Ralph Hanna III, '"Meddling with Makings" and Will's Work'.
[51] BL MS Add. 37049, fol. 52v.
[52] Ibid., fols 46r–66v.
[53] Ibid., fol. 46r.

the function of these pictures be? Their difference from the text on the left is, I believe, borne out by the text which is sometimes found on the pictures themselves. While the poems are obviously didactic, the small texts on the pictures are more dialogic in form. Looking at the picture of Richard Rolle, we see beneath his feet a speech bubble coming from his mouth in which he says: 'I syt & singe. Of luf langyng. þat in my brest is bred. Ihu my kynge/ & my ioyinge. When won is to / ye ledde. Richard hampole'. Five angels above him bear a book or tablet in which is written: 'Sanctus sanctus sanctus / sanctus deus omnipotens'. Other prayers and words on the pictures also have this quality of dialogicity, using the first or second person, as we have seen in the first example of Paul the Hermit, and describing emotions or physical experiences. The texts on the trees themselves are as simple as possible: each leaf is labelled with its quality or a simple injunction, such as 'chastite', or on the tree of the five wits, 'of eene unleful seying', and so on. This was probably to encourage mnemonic practice, so that each leaf might be memorized and visualized individually within its tree, as each virtue might be memorized and meditated upon within one category of virtues. Lay readers might use such texts to repeat to themselves the words or phrases; the simplicity of the design makes the complexity a visual, rather than a verbal, experience and is hence easier to recall. One might also speculate that the dialogic aspect of these texts bears resemblance to folk songs and rhymes on secular themes, both in their form and due to their subject (emotions, the body) and that this resemblance, like modern-day hymns, enables the lay reader to make an imaginative connection between his own experiences of hunger, love, longing, and so on, and the identification with Jesus which was the aim of many meditative texts.

On another double page there is a depiction of the 'Twelve Degrees of Perfection'.[54] (See Plate 9.1) Here, the image on the verso folio does depict, in a different form, the values described in the poem. Contemplation is the twelfth and final degree of perfection, according to the poem, and is one of the twelve leaves on the Tree of Perfection. However, on the picture to the right of the poem contemplation is depicted as the root and heart of all perfection, out of which the tree of virtue itself grows. Above this picture, Christ stands gazing down at the Carthusian monk who is praying below the heart; Christ's blood pours out of his wounds. The monk is, literally, contemplating Christ, and uniquely, no language is involved. Perhaps the reader is to imagine themselves as a similar figure who, having practised those virtues set out as part of the contemplative life on previous pages, has now achieved the level of contemplation itself and hence no longer requires the assistance of language in their relationship with Jesus.

We might see here a visual representation of the different kinds of language described by Ralph Hanna III, above, and discussed by Dennis Martin. Contemplative texts favour a non-linear approach to words and images: words become, as it were, images which are themselves to be contemplated. Mystical writing tends to use words to depict an experience in which any verbal element

---

[54]   BL MS Add. 37049, fols. 62v and 63r.

might be of less importance than sensory or visual experience (such as sweetness, light and so on), and where the highest type of experience was supposed to go beyond the usual human sense perceptions.[55] In medieval theology and especially among the Carthusians, contemplation is viewed as a higher form of approach to God than linear discourse, which can, says Richard of St Victor, only ever grasp one element of the truth at one time.[56] It is worth considering how far a manuscript such as Additional 37049 can be compared with mystical writings both in terms of form and function.

One obvious difference is that it is a fully anonymous manuscript, and, except in its reference to Rolle and other saints does not make claims to personal experiences of God. Thus, the reader need not deal with the mystic's dilemma, which we have described above, nor is the question of authorship in evidence except in its absence. Like mystic writings, however, it both emphasizes the ideal of contemplation, while being itself highly verbal. One might describe the manuscript almost as an excited text, as it is full to the very edges with a bewildering variety of different types of language and imagery. The central paradox of contemplation remains therefore at its heart, and is not resolved. But this kind of text is important precisely because it provides such a variety of possible answers to the question, 'How do I relate to God?'. Clearly, language remains here in a state of creative possibility.

Conclusion

The books written, collected and disseminated by Carthusians seem to be reaching out to a wider community. And indeed, in the fifteenth century, there may have been a transition towards increased outreach, as exemplified by the 'The Pomander of Prayer'.[57] Such books were available to the laity throughout England, through a number of different networks of lending, owning and borrowing. However, the fact that these are potentially books which the laity of provincial communities such as Kent might have read in the vernacular, may lead us to forget that they were selected and/or written in a setting with its own specific theological and emotive values and vocabulary, and which defined itself in terms of its difference to the lay community. In terms of both reading and writing, the Carthusians were involved in the dissemination of spiritual and theological vocabularies. This chapter shows that it is important to think about the transitions between contemplative and 'mystical' language, and what Dennis Martin and Ralph Hanna describe variously as 'scholastic' and 'discursive' language; and also about the transitions involved

---

[55]   See *Cloud of Unknowing*, pp. 117–21, for warnings against evaluating contemplative experience in terms of sense perceptions or sensory 'reward'.

[56]   Quoted in Assunto, *Die Theorie des Schönen im Mittelalter*, p. 37.

[57]   Horsfield, 'The Pomander of Prayer', p. 208.

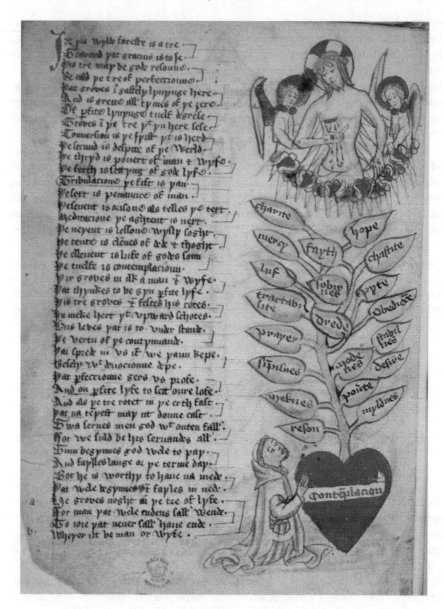

**Plate 9.1 'The Tree of Contemplation', BL MS Additional 37049, fol. 62v
Reproduced with kind permission of the British Library**

where these 'languages' are read by people who are neither contemplatives nor theologians.

The use of language and imagery in Additional 37049 is an example of possible attempts to solve the contemplative dilemma through providing the reader with a spectrum of possibilities for reading and looking. Some pictures show monks or other religious who are apparently silent, lost in contemplation; others, however, provide the pictured subject with representations of dialogic speech. The written discourses in the manuscript, on the other hand, represent a more obviously prescriptive form of writing, which the reader is to follow if they wish to make spiritual progress. However, this means that the manuscript also embodies some of the conflicts and disjunctions between the different requirements of piety. Silence may be enough for some, but is evidently not enough for many. Additional 37049's intense use of the dialogue form and of different vocabularies may represent the wish, and the attempt, to overcome the problem by presenting the reader with the possibility of dialogue as well as authority. What the reader does with this, however, is a different story.

Afterword

Alexandra Walsham

This richly textured collection of essays is the by-product of a thriving scholarly industry that shows little sign of declining in vitality or losing momentum or steam. Over the past three decades the study of religious practice, belief and experience in the late medieval and early modern periods has become one of the most lively, contentious and crowded arenas of academic enquiry. The historiography of this subject is like a swiftly moving stream, ever prone to alter direction and engender new tributaries, and full of swirling eddies and undercurrents. Within the context of England (the chief focus of the present volume), earlier claims about a rapid and popular Reformation that put down deep and penetrating roots within a generation were eclipsed in the 1980s by an emphasis on the slow, halting and haphazard progress of a state-led revolution in doctrine and worship, and the considerable resistance, both active and passive, which it encountered in parishes, communities and neighbourhoods. Reflecting a sharp backlash against a paradigm that concentrated attention on the later phases of this long and protracted movement, recent years have witnessed renewed investigation of the heady religious ferment of the mid-sixteenth century, when Protestantism was a novel, defiant and infectious phenomenon with the power to make immediate and genuine converts. Perceptions of the late medieval Church and the devotional life of the laity have also changed course capriciously: once characterized as corrupt, worldly and out of touch with the spiritual needs of the constituency it served, both the institution and its ecclesiastical hierarchy and personnel have been substantially rehabilitated by detailed revisionist work in local archives. In contrast with previous suggestions about the decadent and burdensome quality of Roman Catholicism prior to its demise, such accounts have underlined the striking vigour and vibrancy of popular piety on the eve of Henry VIII's decisive break with Rome in 1529 and the paucity of evidence for mass disillusionment or pervasive antagonism towards the priesthood. Yet, even as I write, some historians are articulating suspicion about the validity of this picture and re-examining the 'perplexing fragility' and vulnerability late medieval religion seems to have exhibited in the face of the challenge presented by Protestant polemic and theology. Any attempt to capture the current state of consensus on the origins, impact and long-term legacies of the Reformation appears predestined to fail – doomed to appear antiquated and obsolete even before it is further fossilized in print.[1]

The value of the current volume is twofold. It both extends and reinforces certain discernible trends in interpretation and simultaneously attempts to transcend some of the assumptions and preoccupations that have dictated (if not distorted) the shape of the historiographical landscape as it has emerged to date. Adopting a chronology that deliberately defies the boundary that has conventionally been erected between the 'late medieval' and 'early modern' eras around 1500, it invites us to reassess 1400–1640 as a period in its own right, one in which the advent and entrenchment of Protestantism is presented less as a dramatic watershed than as part of a more complex system of shifts and transitions in religious culture that were already underway in pre-Reformation society.

Despite their diversity, a second conceptual thread that links this set of essays is a distinctive, interdisciplinary approach and philosophy. Whether their authors are engaged in scrutinizing testamentary records, court depositions, funeral monuments, monastic manuscripts or annotated liturgical books, they do so animated by the conviction that such sources can provide historians with insight not merely into the intellectual convictions of their producers and consumers, but also, if imaginatively handled, with clues about their psychological ethos, identity and consciousness. Drawing inspiration eclectically from literary theory, anthropology and cognitive psychology, they approach such artefacts not merely as mirrors of past experience, but also as social agents in its making. Parting company with older quantitative methodologies that sought to subject mentalities to the laws of mathematical calculation, they adopt instead more oblique, sophisticated and theoretically informed strategies for deciphering and decoding the texts and objects they place under the microscope. In this regard, they betray the influence of Andrew Butcher, under whose gifted teaching and tutelage at Canterbury much of the research embodied here was originally conceived and nurtured. It is by no means coincidental that the geographical locus of this volume is the county of Kent.

One of the most conspicuous themes to emerge from this collection is the assertion that the noun 'piety' in its singular form fails to do justice to the 'idiosyncratic heterogeneity' of religious belief and practice in both the pre- and post-Reformation era. Only a plural rendering of the term, it is argued, can fully

---

[1]   See the recent surveys by Peter Marshall, *Reformation England 1480–1642* (London, 2003); Felicity Heal, *Reformation in Britain and Ireland* (Oxford, 2003); Alec Ryrie, 'Britain and Ireland', in Ryrie (ed.), *Palgrave Advances in the European Reformations* (Basingstoke, 2006), as well as Peter Marshall and Alec Ryrie (eds), *The Beginnings of English Protestantism* (Cambridge, 2002). Recent straws in the wind include G.W. Bernard, 'Vitality and Vulnerability in the Late Medieval Church: Pilgrimage on the Eve of the Break with Rome', in John L. Watts (ed.), *The End of the Middle Ages? England in the Fifteenth and Sixteenth Centuries* (Stroud, 1998); Peter Marshall, 'Forgery and Miracles in the Reign of Henry VIII', *Past and Present*, 178 (2003): 39–73, quotation at p. 40.

comprehend the multiplicity and mutability of religious experience over these two and a half centuries. Here one implicit target is the rather consensual and harmonious picture of late medieval Catholicism that has been the lasting impression left on many readers of Eamon Duffy's seminal *The Stripping of the Altars* – a picture in which distinctions between literate and illiterate, élite and popular, clerical and lay, communal and individual are accorded relatively little relevance and in which the presence of frictions and fault-lines is so subdued and muted as to be barely perceptible. Duffy's sympathetic evocation of pre-Reformation religious culture does not ignore or overlook – indeed it positively celebrates – its adaptability and flexibility to new conditions, but it remains true that he depicts the official imposition of Protestantism as 'a violent disruption' of enduring patterns of piety which continued to command the respect and loyalty of the laity and which showed 'no particular marks of exhaustion or decay' in the decades preceding the Henrician schism.[2]

Shifting the emphasis slightly, some contributors to this volume are concerned to reassess the significance of the subtle but unsettling transformations that occurred *within* orthodox Catholicism in the fifteenth and early sixteenth centuries, and to combat any suggestion that it was a static or monolithic entity. Rob Lutton's painstaking research on surviving wills from Tenterden, discussed briefly here and explored more fully in his recent book, traces the evolution of strands of piety that were frugal and 'parsimonious' by contrast with the more elaborate and extravagant devotional impulses displayed by others within the town and its close neighbour Cranbrook, and which drew back from lavishing money on traditional cults in favour of sponsoring newer devotions like the Jesus Mass. Adding weight to recent work by Susan Wabuda and Christine Peters which has underlined the capacity of a Christocentric piety rooted in humanism and mysticism to bridge and facilitate the transition to Protestantism, Lutton's work points up the 'powerful polyvalency' of the increasingly personal preoccupation with the passion of Christ and his Holy Name that marked the fifteenth century. What Wabuda calls an emblem of 'the religious bifurcation of western Europe', the IHS could serve both as a focus for old-fashioned cultic devotion and as a potent symbol of a moderate evangelicalism rooted in a culture of spiritual abstraction.[3] Qualifying claims about 1520 as a landmark in the religious history of the Low Countries, in the only chapter to venture beyond the borders of England (and indeed its south-eastern corner), Annemarie Speetjens alludes to similarly delicate transpositions in the culture of commemoration and intercession for the dead which took place after 1450. She interprets the growing involvement of women and of families in chantry foundation

---

[2]   Eamon Duffy, *The Stripping of the Altars: Traditional Religion in England 1400–1580* (London, New Haven, 2005, first published 1992), p. 4.

[3]   Susan Wabuda, *Preaching During the English Reformation* (Cambridge, 2002), ch. 4, and p. 148; Christine Peters, *Patterns of Piety: Women, Gender and Religion in Late Medieval and Reformation England* (Cambridge, 2003), esp. pp. 3, 4, 345. Robert Lutton, this volume, p. 29. Also, G.M. Draper's interesting remarks in passing, this volume, p. 80.

as a sign of their declining status and developing tendency to evade clerical supervision. The displacement of attention from liturgical memorial services to charity is likewise seen as symptomatic of changes that long predated, and therefore cannot be ascribed to, the assault on purgatory launched by the Protestant reformers. Such findings raise further questions about the descriptive utility of the label Duffy employed – with some reservations and in the absence of a more satisfactory alternative – as a shorthand for pre-Reformation piety: 'traditional religion'. They help to focus fresh attention on the ongoing, organic transmutation of 'tradition' and the interesting tensions and divergences that lay hidden beneath the surface of late medieval Christianity.

This provides a stepping stone to the argument, embedded especially in Lutton's chapter, that it may be within devout Catholicism (and its subcultures) that we must look for the seeds of Protestantism, rather than the exotic soil of the Wycliffite heresy that has so often been seen as its ideal germinating environment. In different ways, both he and Andrew Hope cast doubt on the influential thesis posited by A.G. Dickens and John F. Davis that lollardy both paved the way for and fused with the early Reformation, as well as predisposed its adherents to receive it. Richard Rex's recent observation that most early evangelicals came not from lollard but from orthodox stock is one of the springboards for Lutton's suggestion that some forms of late medieval piety had the potential to render its exponents susceptible to key Protestant ideas like the doctrine of justification by faith, helping to bring them to spectacular moments of spiritual insight and epiphany as well as 'less violent journeys' from the 'old religion' to the new.[4] Unlike Rex, though, Lutton is not willing to sever the link between lollardy and the Reformation completely and to dismiss it simply as a fiction retrospectively forged by Protestant polemicists intent upon creating for themselves a plausible history and lineage. Indeed, his work, along with that of Shannon McSheffrey and other scholars, serves to highlight the permeability of the boundary between orthodoxy and heterodoxy and the need for nuanced investigation of the porous interfaces between bodies of belief and practice that were by no means incompatible or mutually exclusive.[5] As Patrick Collinson has recently stressed, lollardy never

---

[4]   A.G. Dickens, *Lollards and Protestants in the Diocese of York* (London, 1959); John F. Davis, *Heresy and Reformation in the South East of England, 1520–1559* (London, 1983). Richard Rex, *The Lollards* (Basingstoke, 2002), pp. 119, 133–7; Rex, 'The Friars in the English Reformation', in Marshall and Ryrie (eds), *Beginnings of English Protestantism*, pp. 38–59. Robert Lutton, this volume, p. 34.

[5]   Shannon McSheffrey, 'Heresy, Orthodoxy and English Vernacular Religion, 1480–1525', *Past and Present*, 186 (2005): 47–80. See also Alec Ryrie, *The Gospel and Henry VIII: Evangelicals in the Early English Reformation* (Cambridge, 2003), ch. 7, for renewed appreciation (drawing on Kentish material) of the overlapping circles of later lollardy and early evangelicalism. But cf. Duffy's preface to the second edition of *Stripping of the Altars*, which reasserts the marginality of lollardy in assessments of fifteenth- and early sixteenth-century religion.

conceived of itself ecclesiologically as a separate church or sect:[6] both the outward conformity and social integration that were its hallmarks and the widespread informal tolerance displayed toward individual lollards in the Kentish Weald, as in other counties and regions, suggests that it may be anachronistic to situate these strands of piety at opposite ends of the ecclesiastical spectrum.

Hope's intriguing piece of historical detective work, meanwhile, questions the same paradigm by focusing on one well-known radical Kentish woman, Joan Bocher (alias Knell), whose extreme anti-Trinitarian opinions and aberrant views on Christ's celestial flesh so horrified the Edwardian establishment that she was burnt at the stake in 1550. Contrary to the claims made by some previous commentators, Bocher did not have lollard ancestry. Rather, she came from and sought to 'get aback' of a family that had yielded up a Catholic martyr for speaking words in support of the papacy, in contravention of the Treason Act of 1534 – a man who seems, moreover, to have been deeply affected by the career of the ill-fated nun and visionary Elizabeth Barton. The hitherto unsuspected connections Hope uncovers between the two women and the pious circles from which they emanated also suggest that it is a mistake to see Barton as a reactionary conservative: initially endorsed by leading churchmen, the spirituality that inspired her political protests against Henry's divorce was in the vanguard of late medieval female mysticism in the mould of Catherine of Siena and Bridget of Sweden.[7] The trajectories and polarities that have been the legacy of denominational and confessional history, his chapter reminds us, may blind us to the beguiling contradictions that are an intrinsic feature of pieties in transition.

This is not to say, however, that the contributors to this collection are unsympathetic to the suggestion – most closely linked with Margaret Spufford and her pupils – that some communities exhibited hereditary traditions of religious orthodoxy and dissent, traditions passed along blood-lines and descending down from generation to generation.[8] Several of these chapters employ genealogy as a methodological tool and adopt the family, rather than the parish, as the primary unit of analysis. Lutton's investigation of the testamentary strategies of Tenderden families is a pioneering experiment in identifying the genetic fingerprint of a distinctive species of piety, while Paula Simpson also detects a 'continuum of resistance' to tithe in woodland and marshland regions of the diocese of Canterbury by paying close attention to the surnames that reappear as defendants in suit after suit across the long curve of the fourteenth, fifteenth and sixteenth centuries.

---

[6]   Patrick Collinson, 'Night Schools, Conventicles and Churches: Continuities and Discontinuities in Early Protestant Ecclesiology', in Marshall and Ryrie (eds), *Beginnings of English Protestantism*, pp. 209–35.

[7]   A recent discussion that emphasizes the medieval pattern of Elizabeth Barton's prophecies can be found in Ethan H. Shagan, *Popular Politics and the English Reformation* (Cambridge, 2003), ch. 2.

[8]   As embodied in Margaret Spufford (ed.), *The World of Rural Dissenters, 1520–1725* (Cambridge, 1995).

Examining piety as a vertical rather than horizontal structure, as an organism evolving over time rather than a cross-section or specimen frozen and dissected at a particular moment in history, such studies are designed to highlight the dynamic but gradual processes of adaptation and modification that characterized the period and culture under consideration.

In this, as in other respects, *Pieties in Transition* moves beyond the dominant priorities of recent Reformation scholarship. This is not a volume that seeks to re-trace the contours of familiar and increasingly tired debates about 'success' and 'failure', to pursue the still elusive question of origin or to enter the fray in heated debates about its long-term repercussions. Its contributors have a limited appetite for historiographical controversy: Dr Simpson, for instance, eschews the opportunity to harness the potential implications of her interesting findings about the high level of clerically inspired tithe litigation to the heated debate precipitated by Christopher Haigh's tendentious claim that anti-clericalism was a consequence rather than cause of the Reformation.[9] Nor are they concerned to try to solve what Chris Marsh has called the 'compliance conundrum': the apparent paradox of '... majority acquiescence in an unwanted religious transformation'.[10] The concept of 'collaboration' Ethan Shagan has invoked in his recent effort to unravel this riddle finds no mention in a collection that not only sidesteps, but implicitly encourages its readers to rethink the revisionist premises on which such an enterprise is predicated – to ask if Protestantism was in fact an inherently unpopular religion and to question the internal coherence and stability of late medieval Catholicism. One of the logical consequences of the assertion that pieties were proliferating and fragmenting in the fifty or so years before the Reformation is perhaps to reduce this knotty problem to something of an optical illusion.[11]

In identifying continuities that helped to temper disruptive theological and liturgical changes, then, the chapters in this volume are less concerned to explain *why* the Reformation took root in English society than to consider *how* these processes perpetuated even as they reconstituted the meaning of older practices and beliefs. In her careful study of the tomb of the Sandwich MP Sir Roger Manwood, Claire Bartram speaks of the capacity of such monuments '... to reinvent pre-Reformation media in a reformed world'.[12] Arguing that the display of social status retained a strong moral and spiritual dimension in a culture of remembrance infused by classical rhetoric and biblical resonances, she persuasively qualifies assumptions about the creeping 'secularization' of funeral art. Extending the

---

[9]	Christopher Haigh, 'Anticlericalism and the English Reformation', in Haigh (ed.), *The English Reformation Revised* (Cambridge, 1987), pp. 56–74; Shagan, *Popular Politics*, ch. 4.

[10]	Christopher Marsh, *Popular Religion in Sixteenth-Century England* (Basingstoke–London, 1998), ch. 5, at pp. 197–8.

[11]	Shagan, *Popular Politics*.

[12]	Claire Bartram, this volume, p. 143.

insights of Helen White and Eamon Duffy[13] on the para-liturgical literature that emerged to cater for the needs of the semi-literate laity, Elisabeth Salter draws attention to the capacity of primers to operate at the popular level as vehicles of a Reformation by which they were not themselves engendered, while Paula Simpson points to the remarkable continuity of the symbolic forms and arenas of confrontations about tithe across the Catholic–Protestant divide as evidence of the power of collective memory to revive 'forgotten' events. Reinforcing the conclusions of Ian Archer's work on Elizabethan London, Sheila Sweetinburgh finds comparable echoes of traditional charitable practices in later Protestant philanthropy, such as the dispensing of doles of food and clothes to the hungry and poor on ecclesiastical feast days. The increasing discrimination exercised by testators should not be exaggerated. An ancient vocabulary of almsgiving, she concludes, was successfully absorbed into a Protestant setting and used to express and advance the new faith in a manner that reformulated rather than cut the bond of spiritual reciprocity between benefactor and beneficiary fostered by the theology of purgatory and a soteriology that accorded such importance to the performance of good works.[14] Like the reproduction of proscribed liturgical rites in the guise of folk custom and popular pastime studied by Ronald Hutton, we might see such transmutations as an index not of an undercurrent of stubborn resistance to Reformed ideology, but as a compelling symptom of the ways which it was creatively assimilated.[15]

In her reassessment of educational provision in the Romney Marsh region, G.M. Draper is no less attuned to the processes by which Protestantism remoulded older institutions, together with narratives of their origins, to serve its own agendas. Underlining the considerable vitality of education in medieval Kent, Draper's chapter further questions the tendency to see the Reformation as a decisive causal factor in the spread of learning and literacy. Demonstrating how far the roots of enduring commonplaces about the incentive for the foundation of grammar schools lay in pious myths constructed about their foundation by Protestant propagandists like William Lambarde, the chapter is a timely reminder both of the role played by Catholic devotion in the expansion of education and of the distorting effects of focusing on the physical evidence of buildings at the expense of the more ephemeral presence of individual teachers such as local chantry priests.

In other ways too, this volume reflects and augments the increasingly nuanced understanding of the relationship between literacy and orality, reading and writing, word and image that has been the outcome of recent scholarship. Discarding any

---

[13] Helen C. White, *The Tudor Books of Private Devotion* (Madison, WI, 1951); Eamon Duffy, 'Continuity and Divergence in Tudor religion', in R.N. Swanson (ed.), *Continuity and Change in Christian Worship*, *SCH*, 32 (Oxford, 1996), pp. 189–205.

[14] Ian Archer, 'The Charity of Early Modern Londoners', *Transactions of the Royal Historical Society*, 6th series, 12 (2002): 223–44.

[15] Ronald Hutton, 'The English Reformation and the Evidence of Folklore', *Past and Present*, 148 (1995): 89–116.

simple equation between the triumph of Protestantism and the arrival of mass literacy and the mechanical press, its contributors resist the temptation to map a transition from speech and script to print and to superimpose this on the boundary between the medieval and early modern eras.[16] Instead, they draw attention to the complex transactions that characterized a region in which literacy had made precocious advances at least a century before the Reformation. Elisabeth Salter employs the concepts of 'oralization' and 'visualization' to illuminate the manner in which Tudor primers and prayer books mimicked the 'doggerel' rhythms of spoken language and to dispute the suggestion that the Reformation effected any far-reaching transformation in devotional reading practices between 1450 and 1560. Claire Bartram is similarly sceptical about the extent to which Protestantism turned its back on visual media and pictures as didactic vehicles, adding a further string to the bow of recent critiques of Professor Collinson's thesis about a dramatic shift in mentality between the first and second generation of Protestant reformers that effected a drift 'from iconoclasm to iconophobia'.[17] As she shows, debates about the propriety of portraiture did not inhibit the development of a distinctly reformed culture of three-dimensional *memoria*. Emily Richards's discerning chapter on the books produced and disseminated by the Carthusians interrogates a rather different nexus: the paradoxical relationship that pertained between writing and silence in a contemplative order that cloistered itself from secular society, but also believed it had a mission to instruct and succour the devout and literate laity. A mechanism for resolving this tension between retreat and outreach, the Carthusian mode of preaching without speaking encapsulated a series of striking ambivalences: writing was an imperfect surrogate for the state of non-verbal and supra-linguistic union with God to which the mystic aspired; it embodied a form of self-abnegating subjectivity that was at the same time a supreme source of personal authority; and it encouraged meditative practices that fostered the very danger of lay heterodoxy it was officially intended to dispel. Conceived of as an antidote to heresy in the wake of Archbishop Arundel's notorious Constitutions of 1409, Richards implies that Carthusian texts were themselves inadvertent agents of the pluralization of piety.

The final distinguishing feature of the perspective on medieval and early modern religious culture enshrined in this collection is its minute scrutiny of what Rob Lutton calls the 'geographies and materialities of piety'. In various ways, all the contributors are concerned to emphasize the influence exerted by landscape and locality in shaping economy, religion, and culture and to insist that devotional trends are best studied in relation to the natural *pays* or milieu from which they grew. For Lutton, the religious culture of spiritual and fiscal restraint he discerns in Tenterden bears the imprint of a particular type of market town in the Kentish

---

[16]   See Alexandra Walsham and Julia Crick (eds), *The Uses of Script and Print, 1300– 1700* (Cambridge, 2004).

[17]   Patrick Collinson, *From Iconoclasm to Iconophobia: The Cultural Impact of the Second English Reformation* (The Stenton Lecture, Reading, 1985).

Weald, in which population increase, trade, and the rapid growth of agrarian capitalism in its hinterland had created an increasingly wealthy and stratified society. For Simpson, marshland and woodland regions emerge as particular foci for traditions of tithe dispute, and for Draper too the evolution of literacy in Romney Marsh and the nearby Cinque Ports of New Romney and Hythe cannot be understood outside the peculiarities of the local environment. All this does not amount to a crude ecological determinism, but it does have some resonances with David Underdown's study of Civil War Wessex, which controversially correlates distinctive regional cultures with particular patterns in social structure, settlement, cultivation and economic development and uses these to explicate differing responses to the mid-seventeenth-century conflicts between King and Parliament in the chalk and cheese country.[18]

Vigorously reasserting the value of a microhistorical approach to piety, the contributors to this volume insist that large-scale studies and surveys risk skimming over the all-important subtleties that emerge when communities, families and individuals are subjected to finely grained analysis. The preferred tool of their technique is the microscope rather than the telescope. But this is local history with a difference – with a post-modern twist. It does not study Kent in the manner of Peter Clark's classic exploration of *English Provincial Society* between 1500 and 1640,[19] with the implication that the cultures of devotion it uncovers are in any sense emblematic, representative or even subversive of broader trends, but rather with a primarily methodological objective. Its aim is less to offer a revisionist reassessment of piety in a county that has long been regarded as a heartland of zealous, progressive and radical Protestantism, as a laboratory for testing the links between lollardy and early evangelicalism, and as a forum for analysing the strength of late medieval anti-clericalism, than to ask its readers to reflect critically on how we can reconstruct the full complexity of religious culture and experience through documents and archives that are inherently slippery, opaque, ambiguous and deceptive.

Even so, the decision to focus principally on the internal dynamics of the pieties under discussion carries with it certain risks and creates some hostages to fortune. One side-effect of stressing the power of place and location on devotional developments may be to perpetuate (albeit unintentionally) the notion of an English, even a Kentish exceptionalism – notwithstanding Dr Speetjens's solitary foray into Flanders and the Netherlands. To speak of the indigenous religious cultures that evolved in this region and of the evolution of 'a particularly English evangelicalism'[20] may inadvertently encourage the opinion that religious change in England owed far more to native conditions that it did to contact with, or infusion

---

[18]   David Underdown, *Revel, Riot and Rebellion: Popular Politics and Culture in England 1603–1660* (Oxford, 1985), ch. 4 and passim.

[19]   Peter Clark, *English Provincial Society from the Reformation to the Revolution: Religion, Politics and Society in Kent, 1500–1640* (Hassocks, 1977).

[20]   Robert Lutton, this volume, p. 29.

by Continental reforming trends and that the Reformation that emerged in this island (if not its constituent regions) had a uniquely vernacular character.[21] It may partially eclipse the international dimension of the transmutations of piety it so carefully scrutinizes and obscure the lesson which Diarmaid MacCulloch's magisterial survey has striven so hard to teach us – that the English experience cannot be extricated from the intersecting movements of Protestant and Catholic renewal that were stirring across so much of northern and southern Europe.[22] In a volume that focuses on a county in close proximity to the melting pot of London and with ready access to ports through which ideas, individuals and texts flowed easily and insidiously to and from the mainland, it is perhaps surprising that we hear so little about the refugees and stranger communities which found asylum in this region and that we catch only occasional glimpses of the ways in which its lay and clerical inhabitants actively participated in a movement to which the Channel by no means acted as an impermeable membrane or impregnable barrier. More attention might also have been paid to the role such variables as gender, age and occupation played in forging and complicating religious culture at a time when social, professional and patriarchal hierarchies were themselves in state of considerable flux.

To point to issues that invite further examination is not, however, to diminish the achievement of this volume. It is to be hoped that this thought-provoking collection will stimulate fresh investigations of these and other aspects of the multiple, malleable and continually evolving pieties that Rob Lutton, Elisabeth Salter and their contributors have compelled us to recognize in late medieval and early modern society. The searching questions they ask of their subjects and sources suggest that there are still many rich insights to be gleaned from the well-tilled soil that is the field of Reformation studies, and new furrows to be ploughed.

---

[21] A tendency present, for example, in Lucy E. C. Wooding, *Rethinking Catholicism in Reformation England* (Oxford, 2000).

[22] Diarmaid MacCulloch, *Reformation: Europe's House Divided 1490–1700* (London, 2003).

Bibliography

Printed Primary Sources

Archdeacon Harpsfield's Visitation, 1557, part I, transcribed by W. Sharp and ed. Rev. L.E. Whatmore (London, Publications of the Catholic Record Society vol. xlv, 1950).

Archdeacon Harpsfield's Visitation, 1557: II together with Visitations of 1556 and 1558, transcribed and ed. Rev. L.E. Whatmore (London, Publications of the Catholic Record Society vol. xlvi, 1951).

Church Life in Kent being Church Court Records of the Canterbury Diocese, 1559–1565, ed. A.J. Willis (London and Chichester, Phillimore, 1975).

Cranmer, Thomas, *Miscellaneous Writings and Letters of Thomas Cranmer*, ed. J. Edmund Cox (Cambridge, CUP, 1846).

Culmer,* R., *Lawles Tythe-Robbers Discovered who make Tythe-Revenue a Mockmayntenance* (London, Thomas Newbery, 1655).

Dering, Edward, A *Briefe and Necessarie Catachisme or Instruction, in Maister Dering's Works* (1590).

Documents of the English Reformation, ed. G. Bray (Cambridge, James Clarke, 1994).

Erasmus, Desiderius, *Collected Works of Erasmus*, 86 vols (Toronto, University of Toronto Press, 1974–), vol. 5 *The Correspondence of Erasmus, Letters 594 to 841, 1517 to 1518*, trans. R.A.B. Mynors and D.F.S. Thomson, annotated by P. G. Bietenholz (Toronto, 1979).

———, *Collected Works of Erasmus*, 86 vols (Toronto, University of Toronto Press, 1974–), vol. 6, *The Correspondence of Erasmus, Letters 842 to 992, 1518 to 1519*, trans. R.A.B. Mynors and D.F.S. Thomson, annotated by P.G. Bietenholz (Toronto, University of Toronto Press, 1982).

Foxe, John, *Actes and Monuments of these Latter and Perilous Dayes*, 8 vols (London, 1583).

———, *Acts and Monuments*, ed. G. Townsend, 8 vols (London, Seeley, 1843).

Googe, Barnabe, *The Foure Bookes of Husbandry, Collected by M. Conradus Heresbachius Counceller ... Newely Englished and increased by Barnabe Googe* (London, R. Watkins, 1577).

Heresy Trials in the Diocese of Norwich, 1428–31, ed. N.P. Tanner (Camden 4th Series 20, 1977).

Holinshed, Raphael, *Holinshed's Chronicles*, ed. H. Ellis, 6 vols (London, 1807–8; repr. with an introduction by V. Snow, New York, 1965).

Kent Chantries, ed. A. Hussey (Kent Records, vol. 12, Ashford, Kent Archaeological Society, 1936).

Kent Heresy Proceedings, 1511–12, ed. N.P. Tanner (Kent Records, vol. 26, Maidstone, Kent Archaeological Society, 1997).

Kentish Visitations of Archbishop William Wareham and his Deputies, 1511–12, ed. K.L. Wood-Leigh (Kent Records, vol. 24, Maidstone, Kent Archaeological Society, 1984).

Lambarde, William, *A Perambulation of Kent Conteining the Description, Historie and Customes of that Shire* (London, H. Middleton, 1576, repr. Chatham, W. Burrill, 1826).

————, *William Lambarde and Local Government: His Ephemeris and Twenty Nine Charges to the Juries and Commissions*, ed. C. Read (New York, Cornell University Press, 1962).

Letters and Papers Foreign and Domestic in the Reign of Henry VIII, Preserved in the Public Record Office, The British Museum, and Elsewhere in England, ed. J.S. Brewer, J. Gairdner and R.H. Brodie, 21 vols (Kew, List and Index Society, Public Record Society, 1862–1965), various volumes.

Marlowe, Christopher, *The Poems*, ed. Millar Maclure (London: Methuen, 1968).

Parsons, Robert, *A Temperate Ward-Word, to the Turbulent and Seditious Wach-Word of Sir Francis Hastinges Knight, Who Indevoreth to Slaunder the Whole Catholique Cause, & All Professors Therof, Both at Home and Abrode* (Menston, Scolar Press,1599).

Register of Henry Chichele, ed. E. F. Jacob (Canterbury and York Series, vol. 47, 1947).

Registrum Statutorum et Consuetudinum Ecclesiae Cathedralis Sancti Pauli Londensis, ed. W. Sparrow Simpson (London, 1873).

Scot, Reginald, *The Discoverie of Witchcraft* (London, W. Brome, 1584).

Simmons, Menno, *Complete Writings of Menno Simons, c.1496–1561*, trans. L. Verduin, ed. J. Christian Wenger (Scottdale, PA, Herald Press, 1956).

Testamenta Cantiana: East Kent, ed. A. Hussey (London, 1907).

The Chronicle and Political Papers of King Edward VI, ed. W.K. Jordan (London, Allen & Unwin, 1966).

The Correspondence of Sir Thomas More, ed. E.F. Rogers (Princeton, Princeton University Press, 1947).

The Letters of Sir John Hackett, 1526–1534, ed. E.F. Rogers (Morgantown, 1971)

The Life and Letters of Thomas Cromwell, ed. R. Bigelow Merriman, 2 vols (Cambridge, OUP, 1902), vol. 1.

The Lisle Letters, ed. M. St Clare Byrne, 6 vols (Chicago, Chicago University Press, 1981).

The Reports of Sir John Spelman, ed. J.H. Baker, 2 vols (London, Selden Society, 1977–78).

The Statutes of the Realm, 12 vols (London, 1810–28).

Three Chapters of Letters Relating to the Suppression of Monasteries, ed. T. Wright (London, Camden Society, 1843).

Tyndale, William, *The Obedience of a Christian Man*, reprinted in *Doctrinal Treatises*, ed. H. Walter (Cambridge, Parker Society, 1848).

Tyndale, William, *An Answer to Sir Thomas More's Dialogue*, ed. H. Walter (Cambridge, Parker Society, 1850).

Voragine, Jacobus de, *The Golden Legend: Readings on the Saints*, trans. W. Granger Ryan, 2 vols (Princeton, Princeton University Press, 1993).

Wolters, C. (ed.), *The Cloud of Unknowing and other works*, translated with an introduction by C. Wolters (London, Penguin, 1967 and 1978).

Reference Works

Oxford Dictionary of National Biography, ed. H.C.G. Matthew and Brian Harrison, 60 vols (Oxford, Oxford University Press, 2004; online edition May 2005)

Secondary Sources

Ackroyd, P., *The Life of Thomas More* (London, Chatto and Windus, 1999).

Adamson, J.W., 'The Extent of Literacy in England in the Fifteenth and Sixteenth Centuries', *The Library*, 4th Series, 10 (1930): 162–93.

Aers, D., *Sanctifying Signs. Making Christian Tradition in Late Medieval England* (Notre Dame, Indiana, University of Notre Dame Press, 2004).

———, Altars of Power: 'Reflections on Eamon Duffy's *The Stripping of the Altars: Traditional Religion in England, 1400–1580*', *Literature & History*, 3rd Series, 3 (1994): 90–105.

Anderson, J., and Sauer, E. (eds), *Books and Readers in Early Modern England (Material Studies)* (Pensylvania, University of Pennsylvania Press, 2001).

Andrewes, J., 'Industries in Kent, *c.* 1500–1640', in M. Zell, *Early Modern Kent*.

Andriessen, J., 'De vroomheid in het middeleeuwse Vlaanderen', *Ons Geestelijk Erf*, 36 (1962): 423–31.

Angenendt, A., *Geschichte der Religiosität im Mittelalter* (Darmstadt, Primus Verlag, 2000).

Anon., *The Wound of Love: A Carthusian Miscellany* (London, Darton, Longman & Todd, 1994).

Archer, I., 'The Charity of Early Modern Londoners', *Transactions of the Royal Historical Society*, 6th Series, 12 (2002): 223–44.

Assunto, R., *Die Theorie des Schönen im Mittelalter* (2nd edition, Cologne, 1996).

Aston, M., *Lollards and Reformers: Images and Literacy in Late Medieval Religion* (London, Hambledon, 1984).

———, *England's Iconoclasts, I: Laws Against Images* (Oxford, OUP, 1988).

———, 'Gods, Saints and Reformers: Portraiture and Protestant England', in L. Gent (ed.), *Albion's Classicism: The Visual Arts in Britain 1550–1660*.

————, 'Iconoclasm in England: Official and Clandestine', in P. Marshall (ed.), *The Impact of the English Reformation 1500–1640*.

Atchley, E.G.C.F., 'Jesus Mass and Anthem', *Transactions of the St Pauls Ecclesiological Society*, 5 (1905).

Axters, S.M., 'l'Abbé Jacques Toussaert et l'Histoire du *Sentiment Religieux en Flandre à la Fin du Moyen*-Age', *Supplément de la Vie Spirituelle*, 16 (1963): 574–84.

Barry, J., and Jones, C. (eds), *Medicine and Charity Before the Welfare State* (London and New York, Routledge, 1991).

Bassett, S. (ed.), *Death in Towns: Urban Responses to the Dying and the Dead 100–1600* (London, Leicester University Press, 1995).

Bennett, H.S., 'Printers, Authors, and Readers, 1475–1557', *The Library*, 5th Series, 4 (1949): 155–65.

Bennett, M., 'Education and Advancement', in R. Horrox (ed.), *Fifteenth-Century Attitudes: Perceptions of Society in Late Medieval England*.

Bentley, J.H., *Humanists and Holy Writ: New Testament Scholarship in the Renaissance* (Princeton, Princeton University Press, 1983).

Bernard, G.W., 'Vitality and Vulnerability in the Late Medieval Church: Pilgrimage on the Eve of the Break with Rome', in J.L. Watts (ed.), *The End of the Middle Ages? England in the Fifteenth and Sixteenth Centuries*.

Besnier, N., *Literacy, Emotion, Authority: Reading and Writing on a Polynesian Atoll*, Studies in the Social and Cultural Foundations of Language, 17 (Cambridge, New York, Melbourne, CUP, 1995).

Bestul, T.H., *Texts of the Passion: Latin Devotional Literature and Medieval Society* (Philadelphia, University of Philadelphia Press, 1996).

Bietenholz, P.G. (ed.), *Contemporaries of Erasmus: A Biographical Register of the Renaissance and Reformation*, 3 vols (Toronto, University of Toronto Press, 1986).

Blake, H., Egan, G., Hurst, J., and New, E., 'From Popular Devotion to Resistance and Revival in England: the Cult of the Holy Name of Jesus and the Reformation', in D. Gaimster, and R. Gilchrist (eds), *The Archaeology of Reformation, 1480–1580*.

Blickle, P. (ed.), *Resistance, Representation and Community* (Oxford, Clarendon, 1997).

Bloch, M.E.F., *How We Think They Think: Anthropological Approaches to Cognition, Memory, and Literacy* (Boulder, Colorado–Oxford, Westview Press, 1998).

Boffey, J., 'Women Authors and Women's Literacy in Fourteenth and Fifteenth-Century England', in C. Meale (ed.), *Women & Literature in Britain, 1150–1500*.

Bossy, J. (ed.), *Disputes and Settlements: Law and Human Relations in the West* (Cambridge, CUP, 1983).

Bower, J., 'Kent Towns, 1540–1640', in M. Zell (ed.), *Early Modern Kent*.

Bowers, R.H., 'Middle English Verses on the Founding of the Carthusian Order', *Speculum*, 42/4 (October 1967): 710–13.

Boyarin, J. (ed.), *The Ethnography of Reading* (London, University of California Press, 1993).

Bradshaw, B., and Duffy, E. (eds), *Humanism, Reform and the Reformation: The Career of Bishop John Fisher* (Cambridge, CUP 1989).

Bredero, A., *De ontkerstening der middeleeuwen* (Kampen, Pelckmans, 2001).

Brietz Monta, S., *Martyrdom and Literature in Early Modern England* (Cambridge, CUP, 2005).

Brigden, S., *London and the Reformation* (Oxford, Clarendon, 1989).

Brown, A., *Popular Piety in Late Medieval England: The Diocese of Salisbury 1250–1550* (Oxford, OUP, 1995).

Bryson, A., 'The Rhetoric of Status: Gesture, Demeanour and the Image of the Gentleman in Sixteenth and Seventeenth Century England', in L. Gent and N. Llewellyn (eds), *The Human Figure in English Culture c.1540–1660*.

Burgess, C., '"Longing to be prayed for": Death and Commemoration in an English Parish in the Middle Ages', in B. Gordon and P. Marshall (eds), *The Place of the Dead: Death and Remembrance in Late Medieval and Early Modern Europe*.

———, 'London Parishioners in Times of Change: St Andrew Hubbard, Eastcheap, c. 1450–1570', *Journal of Ecclesiastical History*, 53/1 (2002): 38–63.

Burke, P., *The French Historical Revolution. The Annales School, 1929–89* (Cambridge, CUP, 1990).

———, 'How to be a Counter-Reformation Saint', in Kaspar von Greyerz (ed.), *Religion and Society in Early Modern Europe 1500–1800*.

Burns, J.H. (ed.), *The Cambridge History of Medieval Political Thought, c. 350 – c. 1450*, (Cambridge, CUP, 1988).

Butcher, A.F., 'The Hospital of St Stephen and St Thomas, New Romney: the documentary evidence', *AC*, 96 (1980).

———, 'The Functions of Script in the Speech Community of a Late Medieval Town, *c.* 1300–1550', in A. Walsham and J. Crick (eds), *The Uses of Script and Print, 1300–1700*.

Butterworth, C.C., *The English Primers (1529–1545): Their Publication and Connection with the English Bible and the Reformation in England* (Philadelphia, University of Pensylvania Press, 1953).

Carlson, E., 'English Funeral Sermons as Sources: The Example of Female Piety in pre-1640 Sermons', *Albion*, 32/4 (2000): 567–97.

Cavallo, G., and Chartier, R. (eds), *A History of Reading in the West* (Cambridge, Polity, 1997).

Cavello, S., 'The Motivations of Benefactors: An Overview of Approaches to the Study of Charity', in J. Barry and C. Jones (eds), *Medicine and Charity Before the Welfare State*.

Charney, E., and Mack, P. (eds), *England and the Continental Renaissance: Essays in Honour of J.B. Trapp* (Woodbridge, Boydell, 1990).

Chartier, R., *Cultural History: Between Practices and Representations*, trans. L.G. Cochrane (Oxford, Polity in association with Blackwell, 1988).

———— (ed.), *The Culture of Print: Power and the Uses of Print in Early Modern Europe* (Cambridge, Polity, 1989).

Chaunu, P., *La Mort à Paris 16e 17e 18e Siècles* (Paris, Presses Universitaires de France, 1978).

Chiffoleau, J., *La Comptabilité de l'Au-delà: les Hommes, la Mort et la Religion dans la Région d'Avignon à la Fin du Moyen Age (vers 1320–vers 1480)* (Rome, 1980).

Christian, W.A., Jr, *Person and God in a Spanish Valley* (Princeton, New Jersey–Guildford, Princeton University Press, 1989).

Clanchy, M.T., *From Memory to Written Record: England 1066–1377* (2nd edition, Oxford–Cambridge, Mass., Blackwell, 1993).

————, 'Images of Ladies with Prayer Books: What do they Signify?', in R. Swanson (ed.), *The Church and the Book*.

Clark, P., *English Provincial Society from the Reformation to the Revolution: Religion, Politics and Society in Kent 1500–1640* (Hassocks, Harvester Press, 1977).

————, and Slack, P., *English Towns in Transition 1500–1700* (London and New York, OUP, 1976).

Clifford, J., and Marcus, G. (eds) *Writing Culture*: *The Poetics and Politics of Ethnography* (Berkeley, University of California Press, 1986).

Cohn, S., *Death and Property in Siena, 1205–1800: Strategies for the Afterlife* (Baltimore and London, Johns Hopkins University Press, 1988).

Cole, C.R., and Moody, M.E. (eds), *The Dissenting Tradition: Essays for Leland H. Carlson* (Athens, Ohio, Ohio University Press, 1975).

Coleman, J., *Public Reading and the Reading Public in Late Medieval England and France* (Cambridge, CUP, 1996).

Collinson, P., *Godly People: Essays in Protestantism and Puritanism* (London, Hambledon, 1983).

————, *From Iconoclasm to Iconophobia: The Cultural Impact of the Second English Reformation* (The Stenton Lecture, Reading, University of Reading, 1985).

————, '"Not Sexual in the Ordinary Sense": Women, Men and Religious Transactions', in *Elizabethan Essays* (London, Hambledon, 1994).

————, 'A Magazine of Religious Patterns: An Erasmian Topic Transposed in English Protestantism', in D. Baker (ed.), *Renaissance and Renewal in Christian History, SCH*, 14 (1977): 223–49.

————, 'Cranbrook and the Fletchers: Popular and Unpopular Religion in the Kentish Weald', in P. Collinson, *Godly People: Essays in Protestantism and Puritanism*.

————, 'Critical Conclusion' in M. Spufford (ed.), *The World of Rural Dissenters*.

————, 'From Iconoclasm to Iconophobia: The Cultural Impact of the Second English Reformation', in P. Marshall (ed.), *The Impact of the English Reformation 1500–1640*.

————, 'The Protestant Cathedral, 1541–1660', in P. Collinson, N. Ramsay and M. Sparks (eds), *A History of Canterbury Cathedral*.

————, 'Towards a Broader Understanding of the Early Dissenting Tradition', in C.R. Cole and M.E. Moody (eds), *The Dissenting Tradition: Essays for Leland H. Carlson*.

————, 'Truth, Lies and Fiction in Sixteenth Century Protestant Historiography', in D. Kelly and D. Harris Sacks (eds), *The Historical Imagination in Early Modern Britain*.

————, 'Night Schools, Conventicles and Churches: Continuities and Discontinuities in Early Protestant Ecclesiology', in P. Marshall and A. Ryrie (eds), *The Beginnings of English Protestantism*.

Collinson, P., Ramsay, N. and Sparks, M. (eds), *A History of Canterbury Cathedral* (Oxford, OUP, 1995).

Constant, G., *The Reformation in England*, 2 vols (London, Sheed and Ward, 1934), vol. 1, *The English Schism. Henry VIII. (1509–1547)*.

Coogan, R., *Erasmus, Lee and the Correction of the Vulgate: The Shaking of the Foundations* (Geneva, Droz, 1992).

Copenhaver, B.P., and Schmitt, C.B., *Renaissance Philosophy* (Oxford, OUP, 1992).

Coppack, G., and Aston, M., *Christ's Poor Men. The Carthusians in England* (Stroud, Tempus, 2002).

Cornwall, J., *Wealth and Society in Early Sixteenth-Century England* (London, Routledge and Kegan Paul, 1988).

Crankshaw, D.J., 'Knell, Thomas the elder', *ODNB*, vol. 31, pp. 874–5.

Crawford, P., *Women and Religion in England, 1500–1720* (London, Routledge, 1993).

Cressy, D., *Birth, Marriage and Death: Ritual Religion and the Life-Cycle in Tudor and Stuart England* (Oxford, OUP, 1997).

Cross, C., 'The Development of Protestantism in Leeds and Hull, 1520–1640: The Evidence from Wills', *Northern History*, 18 (1982): 230–38.

Darnton, R., *The Kiss of Lamourette: Reflections in Cultural History* (London, Norton, 1990).

Daunton, M. (ed.), *Charity, Self-interest and Welfare in the English Past* (London, University College London Press, 1996).

Davis, J.F., *Heresy and Reformation in the South East of England 1520–1559* (London, Swift Printers, 1983).

————, 'Lollard Survival and the Textile Industry in the South-East of England', in G.J. Cuming (ed.), *SCH*, 3 (1966): 191–201.

————, 'Joan of Kent, Lollardy, and the English Reformation', *Journal of Ecclesiastical History*, 32/2 (1982): 225–33.

Day, M., *The Wheatley Manuscript, Early English Text Society*, Original Series, No. 155 (London, Early English Text Society, 1921).

Deanesly, M., 'Vernacular Books in the Fourteenth and Fifteenth Centuries', *Modern Language Review*, 15 (1920): 349–58.

Decavele, J., 'Vroege Reformatorische bedrijvigheid in de grote Nederlandse steden. Claes van de Elst te Brussel, Antwerpen, Amsterdam en Leiden (1524–1528)', *Nederlands archief voor kerkgeschiedenis*, 70 (1990).

Derrett, J.D.M., 'Sir Thomas More and the Nun of Kent', *Moreana*, 15 and 16 (1967).

Despres, D.L., 'Ecstatic Reading and Missionary Mysticism: *The Orchard* of Syon', in R.Voaden (ed.), *Prophets Abroad: the Reception of Continental Holy Women in Late-Medieval England.*

Devereux, E.J., 'Elizabeth Barton and Tudor Censorship', *Bulletin of the John Rylands Library*, 49 (1966): 91–106.

Dickens, A.G., *Lollards and Protestants in the Diocese of York* (London, University of Hull, 1959)

———, *The English Reformation* (2nd edition, London, Hambledon Press,1989)

———, 'The Early Expansion of Protestantism in England, 1520–1558', *Archiv fur Reformationsgeschichte*, 78 (1987): 187–90.

Dierickx, S.J., 'Beoordeling van *Le sentiment Religieux à la Fin du Moyen-Age* van Jacques Toussaert', *Handelingen van de Koninklijke Zuidnederlandse Maatschappij voor Taal- en Letterkunde en Geschiedenis*, 19 (1965): 319–37.

Dieterich, D.H., *Brotherhood and Community on the Eve of the Reformation: Confraternities and Parish life in Liege, 1450–1540* (Michigan, 1982).

Dowling, Maria, *Fisher of Men: a Life of John Fisher, 1469–1535* (Basingstoke, Macmillan, 1999).

Draper, G.M., 'The Farmers of Canterbury Cathedral Priory and All Souls College Oxford on Romney Marsh c.1443–1545', in J. Eddison, M Gardiner and A. Long (eds), *Romney Marsh: Environmental Change and Human Occupation in a Coastal Lowland.*

———, and Meddens, F., *The Sea and the Marsh; the Medieval Cinque Port of New Romney* (Pre-Construct Archaeology monograph, forthcoming).

———, 'Church, Chapel and Clergy on Romney Marsh after the Black Death', *Romney Marsh Irregular*, 16 (October 2000): 6–8.

———, 'Small Fields and Wet Land: Inheritance Practices and the Transmission of Real Property in the Romney Marshes c.1150–1390', *Landscapes*, 6 (Spring 2005): 18–45.

Du Boulay, F.R.H., *The Lordship of Canterbury: An Essay on Medieval Society* (London, Nelson, 1966).

Duffy, E., *The Stripping of the Altars: Traditional Religion in England, 1400–1580* (London, New Haven, 1992, revised edition 2005).

———, *The Voices of Morebath: Reformation and Rebellion in an English Village* (New Haven–London, Yale University Press, 2001).

————, 'Continuity and Divergence in Tudor Religion', in R.N. Swanson (ed.), *Continuity and Change in Christian Worship*, *SCH*, 32 (1996).

————, 'The Spirituality of John Fisher', in B. Bradshaw and E. Duffy, E. (eds), *Humanism, Reform and the Reformation: The Career of Bishop John Fisher* (Cambridge, CUP 1989).

Eddison, J., *The World of the Changing Coastline* (London, Faber, 1979).

————, Gardiner, M., and Long, A. (eds), *Romney Marsh: Environmental Change and Human Occupation in a Coastal Lowland* (Oxford, Oxford University, Committee for Archaeology, 1998).

Edwards, E., 'Education 1500–1700', in T. Lawson and D. Killingray, *An Historical Atlas of Kent*.

Eisenstein, E., *Printing Press as an Agent of Change: Communications and Cultural Transformations in Early Modern Europe* (Cambridge, CUP, 1980).

Elton, G., *Star Chamber Stories* (London, Methuen & Co., 1958).

————, *Policy and Police: The Enforcement of the Reformation in the Age of Thomas Cromwell* (Cambridge, CUP, 1972).

Erler, M.C., 'Devotional Literature', in L. Hellinga and J.B. Trapp (eds), *The Cambridge History of the Book in Britain, 1400–1557*.

Evans, N., 'The Descent of Dissenters in the Chiltern Hundreds', in M. Spufford (ed.), *The World of Rural Dissenters*.

Everitt, A.M., *Continuity and Colonization: The Evolution of Kentish Settlement*, (Leicester, Leicester University Press, 1986).

————, 'Nonconformity in Country Parishes', *The Agricultural History Review*, 18, *Land, Church and People: Essays Presented to Professor H. P. R. Finberg*, ed. J. Thirsk (1970 supplement): 178–99.

————, 'The Making of the Agrarian Landscape of Kent', *AC*, 92 (1976): 1–31.

Fabian, J., 'Keep Listening: Ethnography and Reading', in J. Boyarin (ed.) *The Ethnography of Reading*.

Faith, R.J., 'The "Great Rumour" of 1377 and Peasant Ideology', in R.H. Hilton and T.H. Aston (eds), *The English Rising of 1381*.

Finch, J., '"According to the Quality and Degree of the Person Deceased": Funeral Monuments and the Construction of Social Identities 1450–1700', *Scottish Archaeological Review*, 8 (1991): 105–14.

Fleming, P., 'Charity, Faith and the Gentry of Kent 1422–1529', in A. Pollard (ed.), *Property and Politics: Essays in Late Medieval English History*.

Fletcher, A., 'The Protestant Idea of Marriage in Early Modern England', in A. Fletcher and P. Roberts (eds), *Religion, Culture and Society in Early Modern Britain. Essays in Honour of Patrick Collinson*.

————, and Roberts, P. (eds), *Religion, Culture and Society in Eearly Modern Britain. Essays in Honour of Patrick Collinson* (Cambridge, CUP, 1994).

Fox, A., *Oral and Literate Culture in England, 1500–1700* (Oxford, OUP, 2000).

Freeman, T.S., 'Early Modern Martyrs', *Journal of Ecclesiastical History*, 52/4 (2001): 696–701.

Gaimster, D, and Gilchrist, R. (eds), *The Archaeology of Reformation, 1480–1580* (London, Society for Post-Medieval Archaeology Monograph, 2003).

Gaillard, L. Review in *Revue d'Histoire Ecclésiastique*, 59 (1964): 307–8.

Garner, A., *Granny Reardun* (London, Collins, 1983).

Genard, P. 'Personen te Antwerpen in de XVIe eeuw, voor het "feit van religie" Gerechtelijk Vervolgd', *Antwerpsch Archievenblad*, 7 (n.d.).

Gent, L. (ed.), *Albion's Classicism: The Visual Arts in Britain 1550–1660* (London, Yale University Press, 1997).

———, and Llewellyn, N. (eds), *Renaissance Bodies: The Human Figure in English Culture c.1540–1660* (London, Reaction, 1990).

Gillespie, V., 'Vernacular Books of Religion', in J. Griffiths, and D. Pearsall (eds), *Book Production and Publishing in Britain, 1375–1475*.

———, 'Cura Pastoralis in Deserts', in M. Sergent (ed.), *De Cella in Seculum: Religious Secular Life and Devotion in Late Medieval England*.

———, 'Mystic's Foot: Rolle and Affectivity', in M. Glascoe (ed.), *The Medieval Mystical Tradition in England*.

———, and Doyle, I., (eds) *Catalogue of Syon Abbey with the Libraries of the Carthusians*, Corpus of British Medieval Library Catalogues, 9 (London, The British Library in association with the British Academy, 2001).

Gilmont, F., 'Protestant Reformations and Reading', in G. Cavallo and R. Chartier (eds), *History of Reading in the West*.

Ginzburg, C., *The Cheese and The Worms: The Cosmos of a Sixteenth Century Miller*, trans. J. and A. Tredeschi (London, Johns Hopkins University Press, 1981).

Gittings, C., *Death Burial and the Individual in Early Modern England* (London, Routledge, 1984).

———, 'The Urban Funeral in Late Medieval and Reformation England', in S. Bassett (ed.), *Death in Towns: Urban Responses to the Dying and the Dead 100–1600*.

Glascoe, M. (ed.), *The Medieval Mystical Tradition in England* (Exeter, Exeter University Press, 1982).

Gordon, B., and Marshall, P. (eds), *The Place of the Dead: Death and Remembrance in Late Medieval and Early Modern Europe* (Cambridge, CUP, 2000).

Goudriaan, K., 'Het einde van de Middeleeuwen ontdekt?', *Madoc*, 8 (1994): 66–75.

Green, I., *Print and Protestantism in Early Modern England* (Oxford, OUP, 2000).

Gregory, B.S., *Salvation at Stake: Christian Martyrdom in Early Modern Europe* (Cambridge, Mass., Harvard University Press, 1999).

Griffiths, J., and Pearsall, D. (eds), *Book Production and Publishing in Britain, 1375–1475* (Cambridge, CUP, 1989).

Haigh, C., *Reformation and Resistance in Tudor Lancashire* (London, CUP, 1975).

———, *English Reformations: Religion, Politics, and Society under the Tudors* (Oxford, Clarendon, 1993).

————, (ed.), *The English Reformation Revised* (Cambridge, CUP, 1987).

————, 'The Recent Historiography of the English Reformation', *Historical Journal*, 25 (1982): 995–1007.

————, 'Anticlericalism and the English Reformation', in C. Haigh (ed.), *The English Reformation Revised*.

————, Review of M. Bowker, *The Henrician Reformation. The Diocese of Lincoln under John Longland, 1521–1547* (Cambridge 1981), *English Historical Review*, 48 (1983): 371.

Halkin, L., *De biografie van Erasmus* (Baarn, 1987).

————, *Erasmus: A Critical Biography*, trans. J. Tonkin (Oxford, Blackwell 1993).

Hanna III, R., '"Meddling with Makings" and Will's Work', in A.J. Minnis (ed.), *Late Medieval Religious Texts and their Transmission. Chapters in Honour of A.I. Doyle*.

Hasted, E., *The History and Topographical Survey of the County of Kent* (Canterbury, 1797–1801).

Heal, F., *Reformation in Britain and Ireland* (Oxford, OUP, 2003).

Heath, P., *The English Parish Clergy on the Eve of the Reformation* (London, Routledge, 1969).

Hellinga, L., and Trapp, J.B. (eds), *The Cambridge History of the Book in Britain 1400–1557*, 5 vols (Cambridge, CUP, 1999).

Henderson, J., *Piety and Charity in Late Medieval Florence* (Chicago and London, University of London Press, 1997).

Hickman, D., 'From Catholic to Protestant: The Changing Meaning of Testamentary Religious Provisions in Elizabeth London', in N. Tyacke (ed.), *England's Long Reformation 1500–1800*.

Higgs, L.M., *Godliness and Governance in Tudor Colchester* (Michigan, University of Michigan Press, 1998).

Hill, C., 'From Lollards to Levellers', in *Collected Essays of Christopher Hill, II: Religion and Politics in Seventeenth-Century England*, vol. 3 (Brighton, Harvester Press, 1986).

Hilton, R.H., and Aston, T.H (eds), *The English Rising of 1381* (Cambridge, CUP, 1984).

Hoeppner Moran, J.A., *The Growth of English Schooling, 1340–1548: Learning, Literacy, and Laicization in Pre-Reformation York Diocese* (Princeton, Princeton University Press, 1985).

Hogg, J., 'Richard Methley – To Hew Heremyte a Pystyl of Solytary Lyfe Nowadayes', *Analecta Cartusiana*, 31 (1977): 91–119.

Honée, E., 'Image and Imagination in the Medieval Culture of Prayer: A Historical Perspective', in H. Van Os (ed.), *The Art of Devotion*.

Hope, A., 'Plagiarising the Word of God: Tyndale between More and Joye', in P. Kewes (ed.), *Plagiarism in Early Modern England*.

————, 'Bocher, Joan (d.1550)', *ODNB*, vol. 6, pp. 387–8.

Hoppenbrouwers, R.C.M.,'De broederschap van Onze-Lieve-Vrouw te Heusden', in D.E.H. de Boer & J.W. Marsilje (ed.), *De Nederlanden in de late middeleeuwen* (Utrecht, Het Spectrum,1987).

Horden, P., 'A Discipline of Relevance: The Historiography of the Later Medieval Hospital', *Social History of Medicine*, 1 (1988): 359–74.

Horrox, R. (ed.), *Fifteenth-Century Attitudes: Perceptions of Society in Late Medieval England* (Cambridge, CUP, 1994).

Horsfield, Rev. R.A., 'The Pomander of Prayer: Aspects of Late Medieval Carthusian Spirituality and its Lay Audience', in M. G. Sargent, *De Cella in Seculum: Religious and Secular Life and Devotion in Late Medieval England*.

Houston, R., *Literacy in Early Modern Europe: Culture and Education 1500–1800* (London, Longman, 1998, this edition 2002).

Howarth, D, *Images of Rule: Art and Politics in the English Renaissance 1485–1649* (London, Macmillan, 1997).

Hudson, A., *The Premature Reformation: Wycliffite Texts and Lollard History* (Oxford, OUP, 1988).

———, 'The Examination of Lollards', *BIHR*, 46 (1973): 145–59.

Hugenholtz, F.W.N., "Le Déclin du Moyen Age (1919–1969)", *Acta historiae neerlandica*, 5 (1971): 40–51.

———, 'The Fame of a Masterwork', in W.R.H. Koops, E.H. Kossman, van der Plaat, G. (ed.), *Johan Huizinga 1872–1972: Papers Delivered to the Johan Huizinga Conference, Groningen 11–15 December 1972* (Den Haag, Nijhoff, 1973), pp. 91–3.

Hughes, P., *The Reformation in England*, 3 vols (London, 1950, 5th edition, 1963), vol. 1, *The King's Proceedings*.

Huizinga, J., *Herfsttij der Middeleeuwen. Studie over Levens– en gedachtenvormen der veertiende en Vijftiende Eeuw in Frankrijk en de Nederlanden* (Haarlem, 1919).

———, *The Autumn of the Middle Ages*, trans. Rodney J. Payton and Ulrich Mammitzsch (Chicago, University of Chicago Press, 1996).

———, *Verzamelde werken* III (Haarlem, 1949), pp. 180–278.

Humphrey, C., and Laidlaw, J., *The Archetypal Actions of Ritual: A Theory of Ritual Illustrated by the Jain Rite of Worship* (Oxford, OUP, 1994).

Hussey, S.S., 'The Audience for the Middle English Mystics', in M.G. Sargent (ed.), *De Cella in Seculum: Religious and Secular Life and Devotion in Late Medieval England*.

Hutchinson, A., 'Devotional Reading in the Monastery and in the Household', in M. G. Sargent (ed.), *De Cella in Seculum: Religious Secular Life and Devotion in Late Medieval England*.

Hutchinson, R., *The Image of God or Layman's Book*, in *The Works of Roger Hutchinson*, ed. J. Bruce (Cambridge, 1842).

Hutton, R., 'The English Reformation and the Evidence of Folklore', *Past and Present*, 148 (1995): 89–116.

Hyde, P., and Zell, M., 'Governing the County', in M. Zell, *Early Modern Kent*.

Jack, S.M., 'Manwood, Sir Roger (1524/5–1592)', *ODNB* (online edition May 2005).

Jansen, S.L., *Dangerous Talk and Strange Behaviour: Women and Popular Resistance to the Reforms of Henry VIII* (Basingstoke, Macmillan, 1996).

Jardine, L., and Grafton, A., *From Humanism to Humanities: Education and the Liberal Arts in Fifteenth- and Sixteenth-Century Europe* (London, Duckworth, 1986).

Jones, C., 'Some Recent Trends in the History of Charity', in M. Daunton (ed.), *Charity, Self-interest and Welfare in the English Past.*

Jones, N., *The English Reformation: Religion and Cultural Adaptation* (Oxford, Blackwell, 2002).

Jordan. W.K., *Philanthropy in England 1460–1660. A Study of the Changing Pattern of English Social Aspirations* (London, Russell Sage Foundation, 1959).

———, 'Social Institutions in Kent, 1480–1660: A Study of the Changing Patterns of Social Aspiration', *AC*, 75 (1961): 45–61.

Kelly, D., and Harris Sacks, D. (eds), *The Historical Imagination in Early Modern Britain* (Cambridge, Woodrow Wilson Center Press and CUP, 1997).

Kewes, P. (ed.), *Plagiarism in Early Modern England* (Basingstoke, Palgrave Macmillan, 2003).

Killingray, D. (ed.), *Sevenoaks People and Faith: Two Thousand Years of Religious Belief and Practice* (Chichester, Phillimore & Co, 2004).

Knowles, D., *The Religious Orders in England*, 3 vols (Cambridge, CUP, 1959), vol. 3, *The Tudor Age.*

Kruisheer, C.I., *De Onze Lieve Vrouwe-Broederschap, c. 1397-1580* (Annheim, Gysbers & Vanloon, 1976).

Krul, W.E., *Historicus tegen de tijd. Opstellen over Leven en Werk van J. Huizinga* (Groningen, Historische Uitgeverij, 1990).

Lambert, M., *Medieval Heresy: Popular Movements from the Gregorian Reform to the Reformation* (3rd edition, Oxford, OUP, 2002).

Latreille, A., Review in *Le Monde*, 5 October 1963.

Lawson, T., and Killingray, D., *An Historical Atlas of Kent* (Chichester: Phillimore & Co, 2004).

Le Goff, J. *La Civilisation de l'Occident Médiéval* (Paris, Blackwell, 1984).

———, *Medieval Civilisation 400–1500* (Oxford, Blackwell, 1988).

Lee, P., *Nunneries, Learning and Spirituality in Late Medieval English Society: The Dominican Priory of Dartford* (Woodbridge, Boydell, 2001).

Lewis, K.J., Menuge, N.J., and Phillips, K.M. (eds), *Young Medieval Women* (Stroud, Sutton, 1999).

Lewis, K.J., 'Model Girls? Virgin-Martyrs and the Training of Young Women in Late Medieval England', in K.J. Lewis, N.J. Menuge, and K.M. Phillips (eds), *Young Medieval Women.*

Llewellyn, N., *Art of Death: Visual Culture in the English Death Ritual c.1500–c.1800* (London, Reaktion, 1991).

——, '"Plinie is a Weyghtye Witnesse": The Classical Reference in Post-Reformation Funeral Monuments', in L. Gent (ed.), *Albion's Classicism: The Visual Arts in Britain 1550–1660*.

——, 'Accident or Design? John Gildon's Funeral Monuments and Italianate Taste in Elizabethan England', in E. Charney and P. Mack (eds), *England and the Continental Renaissance: Essays in Honour of J.B. Trapp*.

——, 'Claims to Status through Visual Codes: Heraldry on post-Reformation Funeral Monuments', in S. Anglo (ed.), *Chivalry in the Renaissance* (Woodbridge, Boydell, 1990).

——, 'Honour in Life, Death and Memory: Funeral Monuments in Early Modern England', *Transactions of the Royal Historical Society* 6th Series, 6 (1996): 179–200.

Lockhart, R.B. (ed.), *"O bonitas!" Hushed to Silence: a Carthusian Monk* (Salzburg, University of Salzburg Press, 2000).

Lutton, R., *Lollardy and Orthodox Religion in Pre-Reformation England: Reconstructing Piety* (Woodbridge, Boydell, 2006).

——, 'Godparenthood, Kinship, and Piety in Tenterden, England 1449–1537', in I. Davis, M. Müller and S. Rees Jones (eds), *Love, Marriage and Family Ties in the Later Middle Ages* (Turnhout, Brepols. 2003).

MacCulloch, D., *Thomas Cranmer, A Life* (New Haven, Yale University Press, 1996).

——, *Tudor Church Militant: Edward VI and the Protestant Reformation* (London, Allen Lane, 1999).

——, *Reformation: Europe's House Divided 1490–1700* (London, Allen Lane, 2003).

Maclean, I., *The Renaissance Notion of Woman: A Study in the Fortunes of Scholasticism and Medical Science in European Intellectual Life* (Cambridge, CUP, 1980).

Marks, R., *Image and Devotion in Late Medieval England* (Stroud, Sutton, 2004).

Marsh, C., *Popular Religion in Sixteenth-Century England* (Basingstoke–London, Macmillan, 1998).

Marshall, P., *Beliefs and the Dead in Reformation England* (Oxford, OUP, 2002).

——, *Reformation England, 1480–1642* (London, Arnold, 2003).

——, (ed.), *The Impact of the English Reformation 1500–1640* (London, Arnold, 1997).

——, and Ryrie, A. (eds), *The Beginnings of English Protestantism* (Cambridge, CUP, 2002).

——, 'Evangelical Conversion in the Reign of Henry VIII', in P. Marshall and A. Ryrie (eds), *The Beginnings of English Protestantism*.

——, and Ryrie, A., 'Protestantisms and their Beginnings', in P. Marshall and A. Ryrie (ed.), *The Beginnings of English Protestantism*.

——, 'Forgery and Miracles in the Reign of Henry VIII', *Past and Present*, 178 (2003): 39–73.

Martin, D., and Martin, B., *New Winchelsea, Sussex: A Medieval Port Town* (London, Heritage Marketing and Publications, 2004).

Martin, D.M., *Fifteenth Century Carthusian Reform. The World of Nicholas Kempf* (Leiden–New York–Cologne, Brill, 1992).

Mayhew, G., 'The Progress of the English Reformation in East Sussex 1530–1559: The Evidence from Wills', *Southern History*, 5 (1983): 38–67.

McConica, J.K., 'Warden Hovenden', *Unarmed Soldiery: Studies in the Early History of All Souls College Oxford*, The Chichele Lectures, 1993–4 (Oxford, All Souls College, 1996).

———, 'John Fisher of Beverley, 1469–22 June 1535', in P.G. Bietenholz (ed.), *Contemporaries of Erasmus: A Biographical Register of the Renaissance and Reformation* (Toronto, Buffalo, University of Toronto Press, 1985–87).

McSheffrey, S., 'Heresy, Orthodoxy and English Vernacular Religion 1480–1525', *Past and Present*, 186 (2005): 47–80.

Meale, C.(ed.), *Women & Literature in Britain, 1150–1500* (Cambridge, CUP, 1993).

———, *Readings in Medieval English Romance* (Cambridge, CUP, 1994).

Meale, C., '"…alle the bokes that I have of latyn, englisch, and frensch": Laywomen and their Books in Late Medieval England', in C. Meale (ed.), *Women & Literature in Britain, 1150–1500*.

———, '"gode men/ Wiues maydnes and alle men": Romance and its Audiences', in C. Meale (ed.), *Readings in Medieval English Romance*.

Meyers-Reinquin, A-M., 'Repertorium van de kerkfabrieksrekeningen in Oost- en West-Vlaanderen. Einde 14de eeuw tot 1630', *De Leiegouw*, 12 (1970): 29–48.

———, 'Proeve tot statistische benadering van de godsdienstpraktijk in de Late middeleeuwen en de moderne tijden (tot 1630) aan de hand van de Kerkfabrieksrekeningen', in *Handelingen der Koninklijke Zuidnederlandse Maatschappij voor Taal- en Letterkunde en Geschiedenis*, 23 (1969): 205–273.

Milis, L., 'De devotionele praktijk in de Laat-middeleeuwse Nederlanden', in J.D. Janssen (ed.), *Hoofsheid en devotie in de middeleeuwse maatschappij. De Nederlanden van de 12^e tot de 15^e eeuw. Handelingen van het Wetenschappelijk Colloquium te Brussel 21–24 Oktober 1981* (Brussels, Amsterdam University Press, 1982).

Minnis, A.J. (ed.), *Late Medieval Religious Texts and their Transmission. Chapters in Honour of A.I. Doyle* (Cambridge, CUP, 1994).

Mol, J.A., 'Friezen en het hiernamaals. Zielheilsbeschikkingen ten gunste van kerken, kloosters en armen in testamenten uit Friesland tot 1580', in N. Lettinck and J.J. van Moolenbroek (eds), *In de schaduw van de eeuwigheid. Tien studies aangeboden aan prof. dr A.H. Bredero* (Utrecht, 1986), revised reprint in J.A. Mol (ed.), *Zorgen voor Zekerheid. Studies over Friese Testamenten in de Vijftiende en Zestiende Eeuw* (Leeuwarden, 1994).

Mols, S.J., 'Emploi et Valeur des Statistiques en Histoire Religieuse, *Nouvelle Revue Théologique*, 86 (1964).

Moran, J. *Education and Learning in the City of York, 1300–1560* (York, Borthwick Institute of Historical Research, 1979).

Neame, A., *The Holy Maid of Kent: The Life of Elizabeth Barton, 1506–1543* (London, Hodder and Stoughton, 1971).

Neveux, H., and Osterburg, E., 'Norms and Values of the Peasantry in the Period of State Formation: a Comparative Interpretation', in P. Blickle (ed.), *Resistance, Representation and Community*.

Noordegraaf, J., *Hollands welvaren? Levensstandaard in Holland 1450–1650* (Bergen, Octavo, 1985).

Norris, M., 'Late Medieval Monumental Brasses: An Urban Funerary Industry and its Representation of Death', in S. Bassett (ed.), *Death in Towns: Urban Responses to the Dying and the Dead 100–1600*.

O'Hara, D., *Courtship and Constraint. Rethinking the Making of Marriage in Tudor England* (Manchester, Manchester University Press, 2000).

Orme, N., *English Schools in the Middle Ages* (London, Methuen, 1973).

————, *Education in the West of England, 1066–1548: Cornwall, Devon, Dorset, Gloucestershire, Somerset, Wiltshire* (Exeter, Exeter University Press, 1976).

Pacaut, M., Review in *Revue du Nord*, 46 (1964): 107–110.

Page, W. (ed.), *Victoria County History, Kent*, 3 vols (London, 1926), vol. 2.

Parker Pearson, M., *The Archaeology of Death and Burial* (Stroud, Sutton, 1999).

————, 'Mortuary Practices, Society and Ideology: An Ethnoarchaeological Study', in I. Hodder (ed.), *Symbolic and Structural Archaeology* (Cambridge, CUP, 1982).

Parkin, E., 'The Ancient Cinque Port of Sandwich', *AC*, 100 (1984): 189–216.

Peacey, J.T., 'Knell, Paul', *ODNB*, pp. 873–4.

Peacock, John, 'The Politics of Portraiture', in K. Sharpe and P. Lake (eds), *Culture and Politics in Early Stuart England* (London, Macmillan, 1994).

Penny, D.A., *Freewill or Predestination: The Battle Over Saving Grace in Mid-Tudor England* (Woodbridge, Boydell, 1990).

Personen G.P., te Antwerpen in de XVIe eeuw, voor het "feit van religie" Gerechtelijk Vervolgd', *Antwerpsch Archievenblad*, 7 (no date): 176.

Peters, C., *Patterns of Piety: Women, Gender and Religion in Late Medieval and Reformation England* (Cambridge, CUP, 2003).

Peters, E., and Simons, W.P., 'The New Huizinga and the Old Middle Ages', *Speculum*, 74 (1999): 587–620.

Pettegree, A., *Reformation and the Culture of Persuasion* (Cambridge, CUP 2005).

Pfaff, R.W., *New Liturgical Feasts in Later Medieval England* (Oxford, Clarendon, 1970).

Plumb, D., 'The Social and Economic Status of the Later Lollards', in M. Spufford (ed.), *The World of Rural Dissenters, 1520–1725*.

Polito, Mary, *Governmental Arts in Early Tudor England* (Aldershot, Ashgate, 2005).

Pollard, A. (ed.), *Property and Politics: Essays in Late Medieval English History* (Gloucester, Sutton, 1984).

Porter, H.C., 'Fisher and Erasmus', in B. Bradshaw and E. Duffy (eds), *Humanism, Reform and the Reformation*.

Purvis, J.S., *Select 16th Century Causes in Tithe* (London, York Archaeological Society, 1949).

Rapp, F., *L'Eglise et la Vie Religieuse en Occident à la Fin du Moyen Age* (Paris, Presses Universitaires de France, 1971).

Rex, R., *The Lollards* (Basingstoke, Palgrave Macmillan, 2000).

———, 'Gold, Henry (d.1534)', *ODNB*, vol. 22, p. 645.

———, 'The English Campaign against Luther in the 1520s', *Transactions of the Royal Historical Society*, 5th Series, 39 (1989): 85–106.

———, 'The Friars in the English Reformation', in P. Marshall and A. Ryrie (eds), *The Beginnings of English Protestantism*.

———, 'The Polemical Theologian', in P. Bradshaw and E. Duffy (eds) *Humanism, Reform and the Reformation*.

———, 'The Friars in the English Reformation', in P. Marshall and A. Ryrie (eds), *The Beginnings of English Protestantism*.

Reynolds, M., 'Reformation and Reaction, 1534–69', in D. Lawson and H. Killingray, *An Historical Atlas of Kent*.

Riddy, F., '"Women talking about the things of God": A Late Medieval Sub-Culture', in C. Meale (ed.) *Women & Literature in Britain, 1150–1500*.

Rigold, S., 'Two Kentish Hospitals Re-examined', *AC*, 79 (1964): 47–69.

Riley, H.T., 'The Manuscripts of New Romney Corporation', in *Fifth Report of the Royal Commission on Historical Manuscripts* (London, 1876)

Rosenthal, J.T., *The Purchase of Paradise. Gift Giving and the Aristocracy, 1307–1485* (London & Toronto, Routledge, 1972).

———, 'Aristocratic Cultural Patronage and Book Bequests, 1350–1500', *Bulletin of John Rylands University Library of Manchester,* 64 (1982): 522–48.

Ross, T.W., 'Five Emblem Verses in BL Additional 37049', *Speculum*, 32 (1957): 276–9.

Rublack, U., *Reformation Europe*. (Cambridge, CUP, 2005).

Ryrie, A., *The Gospel and Henry VIII: Evangelicals in the Early English Reformation* (Cambridge, CUP, 2003).

———, 'Britain and Ireland', in A. Ryrie (ed.), *Palgrave Advances in the European Reformations* (Basingstoke, Palgrave Macmillan, 2006).

Saenger, P., 'Books of Hours and the Reading Habits of the later Middle Ages', in R. Chartier (ed.), *The Culture of Print: Power and the Uses of Print in Early Modern Europe*.

Salter, E., *Cultural Creativity in the Early English Renaissance: Popular Culture in Town and Country* (London, Palgrave Macmillan, 2006).

Sargent, M.G., (ed.), *De Cella in Seculum: Religious and Secular Life and Devotion in Late Medieval England* (Cambridge, CUP, 1989).

———, 'The Transmission by the English Carthusians of some Late Medieval Spiritual Writings', *Journal of Ecclesiastical History,* 27/3 (1976): 225–40.

Scarisbrick, J.J., *The Reformation and the English People* (Oxford, Blackwell, 1984).

Scott, J.C., *Weapons of the Weak: Everyday Forms of Peasant Resistance* (Yale, Yale University Press, 1985).

―――, 'Resistance without Protest and without Organization: Peasant Opposition to the Islamic Zakat and the Christian Tithe', *Comparative Studies in Society and History*, 29 (1987): 417–52.

Scragg, B., *Sevenoaks School: A History* (Bath, Ashgrove,1993).

Selwyn,D.G., *The Library of Thomas Cranmer* (Oxford, Oxford Bibliographical Society, 1996).

Shagan, E.H., *Popular Politics and the English Reformation* (Cambridge, CUP, 2003).

Sharpe, J.A., '"Such Disagreement betwyx Neighbours": Litigation and Human Relations in Early Modern England', in J. Bossy (ed.), *Disputes and Settlements: Law and Human Relations in the West.*

Sharpe, K., and Zwicker, S. (eds), *Reading, Society and Politics in Early Modern England* (Cambridge, CUP, 2003).

Sheils, W.J., 'The Right of the Church: The Clergy, Tithe and the Courts at York 1540–1640', in W.J. Sheils and D. Wood (eds), *The Church and Wealth.*

―――, and Wood, D. (eds), *The Church and Wealth* (Oxford, Blackwell, 1987).

Simon, J., *Education and Society in Tudor England* (Cambridge, CUP, 1979).

Simpson, P., 'Tithe Litigation on Romney Marsh, 1371–1600', *Romney Marsh Irregular*, 22 (2003): 10–14.

Slootmans, K., 'De Hoge Lieve Vrouwe van Bergen op Zoom', in *Jaarboek Oudheidkundige Kring 'De Ghulden Roos'*, 24 (1964).

Spufford, M., *Small Books and Pleasant Histories: Popular Fiction and its Readership in Seventeenth-Century England* (Cambridge, CUP, 1981).

―――, (ed.), *The World of Rural Dissenters* (Cambridge, CUP, 1995).

―――, 'The Importance of Religion in the Sixteenth and Seventeenth Centuries', in M. Spufford (ed.), *The World of Rural Dissenters.*

Street, B., *Literacy in Theory and Practice,* Cambridge Studies in Oral and Literate Culture (Cambridge, CUP, 1984).

Strype, J., *Ecclesiastical Memorials*, 3 vols (Oxford, 1822).

Swanson, R.N., *Religion and Devotion in Europe, c. 1215–c. 1515* (Cambridge, CUP, 1995).

―――, (ed.), *Continuity and Change in Christian Worship*, SCH, 32 (Ecclesiastical History Society, Oxford, Boydell, 1996).

―――, (ed.), *The Church and the Book*, SCH, 38 (Ecclesiastical History Society, London, Boydell, 2004).

Sweetinburgh, S., *The Role of the Hospital in Medieval England. Gift-giving and the Spiritual Economy* (Dublin, Four Courts Press, 2004).

―――, 'Joining the Sisters: Female Inmates of the Late Medieval Hospitals in East Kent, *AC,* 123 (2003): 27–33.

———, 'Medieval Hospitals and Almshouses', in T. Lawson and D. Killingray (eds), *An Historical Atlas of Kent*.

———, 'The Territorial Organisation of the Church', in T. Lawson and D. Killingray (eds), *An Historical Atlas of Kent*.

Tanner, N.P., 'The Reformation and Regionalism: Further Reflections on the Church in Late Medieval Norwich', in J.A.F. Thomson (ed.), *Towns and Townspeople in the Fifteenth Century*.

Tanner, N.P., *The Church in Late Medieval Norwich* (Toronto, University of Toronto Press, 1984).

Taylor, A., 'Into his Secret Chamber', in J. Raven, H. Small, and N. Tadmor (eds), *The Practice and Representation of Reading in England* (Cambridge, CUP, 1996).

Taylor, A.H., 'The Rectors and Vicars of St Mildred's Tenterden. With an Appendix.' *AC*, 31 (1915): 207–24.

Thirsk, J. (ed.), *The Agrarian History of England and Wales 1500–1640* (Cambridge, CUP, 1967).

Thomas, K., 'Age and Authority in Early Modern England', *Proceedings of the British Academy*, 62 (1976): 205–248.

Thompson, E.M., *The Carthusian Order in England* (London, Society for Promoting Christian Knowledge, 1930).

Thomson, J.A.F., *The Later Lollards, 1414–1520* (Oxford, OUP, 1965).

———, (ed.), *Towns and Townspeople in the Fifteenth Century* (Gloucester, Sutton, 1987).

Todd, M., *Christian Humanism and the Puritan Social Order* (Cambridge, CUP, 1987).

Toussaert, J., *Le Sentiment Religieux en Flandre à la fin du Moyen-Age* (Paris, 1963).

Trio, P., 'Friese Testeerpraktijken', review of J.A. Mol (ed.), *Zorgen voor zekerheid. Studies over Friese testamenten in de vijftiende en zestiende eeuw* (Leeuwarden, 1994), *Signum*, 8 (1996): 47–58.

Trio, P., *Volksreligie als spiegel van een stedelijke samenleving. De broederschappen te Gent in de late middeleeuwen* (Leuven, Universitaire Pers Leuven, 1993).

Tyacke, N. (ed.), *England's Long Reformation 1500–1800* (London, University College London, 1998).

Underdown, D., *Revel, Riot and Rebellion: Popular Politics and Culture in England 1603–1660* (Oxford, Clarendon, 1985).

Usher, B., 'Knell, Thomas the younger', *ODNB*, vol. 31, pp. 875–6.

Van Dijck, G.C.M., *De Bossche Optimaten, Geschiedenis Van de Illustere Lieve Vrouwebroedershap te 's-Hertogenbosch, 1318-1973* (Tilburg, Stichting Zuidelijk Historisch Contact, 1973)

Van Engen, J., The Christian Middle Ages as an Historiographical Problem', *The American Historical Review*, 91 (1986): 519–52.

Van Herwaarden, J., 'Religion and Society: The Cult of the Eucharist and the Devotion to Christ's Passion', in J. Van Herwaarden, *Between Saint James and Erasmus: Studies in Late-Medieval Religious Life: Devotion and Pilgrimage in the Netherlands* (Leiden, Brill, 2003).

———, 'Medieval Indulgences and Devotional Life', in J. Van Herwaarden, *Between Saint James and Erasmus. Studies in Late-Medieval Religious Life: Devotion and Pilgrimage in the Netherlands* (Leiden, Brill, 2003).

———, and de Keyser, R., 'Het Gelovige Volk in de Late Middeleeuwen', *Algemene Geschiedenis der Nederlanden*, 4 (Haarlem,1980).

Van Os, H. (ed.) et al, *The Art of Devotion in the Late Middle Ages in Europe 1300–1500*, trans. from the Dutch by Michael Hoyle (London, Merrell Holberton, 1994).

Van Tongerloo, L., 'De financiering van de Dom', *Maandblad Oud-Utrecht*, 54 (1981): 167–9.

Verhoeven, G., *Devotie en negotie. Delft als bedevaartplaats in de Late middeleeuwen* (Amsterdam, Vu, 1992).

Viaene, A., 'Lichten op rood. Aantekeningen bij een werk van Jacques Toussaert', *Biekorf*, 64 (1963): 145–296.

Visser, C.Ch.G., *Luther's geschriften in de Nederlanden tot 1546* (Amsterdam, 1969).

Voaden, R. (ed.), *Prophets Abroad: the Reception of Continental Holy Women in Late-Medieval England* (Cambridge, CUP, 1996).

von Greyerz, K. (ed.), *Religion and Society in Early Modern Europe 1500–1800* (London, German Historical Institute, 1984).

Vovelle, M., *Piété Baroque et Déchristianisation en Provence au XVIIIe Siècle. Les Attitudes Devant la Mort d'Après les Clauses des Testaments* (Paris, Editions du C.T.H.S., 1973).

Vroom, W.H., *De financiering van de kathedraalbouw in de middeleeuwen, in het bijzonder van de dom van Utrecht* (Maarssen, Schwartz, 1981).

———, *De Onze-Lieve-Vrouwekerk te Antwerpen. De financiering van de Bouw tot de Beeldenstorm* (Antwerpen, 1983).

Wabuda, S., *Preaching During the English Reformation* (Cambridge, CUP, 2002).

Walsham, A., and Crick, J. (eds), *The Uses of Script and Print, 1300–1700* (Cambridge, CUP, 2004).

———, '"Frantick Hacket": Prophecy, Sorcery, Insanity and the Elizabethan Puritan Movement', *The Historical Journal*, 41/1 (1998): 27–66.

———, 'Preaching Without Speaking: Script, Print, and Religious Dissent', in A. Walsham and J. Crick (eds), *The Uses of Script and Print, 1300–1700*.

Watson, N., *Richard Rolle and the Invention of Authority* (Cambridge, CUP, 1991).

Watt, D., *Secretaries of God: Women Prophets in Late Medieval and Early Modern England* (Woodbridge, D.S. Brewer, 1997).

———, 'Barton, Elizabeth (c.1506–1534)', *ODNB*, vol. 4, pp. 201–4.

————, 'Reconstructing the Word: the Political Prophecies of Elizabeth Barton (1506–1534)', *Renaissance Quarterly*, 50 (1997): 136–63.

————, 'The Prophet at Home: Elizabeth Barton and the Influence of Bridget of Sweden and Catherine of Siena', in R. Voaden (ed.), *Prophets Abroad: The Reception of Continental Holy Women in Late-Medieval England.*

Watt, J.A., 'Spiritual and Temporal Powers', in J.H. Burns (ed.) *The Cambridge History of Medieval Political Thought, c. 350 – c.1450.*

Watt, T., *Cheap Print and Popular Piety, 1550–1640* (Cambridge, CUP, 1991).

Watts, J.L. (ed.), *The End of the Middle Ages? England in the Fifteenth and Sixteenth Centuries* (Stroud, Sutton, 1998).

Whatmore, L.E., 'The Sermon Against the Holy Maid of Kent and her Adherents, Delivered at Paul's Cross, November the 23rd, 1533, and at Canterbury, December the 7th', *English Historical Review*, 58 (1943): 263–75.

————, 'A Sermon of Henry Gold, Vicar of Ospringe, 1525–27, Preached Before Archbishop Warham', *AC*, 57 (1944): 37–8.

White, H.C., *The Tudor Books of Private Devotion* (Madison, WI, University of Wisconsin Press, 1951, 2nd edition, 1979).

Whitehouse, H., *Arguments and Icons: Divergent Modes of Religiosity* (Oxford, OUP, 2000).

Wilson, C., 'The Medieval Monuments', in Patrick Collinson et al. (eds), *A History of Canterbury Cathedral.*

Wogan-Browne, J., Watson, N., Taylor, A., and Evans, R. (eds), *The Idea of the Vernacular: An Anthology of Middle English Literary Theory, 1280–1520*, Exeter Middle English Texts and Studies (Exeter, Exeter University Press, 1999).

Wooding, L.E.C., *Rethinking Catholicism in Reformation England* (Oxford, Clarendon, 2000).

Woodruff, U.E., 'Inventory of the Church Goods of Maidstone', *AC,* 22 (1897): 29–33.

Zell, M., *Industry in the Countryside: Wealden Society in the Sixteenth Century* (Cambridge, CUP, 1994)

————, (ed.), *Early Modern Kent 1540–1640* (London, Boydell, 2000).

————, 'The Coming of Religious Reform', in M. Zell (ed.), *Early Modern Kent, 1540–1640.*

————, 'The Establishment of a Protestant Church', in M. Zell, (ed.), *Early Modern Kent 1540–1640.*

————, 'A Wood–Pasture Agrarian Regime: the Kentish Weald in the Sixteenth Century', *Southern History*, 7 (1985): 72–86.

Unpublished Secondary Sources

Acheson, R.J., 'The Development of Religious Separatism in the Diocese of Canterbury, 1590–1660', unpublished Ph.D Thesis, University of Kent at Canterbury (1983).

Bartram, C., 'The Reading and Writing Practices of the Kentish Gentry: The Emergence of a Protestant Identity in Elizabethan Kent', unpublished Ph.D Thesis, Canterbury Centre for Medieval & Tudor Studies, University of Kent (2004).

Butcher, A.F., '"The Micro-Mechanisms of Cognition and Communication" and Changing Modes of Religiosity', unpublished paper given at the 'Pieties in Transition' colloquium, University of Kent, September, 2004.

Daly, C., 'The Hospitals of London: Administration, Reformation and Benefaction c. 1500–1572', unpublished D.Phil. Thesis, University of Oxford (1993).

Dinn, R.B., 'Popular Religion in Late Medieval Bury St Edmunds', unpublished Ph.D Thesis, University of Manchester (1990).

Draper, G.M., 'Literacy and its Transmission in the Romney Marsh Area, *c*. 1150–1550', unpublished Ph.D. Thesis, University of Kent (2003).

Durkin, G., 'The Civic Government and Economy of Elizabethan Canterbury', Unpublished Ph.D Thesis, University of Kent (2001).

Higgs, L.M.A., 'Lay Piety in the Borough of Colchester, 1485–1558', unpublished Ph.D Thesis, University of Michigan (1983).

Lee, P., 'Monastic and Secular Religion and Devotional Reading in Late Medieval Dartford and West Kent', unpublished Ph.D Thesis, University of Kent (1998).

Salter, E., 'Cultural Appropriation and Transmission in Town and Country in Late Medieval England', unpublished Ph.D Thesis, Canterbury Centre for Medieval & Tudor Studies, University of Kent (2003).

Simpson, P., 'Custom and Conflict: Disputes over Tithe in the Diocese of Canterbury, 1501–1600', unpublished Ph.D Thesis, University of Kent (1997).

Index

Index

Index

communication of 165
English 190
mirrors of 182
popular 161
religious 122, 183
sensory or visual 177
spiritual 8, 38, 167
visual and verbal 176

Fabian, Johannes 150, 152, 158–9
fabric of the building 130
fabric, physical, of devotion 21, 24
faith, justification through 122
families 36, 37, 38, 39, 183, 189
    Cranbrook 31
    Lollard 35
    religiously frugal 34
    Tenterden 31, 37, 185
    will-making 30
family 3, 5, 7, 16, 18, 19, 31, 34, 35, 37,
        50, 55, 72, 185
    and kin 19
    duty 2
    dynamics 54
    generations of 25
    nuclear 30
    pieties 30, 31, 39
    small farms of 34
    status 90
    ties 2, 126
    tradition 5
farmers 34, 100
    yeomen 31
farming, commercial livestock 34
farms, small family 34
Faversham 20, 86
    chantries 77
feast days 64
feeding the hungry 64
financial dues 101
Finch, John 133, 134, 143
Fisher, John, Bishop of Rochester 41, 45,
        46, 47
    De unica Magdalena 46
fishing settlements 100
Flanders 1, 111–12, 114, 189
Flemings 52
Fogge, John 84

Folkestone 20, 78
forgotten events 187
Forstall, David 105
foundation 76
founders 86
    post-Reformation 85
Four Books of Husbandry, Heresbach
        135
Foxe, John 136–7
    Acts and Monuments 131, 135–6
fragmentary evidence 146–7, 160
fragmentation 34
Franciscans 121
Fraternity 30
    Corpus Christi 67
friaries 66
friars 25, 61
Frisia, late medieval 117
Frisians, Catholic 120
Frittenden 98
frugality 25, 31, 34, 35, 36, 183
functionalism 45
funeral art, secularization of 186
funeral ceremonies 123
    days 67
    effigy 138
    giving 31
    heraldic 135
    monument, elite 133
        Elizabethan 129
    sermon 22, 132
    services 24–5, 63, 70, 117, 132
funerary ritual 24, 134
Fyshare, John 79

Galen 51, 52, 53
Garner, Alan 50
gender 126
genealogy 185
generations 30, 185
generosity 31
Genesis 52
gentlemen 100, 143
gentry 4, 30, 34, 45, 49, 134, 138
    culture 130
    Kentish 135
    monuments 130

Index